THE NEW NATURALIST
A SURVEY OF BRITISH NATURAL HISTORY

MAMMALS
IN THE BRITISH ISLES

THE NEW NATURALIST

MAMMALS
IN THE BRITISH ISLES

L. HARRISON MATTHEWS
M.A., Sc.D., F.R.S.

COLLINS
ST JAMES'S PLACE, LONDON

William Collins Sons & Co Ltd
London · Glasgow · Sydney · Auckland
Toronto · Johannesburg

First published 1982
© L. Harrison Matthews 1982
ISBN 0 00 219738 3
Filmset by Servis Filmsetting Ltd, Manchester
Black and white reproduction by
Adroit Photo-Litho Ltd, Birmingham
Made and printed in Great Britain by
William Collins Sons & Co Ltd, Glasgow

CONTENTS

PLATES

EDITORS' PREFACE

IT IS NOW over 30 years since Dr Matthews wrote his *British Mammals*, which was No. 21 in the *New Naturalist* series. The Editors then described it as 'the most important book on British mammals that has ever been published, bringing together as it does an enormous number of facts into a new synthesis'. The reviewers and our public fully endorsed this opinion, and the book has been a continuing success ever since it was published. It is still the most useful volume in its field, and owners of copies will treasure them on their shelves, and make use of them in their studies, for many years to come.

British Mammals, when it was published, was topical and very up to date, bringing together the results of Dr Matthews' own observations and the research of many other mammalogists. Since then the subject has made great progress, often stimulated by Dr Matthews' own writings. As a result there was need for considerable addition to the original text, even though there was little that newer investigations had shown to require correction. *British Mammals* was already a long book, though every word of its text was interesting and worth reading. Further extensions and revisions would have produced a volume which, in today's circumstances, would have been so expensive as to have been out of reach of many of those for whom it was intended – 'the general reader interested in wildlife'.

It was for this reason that we persuaded Dr Matthews to produce an entirely new book. It is in no way a revision of the 1952 publication. Although considerably shorter than its predecessor, it covers all facets of the life of the mammals of the British Isles. Like others in this series, it is not a text book. Several admirable volumes of this nature are now available; this has made it possible to reduce the description of the species to a minimum. Once more the author has produced a synthesis of modern knowledge, which treats mammals as living creatures, living in and adapted to their environment. We are confident that it will meet a real need of today's readers, and that it is a worthy successor to the author's previous volume.

9

AUTHOR'S PREFACE

THIRTY years have passed since my volume 'British Mammals' was published as No. 21 in the *New Naturalist* series, and a large amount of new information has come to hand during that time. The cost of re-setting a fully revised new edition was too expensive for the publishers to face; I had therefore to insist that it should be allowed to go out of print – I could not let readers be fobbed off with so out-of-date a book. Paradoxically, the publishers then asked me to write a new and different book on our mammals, and here it is.

I have tried to give a general picture of the British mammals and the things influencing their numbers and distribution both now and in the past, together with the history and development of their environment. I then examine various aspects of their biology, dealing with them as living animals in the field rather than as captives in the laboratory or preserved specimens in museums. I have avoided elaborating technical points of anatomical structure unless they are relevant to matters of function and physiology. In a land so densely populated as the British Isles the paths of animal and man inevitably cross at many places, so I conclude with an account of such relationships and a consideration of the measures man has taken for the control and conservation of his fellow mammals.

The growth in knowledge of the British mammals that has occurred since the publication of the previous book is due to the greatly increased number of people taking an active interest in the subject. Most of them are members of the Mammal Society which in bringing them together to present and discuss the results of their researches at its annual conferences and other meetings has greatly stimulated an interest in the scientific study of mammals. Membership is open to anyone interested; its address is Harvest House, 62 London Road, Reading, Berkshire RG1 5AS.

LHM

CHAPTER I

THE MAMMALS OF THE BRITISH ISLES

THE number of different kinds of mammal indigenous to the British Isles, and now living in them, is comparatively small. About four thousand kinds of living mammals are known to science throughout the world, but of these only forty-one indigenous land mammals inhabit our region. In addition two kinds of seal breed on our coasts, and seventeen kinds of whale and dolphin are regular inhabitants of our inshore or offshore seas, making a total of sixty.

This total, however, does not include all the kinds of mammal now living in our islands, for we have no less than fourteen kinds that have been introduced by man and have become established members of the fauna. There are moreover two kinds of bat, six kinds of whale or dolphin, and six kinds of seal that have occasionally wandered to our shores and are regarded as accidental vagrants. In addition five kinds of domestic animal have become feral – that is, have run wild – in various parts of the country, and if we add to these four kinds of indigenous mammal that have been exterminated in historic times, and one introduced but subsequently exterminated, we have a grand total of ninety-eight. This represents about one fortieth of the number of known living mammals, far less than the more than five hundred kinds of bird 'admitted to the British list', which represent about one fifteenth of the known kinds of bird inhabiting the world.

As might be expected in a country so densely populated by man as the British Isles, most of the mammals are small and inconspicuous so that they easily keep out of harm's way. The majority are active only by night; those active during the day live concealed underground, in woodland and hedgerow litter, or among dense vegetation. Forty-five different kinds fall into the category of small mammals, ranging in size from the pygmy shrew to the hedgehog and the pine marten; they include the insectivores, the shrews, mole and hedgehog; the bats; all but one of the rodents, the rats, mice and voles; and six of the smaller carnivores such as the stoat, weasel, and polecat.

The medium-sized mammals are much fewer; they range in size from the rabbit to the fox, and include the leporids, the rabbit and hares; four carnivores, the fox, badger, otter and wild cat; one introduced rodent, the coypu; and one introduced marsupial, the red-necked wallaby – only nine different kinds in all. Most of them are nocturnal or crepuscular – active around dusk and dawn – and all but three lie up in underground burrows for much of the daylight hours. The brown hare lies up in a form, a slight depression among herbage or even in a bare ploughed field, in which it is remarkably difficult to detect; if disturbed it escapes from danger by its speed in running and adroitness in jinking if pursued. The mountain hare digs short burrows but usually sits at the entrance and escapes from danger by running away rather than entering the burrow; it too is remarkably inconspicuous when it sits still unless it is in its white winter coat and the ground is not covered with snow. The wallaby lies up in scrubby woodland when not grazing in the open.

Of the large mammals there are only four kinds that are indigenous to our fauna, two kinds of seal and two of deer. To these must be added five introduced kinds of deer, one semi-domesticated; the semi-feral horse; and the feral sheep and goat. The only enemy these have to fear is man. The seals avoid him by hauling out only on inaccessible ocean beaches, in sea caves, on remote uninhabited islands of the western coasts, or sandbanks such as those of the Wash where no one can approach unobserved within a mile. The native red deer live in the hills and mountains of the north where there is plenty of room to flee from approaching danger, which they are quick to apprehend by scent, hearing and sight in that order. The native roe deer is a woodland animal, and by day remains hidden in thick cover from which it emerges to feed in the open at dusk and dawn. Where these animals have been introduced to other places, or have become established through escapes from parks and enclosures, they are usually nocturnal inhabitants of woodlands. The introduced fallow, sika, muntjac, and Chinese water deer avoid disturbance by man in a similar way, generally emerging from thick cover only by night or at dawn and dusk. Most of these introductions and escapes have increased greatly in numbers and distribution since the end of the war in 1945, and often live close to human habitations where, because of their secretive habits, they are seldom seen unless specially sought for. Their depredations in field and garden are more commonly seen and noticed with disapproval. The feral, miscalled 'wild', horses, goats and sheep live on open moors and mountains where, like the red deer, they can from afar see the approach of danger – that is, man – and can move swiftly away to safety. The feral ponies of the New Forest, however, are so used to the sight of man that they take little notice of his presence, and often approach picnickers to beg for titbits.

The whales and dolphins all fall into the category of large mammals, but as they are creatures of the seas their way of life is so different from that of the land mammals that they cannot usefully be considered as living in the British Isles.

We shall now briefly pass in review the different kinds of mammal, and their taxonomic classification, before going on to consider their habits, habitats and ways of life. We fortunately do not need to enter into minute description of their diagnostic characters and structure, or the basic details of their biology, which are all set forth with great clarity in the second edition of the Handbook of British Mammals, edited for the Mammal Society by G.B. Corbet and H.N. Southern, and published in 1977, a work indispensible to naturalists interested in British Mammals.[39]

Many naturalists have worked out schemes of classification for animals both before and since the Swedish naturalist Carl von Linné, whose name is latinised as Linnaeus, invented the binomial system. He gave each kind of animal and plant a specific name, and grouped the species, 'species' being merely the latin for 'kind', that showed some resemblance to each other into genera, singular 'genus', the latin for a clan or tribe. For example he classified the rats and mice into the genus *Mus*, giving the specific names *Mus rattus* to the black rat, *Mus musculus* to the house mouse, and *Mus sylvaticus* to the wood mouse. Since his time they have been separated into different genera, but still retain their specific names.

Before the time of Linnaeus naturalists distinguished species by using cumbrous compound names often amounting to short descriptive sentences. For example, Linnaeus named the daisy of our lawns and fields *Bellis perennis*, whereas many earlier botanists called it '*Bellis scapo nudo unifloro*'. Early writers in English often used expressions that appear quaint to modern eyes; Edward Topsell whose 'Historie of Foure-footed Beastes' was published in 1607–08, heads his chapter on mice 'Of the vulgar little Mouse' – meaning the 'common house mouse' – to distinguish it from the 'Vulgar Rat, or great domesticall Mouse'.

When species are classified into genera, the genera themselves need to be arranged into convenient groups, the genera in each having some characters in common. Thus genera are gathered into families,

families into orders, orders into classes, and classes into phyla (singular, phylum). Intermediate grades such as superfamily or subfamily are often used for finer divisions of classification. Thus the mammals are put into the Class Mammalia of the sub-phylum Vertebrata of the Phylum Chordata; and the 'vulgar little mouse' becomes *Mus musculus* of the genus *Mus*, of the Family Muridae, of the Order Rodentia, of the class Mammalia.

Although this system of classification is linear it must not be read as though it were a genealogy or family tree in which the successive levels are the descendants of the previous ones. It is merely a convention and a convenience, at least partly determined by the necessity of representing it in only two dimensions on a written or printed sheet of paper. In nature all the living species of animal are on a single level, and can be likened to the tips of the twigs of a three-dimensional tree, of which the dead-wood in the branches, limbs and trunk represents the extinct ancestors of the living species. The analogy is the more apt because the wood ascends continuously from its origin to its utmost ramifications unlike a family tree which is inverted and where the descent is cut up into generations.

The scheme of classification for the mammals now almost universally accepted and adopted by naturalists was worked out by the American zoologist G.G. Simpson and published in 1945.[131] Some minor modifications have been made to it during the last thirty-five years, but it has proved so useful, and is supported by such erudite and convincing arguments, that it has become the standard system adopted by zoologists throughout the world. According to the modified Simpson's system there are 33 orders of mammals, 14 of which are extinct; 257 families, of which 139 or 54 per cent are extinct; and 2,864 genera, of which 1,932 or 67 per cent are extinct. Thus the living species represent only a small fraction of the total that have lived since the class Mammalia evolved. The diversity and number of species in all the orders except perhaps the rodents reached their peak in the Miocene or Pliocene epochs – some twenty-five to three million years ago – since when they have declined to their present level.

In the British Isles, excluding the whales, we have mammals representing nine of the nineteen orders now living, but of these only seven are indigenous, the two others are either introduced and naturalised, or are derived from stocks of domestic animals. Our fauna is therefore no more than a small sample of the mammalian diversity that ornaments the fauna of the world. It has, moreover, not contained a larger number of orders since the land became generally habitable by warm-blooded animals at the end of the great glaciation of the Pleistocene epoch, about half a million years ago. In the preceeding epochs, before the ice ages, several other orders were represented by species of mammal that became extinct long before the present pattern of the fauna evolved.

Before we discuss the problematic origin of the present fauna we should enumerate and specify the species about which we shall be speaking. In following Simpson's arrangement of the orders the indigenous species are necessarily not separated from those that have been introduced or are extinct.

ORDER MARSUPIALIA

The marsupials differ so fundamentally from the other mammals that they are placed in a separate Infraclass, the Metatheria, whereas the other mammals of our fauna are included in the Infraclass Eutheria. The marsupials show many unique anatomical characters, but are popularly known merely by a single one, as the mammals that carry their young in a pouch. This is not universally true, for some of them are pouchless; but in all of them the young are born at a comparatively early stage of development and thus need to be carried attached to the mother's nipples. The marsupials are typically the mammals of the Australasian region, but in addition many species live in South America and one, the Virginian opossum, extends into North America. The living species are divided into eight families of which one, containing the kangaroos and wallabies, is represented in our fauna by a single introduced species.

Family Macropodidae

Macropus rufogriseus, the red-necked wallaby or Bennett's wallaby, is a medium sized kangaroo-like animal weighing up to about 30 pounds, sometimes nearly 50 pounds. It is native to south-eastern Australia and Tasmania; but as it is easily kept in captivity it is commonly exhibited in zoos and parks of many lands, whence it sometimes escapes. Small feral populations of that origin have become established in Sussex and Derbyshire; smaller colonies deliberately introduced on Herm in the Channel Islands, and on Lambay Island off the coast of Co. Dublin in Eire have died out. Although the English populations have been established for over thirty years they remain small because wallabies are liable to suffer heavy mortality in severe winters.

The insectivores are mostly small mammals characterised by many primitive or generalised mammalian characters. They are considered to be descended with least change from the ancestral stock of the mammals, though all living species have various specialised adaptations. Insectivores live in most parts of the world except Australasia and South America; they include the tenrecs, hedgehogs, moles, desmans, and shrews.

Family Erinaceidae

Erinaceus europaeus, the hedgehog, our only mammal with prickles in its skin, is the largest of our insectivores. It is present throughout the mainland of Great Britain and Ireland and is common in lowland areas, particularly in the suburbs of towns. It is also found in many of the islands, but has probably been introduced into most of them by man. It lives in woods and hedgerows, coming into the open to feed as night falls. The hedgehog and the dormouse are our only mammals besides the bats that hibernate in winter.

Family Talpidae

Talpa europaea, the mole, is our only mammal that spends nearly all of its life underground. Its cylindrical body, some five to five and a half inches in length, is covered with black velvety fur. The fore limbs and their muscles are highly adapted for tunnelling in the earth, and the strongly clawed hands are broadened internally by an extra bone, the radial sesamoid. The hind feet are similarly but less conspicuously reinforced by an accessory sesamoid bone. The eyes are minute and hidden by the fur, and there is not an ear pinna, but the long snout is plentifully supplied with special touch organs. The sites of mole burrows are shown by the conspicuous heaps of earth pushed up to the surface as the mole digs its underground tunnels, in which it spends most of its life feeding mainly on earthworms which fall into the burrows. Moles are present throughout Great Britain but not Ireland or the Isle of Man; they are not found on many of the smaller islands except Anglesey and the Isle of Wight, Alderney and Jersey.

Family Soricidae

The shrews are small mouse-like animals with velvety fur, long pointed snouts, small eyes and ears. They are insectivorous and carnivorous, generally seeking their food under thick vegetation and litter below which they have runways; some species dig burrows. The first incisor teeth are large and project forwards, acting like forceps in picking up small food objects; the back teeth bear sharp pointed cusps. Shrews need comparatively large quantities of food, and are consequently active by day and night, alternating short periods of activity and rest throughout the twenty-four hours. They soon die of starvation if denied food for a few hours.

The genus *Sorex* contains two British species, the common shrew, *S. araneus*, and the pygmy shrew *S. minutus*, the latter being our smallest British mammal. The enamel of the tips of the teeth is red in both species, which are distinguished by size, relative length of tail which is longer in the pygmy shrew, and colour of the fur, darker in *S. araneus* but lighter in *S. minutus*. The common shrew is found throughout England, Scotland and Wales and on many of the islands, but is absent from Ireland, Orkney, Shetland, the outer Hebrides and Man. The pygmy shrew, although less abundant, is found throughout the whole of the British Isles except Shetland, the Scilly and Channel Islands. The common shrew is peculiar in showing chromosome polymorphism, that is, the number and form of the chromosomes differs in animals from different parts of the country.[62] Both species are annuals: young born in one summer breed in the next and die in the following autumn, so the winter population consists entirely of immature animals, and none normally lives through a second winter.

The water shrew, *N. fodiens*, is the only British species of the genus *Neomys*, and is easily distinguished by its larger size and the black colour of the fur on the upper parts; it too has red-tipped teeth. Although it is aquatic and has fringes of stiff hairs on feet and tail that aid in swimming, it is nevertheless often found at considerable distances from water in woods and hedgerows in similar places to those inhabited by other shrews. It lives in burrows in the banks of clear streams and ponds; when it enters the water the fur traps air so that it appears silvery. The fur nevertheless soon becomes wet and is dried on landing by squeegeeing through the tight fitting burrow. Its food consists of invertebrates and even creatures as large as itself such as frogs and small fish. It is found throughout the mainland but is absent from Ireland, Isle of Man, and the western and northern islands of Scotland. The water shrew is unique among British mammals in being the only one with a poisonous bite, because the submaxillary salivary glands contain a venom that paralyses small prey.

The other two species of British shrew belong to the genus *Crocidura*, at once distinguished from the rest by their white teeth. Their ears are larger than in the others, and the tails bear a number of long scattered hairs. They are found only in the Scilly and Channel Islands, where they live in habitats similar to those of the common and pygmy shrews. The lesser white-toothed shrew, *C. suaveolens*, is found on most of the Scilly Islands, Jersey and Sark; it was probably unintentionally introduced into Scilly from the continent by man. The greater white-toothed shrew, *C. russula*, is found only on Alderney, Guernsey and Herm in the Channel Islands. The water and greater white-toothed shrews reach a life span of eighteen months or a little more, but the lesser white-toothed shrew is as short-lived as the common and pygmy shrews.

ORDER CHIROPTERA— BATS

All the British bats are comparatively small animals, and all are solely insectivorous, and nocturnal or crepuscular. They generally catch their food on the wing but some carry their larger prey to habitual perches to eat it. During darkness they find their prey by echo-

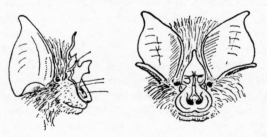

Fig. 1. Side and front views of the head of a horseshoe bat to show the details of the nose-leaf.

location or 'sonar', emitting pulses of high frequency ultrasound which are reflected back from surrounding objects to give a mental image probably similar to that produced by sight in other animals. The horseshoe bats emit pulses through the nostrils, the other species through the open mouth. All species hibernate during the winter, and become torpid for four or five months, though not continuously, for hibernation is interrupted by short periods of activity. Bats are long-lived in comparison with other small mammals, reaching an age of four or five, and sometimes over twenty years.

Family Rhinolophidae

Two species of this family are members of the British fauna, the greater and lesser horseshoe bats, *Rhinolophus ferrumequinum* and *R. hipposideros*. They are characterised by the possession of 'nose leaves', thin fleshy outgrowths arising round the nostrils but overlapping the fur of the face with their free outer parts. Their structure is complex and better described by a drawing than by words; the part over the muzzle and round the nostrils is crescentic in shape, hence the English, Latin, and latinised Greek names of these bats.

The nose leaf is part of the special echolocation system. The greater horseshoe bat has a wingspan of 34 to 39 centimetres and is thus one of our larger bats. Its natural roosts are in caves, but it also uses mines and the cellars and roof spaces of buildings. In the British Isles it is found only in southwest England and south Wales. The lesser horseshoe bat is one of our smaller species, with a wingspan of only 22 to 25 centimetres. It roosts in similar places to those used by the larger species, and has a larger range, being found in southwest England, all of Wales and extending into Yorkshire, and far to the west in western Ireland.

Family Vespertilionidae

All the other British bats belong to this family – fifteen species in seven genera. They are mostly small to medium-sized bats but the serotine and noctule equal the greater horseshoe in wingspan, and one, the rare mouse-eared bat exceeds it by up to six centimetres.

Of the fifteen species, six are common throughout much of the British Isles, though only one, the pipistrelle, is found everywhere except in Shetland; they are the whiskered, Natterer's, Daubenton's, noctule, pipistrelle, and long-eared bats. Five species are rare, or occasional vagrants – Bechstein's, the mouse-eared, parti-coloured, Nathusius' pipistrelle, and the grey long-eared bats. The remaining four species are intermediate, having a limited distribution within the bounds of which they may not be scarce. They are Brandt's, the serotine, Leisler's and the barbastelle bats.

Six species of the genus *Myotis* are British. The whiskered bat, *M. mystacinus*, is a small dark grey bat that roosts in trees and buildings and often hibernates in caves. It is found throughout England, Wales and Ireland, but is less common in southern Scotland and absent from the north. Brandt's bat, *M. brandti*, so closely resembles the whiskered bat that it has only recently been recognised as a separate species, differing slightly in details of the ear and teeth; it is known from many parts of England and Wales but its overall distribution has yet to be ascertained. Natterer's bat, *M. nattereri*, is larger, with a wingspan of up to 30 cm, and the fur brown above and light or white below. It can be distinguished from all others by the fringe of stiff short hairs along the edge of the bare skin joining the legs and tail – the interfemoral part of the patagium or double layer of skin that makes a bat in effect an aerofoil. It roosts in trees, buildings and caves throughout the British Isles as far north as central Scotland. Bechstein's bat, *M. bechsteini*, very similar to Natterer's bat but having longer ears and lacking the fringe of hairs on the interfemoral patagium, is a rare woodland bat that has occasionally been found in southern England, mostly in Dorset. The mouse-eared bat, *M. myotis*, our largest species with wingspan up to 45 centimetres, was known only as a rare vagrant until 1956 when a small colony was found in a cave in Dorset; another was found in Sussex fifteen years later. Daubenton's bat, *M. daubentoni*, is medium in size, dark brown above and pale grey below. The ear is comparatively short, and the feet large. It is often seen catching insects flying low over water, but is by no means confined to this way of feeding and frequently hunts in other places. It roosts in hollow trees and buildings, and often hibernates in caves. It is found throughout the British Isles except the northern parts of Scotland and the Hebrides.

Of the genus *Vespertilio* only the parti-coloured bat, *V. murinus*, has been found in the British Isles, as a very rare vagrant from the continent. It is a medium-sized bat; the dark brown hairs of the back have white or buff tips which give a grizzled or speckled appearance. Similarly, the genus *Eptesicus* has only one British species, the serotine bat, *E. serotinus*, which is, however, a regular though localised member of the fauna. It is a large species with a wingspan of up to 38 centimetres, and has dark brown fur, paler below. It is mainly a woodland species but often roosts in buildings; in England it is found only in the southern and eastern counties as far north as the Wash.

Two species of the genus *Nyctalus*, the noctule *N. noctula*, and Leisler's bat *N. leisleri*, are widespread though not universal in the British Isles; both have comparatively narrow pointed wings. The large noctule with a wingspan of up to 39 centimetres has dark yellowish or reddish brown fur. It is a woodland bat, roosting in holes in trees, and often flies well before dark, hunting high above the trees. It occurs throughout England and Wales, rarely in southern Scotland and is absent from Ireland. The smaller but similar Leisler's bat on the other hand is found throughout Ireland but has a more restricted distribution in central and southern England. It, too, is a woodland bat, differing from the noctule not only in its smaller size but also in the colour of the fur on the back, which is reddish brown at the surface but dark brown at the bases of the hairs.

The pipistrelle, *Pipistrellus pipistrellus*, a small bat with a wingspan not over 25 centimetres, is our commonest species, being found throughout the British Isles with the exception of Shetland. It varies greatly in colour, ranging from rufous through shades of brown to almost black. It roosts commonly in buildings, in which its colonies may number several hundred animals. The closely similar Nathusius' pipistrelle, *P. nathusii*, is slightly larger, but is known only as a vagrant, a single specimen having been found in Dorset in 1959.

The barbastelle, *Barbastellus barbastellus*, the only British member of its genus, is a medium-sized bat with black fur, the lighter tips of the hairs giving a frosted appearance. The ears are short but wide and joined at their bases above the face, thus differing from all other British species except the long-eared bat. Barbastelles roost in hollow trees and buildings, and sometimes hibernate in caves. The species is rather thinly distributed over England and Wales as far north as Cheshire and Yorkshire, and is generally regarded as uncommon.

The long-eared bat, *Plecotus auritus*, is a small species recognised by its enormously long narrow ears which are nearly as long as the head-and-body. When asleep it tucks the ears under the wings leaving the tragus, the lobe representing the ear-cover, of each side sticking up like a pair of spikey horns. It roosts in trees and buildings and frequently hibernates in caves; when feeding it often hovers to pick insects off the leaves of trees. It is widely distributed throughout the British Isles except in northern Scotland and most of the Scotch islands. The very similar grey long-eared bat, *P. austriacus*, slightly larger, greyer, and with broader ears, has only recently been recognised as a separate species. It has been found in the south of Dorset, Hampshire and Sussex, but may prove to be more widely distributed after further study.

ORDER LAGOMORPHA

This order contains the rabbits and hares, easily distinguished from rodents by the presence of a second pair of small upper incisor teeth immediately behind the large first pair. There are three British species. *Oryctolagus cuniculus*, the rabbit, has long been an established member of the fauna although it is not indigenous. It was introduced by man a little before A.D. 1200 from its native Iberian peninsula and north Africa to be raised in confinement for fur and meat; it subsequently escaped, became feral and increased so that it is now found everywhere in the British Isles. The myxomatosis epidemic of the 1950s reduced the population drastically, but numbers have now recovered in many places.

We have two species of hare, the brown hare, *Lepus capensis*, and the mountain hare, *L. timidus*, both considerably larger than the rabbit, and with longer, black-tipped ears and longer legs. Linnaeus named the only hare found in Sweden in his time *L. timidus*, and a species from South Africa *L. capensis*, not knowing that the brown hare of Europe differs from the mountain hare, or that its range extends from South Africa to most of Europe and much of Asia – hence the peculiarity that our native brown hare takes its scientific name from the Cape of Good Hope. The brown hare, distinguished by the black upper side of the tail, is found throughout England and Wales, southern and north-eastern Scotland. It is not native to Ireland, but has been introduced into the north, and also into many of the Scotch islands. The mountain hare is smaller, has shorter ears, and the upper side of its tail is not black. After the autumn and winter moult the coat is wholly or partly white, and becomes brown again with the spring moult. The mountain hare is indigenous to the highlands of Scotland and all of Ireland. The Irish mountain hare is considered to be a distinct subspecies slightly larger than the Scotch, and assuming a white coat incompletely or not at all during winter. Mountain hares have been introduced into parts of southern Scotland and some of the islands, the Peak district and north Wales.

ORDER RODENTIA

The rodents comprise the rats, mice, squirrels, beavers, porcupines, and cavies. They are mostly small to medium-sized animals, the largest, the Capybara, a huge cavy of South America, reaching a weight of over a hundredweight; few others approach this size. There are about 1,500 species of rodents; Simpson[131] remarks that they are 'believed to be as abundant individually and in variety as all other mammals put together.' Fortunately we have only fifteen species living in the British Isles, eight of them introduced; one introduced and one indigenous species are extinct. The incisor teeth of rodents, separated by a long gap from the cheek teeth, are single upper and lower pairs with chisel-like cutting edges and long roots from which growth is continuous so that the loss by wear at the cutting edge is perpetually made good.

Family Castoridae

The beaver, *Castor fiber*, was exterminated in the British Isles about AD 1200, but had been scarce long before. It was abundant in the Fens during prehistoric times.

Family Sciuridae

The red squirrel, *Sciurus vulgaris*, our only indigenous species, is typically an inhabitant of coniferous forests, especially those of our only indigenous pine, *Pinus sylvestris*, though not confined to them. The fur is reddish brown above, white below, the tail is long and bushy, and in winter tufts of long hair on the ears are conspicuous. The hairs of the tail and ear tufts wear and bleach during spring and summer, leaving the tail almost white and the ear tufts sparse. The numbers of red squirrels have varied widely during the last 300 years, but reached a peak at the turn of the century since when they have declined again. It is now widespread in much of Scotland, Ireland, Wales and northern England, but extinct in most of southern and central England. The causes of the fluctuation in the size of the population are not known.

The grey squirrel, *Sciurus carolinensis*, was introduced from North America and irresponsibly released in various places in the last quarter of the nineteenth century and the first of the twentieth. It has spread widely, and is now found in most of England and Wales, central Scotland and central Ireland. It is larger than the red squirrel, and has proportionally larger ears without conspicuous tufts. The fur is grey with yellowish brown streaks on the sides and feet and, in the winter coat, on back and head. The grey squirrel lives in woods of broad-leaved trees as well as of conifers; some town people regard it as an attraction in public parks, but in the country it is so destructive to young trees, fruit, forestry, agriculture and horticulture that it is now illegal to import or to release grey squirrels or keep them in captivity. Legislation, however, came too late to rid us of this pest.

Family Cricetidae

There were five species of voles in the British Isles, one probably introduced, and another that was injudiciously introduced but successfully exterminated. The last was the musk rat, *Ondatra zibethicus*, which escaped from fur farms, to which it had been brought from its native America. It became established in several districts about 1930, but a great official effort of destruction eliminated it seven years later.

The British voles are small mouse-sized animals with one exception, the water vole, often called the water rat from its larger size. The voles are distinguished from the mice by the rounded or blunt rather than pointed profile of the snout, and the comparatively small ears partly concealed in the fur. The diagnostic character of the different species is given by the pattern of the cheek teeth. Our four species are classified into three genera.

The bank vole, *Clethrionomys glareolus*, is recognised by the chestnut red fur of the upper side. It lives mostly in woodland, scrub and hedgerows, under which it makes runways and burrows, but it also habitually climbs among the branches of shrubs and small trees – so much that the late Oliver Hook, the well-known naturalist, nick-named it 'Cleth the Climber', though the wood and yellow-necked mice are at some times and in some places equally or even more arboreal[111a]. The bank vole is often a destructive pest in country gardens. It is found all over the mainland of Great Britain, and on many of the islands, but is not indigenous in Ireland where it has recently been introduced, perhaps by some zoological practical joker, and now occupies a large area in the south-west. Four sub-species are recognised, each confined to a separate island – Raasay, Mull, Skomer, and Jersey. All are larger than the mainland race, and that of Skomer is much brighter in colouration.

The field vole, *Microtus agrestis*, is of smaller size but has greyish brown fur, smaller ears, and a short tail. It lives mainly in rough grassland and less often among scrub and dense cover; it makes runways and builds its nests under the thick mat of grasses, the stems and leaves of which form the greater part of its food. It is found throughout the mainland of Great Britain and on many of the Hebrides, but not in Ireland, the Isle of Man, Orkney or Shetland.

The voles of Orkney and Guernsey are slightly larger and darker, and differ from the field vole by a detail in the pattern of the cheek teeth. They are a separate species, *M. arvalis*, common on the Continent whence they were probably accidentally introduced into the islands long ago.

Our largest vole, the water vole *Arvicola terrestris*, about the size of a rat, lives near rivers, ponds and canals, into the banks of which it burrows to make its nest. Although it feeds mainly upon the grass growing near the banks it readily dives into the water and swims well. Its colour is generally brown, but populations of black water voles are present in north Scotland and East Anglia. The water vole is found throughout the mainland of Great Britain but is rare in north-west Scotland, and is absent from most of the islands and from Ireland. The paradox of a water animal having the scientific name '*terrestris*' is due to the habits of this vole on the Continent, where it is not confined to the neighbourhood of water.

Family Muridae

The mice and rats differ from the voles in having proportionally larger ears and eyes, more pointed snouts, and longer tails. The cheek teeth differ in having low crowns with cusps. We have three indigenous and one introduced species of mouse, and two introduced rats.

The wood mouse, *Apodemus sylvaticus*, brownish yellow above and nearly white below, often with a coloured spot on the chest, was formerly called the 'Long-tailed Field mouse'. It lives wherever there is cover, especially in woodlands and hedgerows and consequently is found throughout the British Isles and off-lying islands into many of which it was probably accidentally introduced by man. A large number of subspecies has been described none of which are now held to be valid. Although primarily vegetarian the diet is very varied and includes many small invertebrates.

A. flavicollis, the yellow-necked mouse, closely resembles the wood mouse but is larger and has a yellow band across the chest joining the colour of the upper side. It is found in many parts of England south of the Humber, and in Wales, but is absent elsewhere. It lives in similar places to the wood mouse, but more frequently comes into houses in autumn and winter. It was not recognised as a member of the British fauna until 1894.

The harvest mouse, *Micromys minutus*, is the smallest British rodent. Gilbert White of Selborne, the first naturalist to note its presence in England, wrote in 1768[152] that he found two of them just counter-balanced 'one copper halfpenny, which is about the third of an ounce avoirdupois' or six to the ounce – they must have been thin mice for the average weight is about 6.0 grams or just over four to the ounce. The fur of the upper parts of the harvest mouse is bright reddish yellow and of the underside white. The nose is rather blunt, the hairy ear rather small, and the tail is prehensile. Harvest mice live among tall ground plants such as long grass and rough herbage among the stems of which they climb to seek their food and where they make globular breeding nests in summer up to about two feet above ground; in winter they live among the litter below. They are found, sometimes in abundance, throughout most of England and much of Wales, but are absent from the greater part of Scotland and the whole of Ireland.

The house mouse, *Mus domesticus**, has dull brownish grey fur, slightly lighter below, occasionally much lighter. Unlike the other mice it has an unpleasant smell resembling that of acetamide. It is found wherever there are human habitations throughout the British Isles, feeding upon and spoiling man's stored foods. It also occurs in hedgerows and fields away from buildings. It was introduced from the continent, no doubt unintentionally, about 2,000 years ago. Both the British species of rat are introduced, the ship or black rat about 900, and the brown or common rat about 250 years ago.

The ship rat, *Rattus rattus*, is commonly black in colour, but also occurs as two other forms, brown with grey underside or brown with

* For latest information on species of house mice see Berry, R.J. 1981. Mammal Rev. 11, 91 (No. 3, September 1981).

nearly white underside. It was once widespread but is now found, with few exceptions, solely in the neighbourhood of sea ports, where it lives only in buildings.

The common rat, *Rattus norvegicus*, is larger than the ship rat and has comparatively smaller eyes and ears; the fur is greyish brown, lighter beneath. It lives in buildings of all sorts but also inhabits rubbish tips and hedgerows far from them. In addition it commonly lives in the open on the coast, especially on the shores of estuaries and salt marshes. It is found throughout the British Isles and off-lying islands, having replaced the once abundant ship rat. Charles Waterton, the early nineteenth century naturalist of Wakefield, expressed[150] his extreme Jacobin loyalty by calling the common rat the 'Hanoverian rat' because it was introduced soon after King George I's accession in 1714 – a name that was sometimes used by other writers.

Family Gliridae

Our only native member of this family is the dormouse, *Muscardinus avellanarius*, distinguished by its orange-brown fur, long whiskers, and hairy, almost bushy tail. It lives in broad-leaved woodlands, coppices and overgrown hedgerows, building a globular nest of bark fibre, grass, and leaves several feet, sometimes yards, above ground among shrubs. Apart from the bats the dormouse and the hedgehog are the only indigenous British mammals that hibernate; the winter nest is usually made underground or among litter at ground level. The dormouse occurs sparsely throughout England and Wales, becoming scarcer in the north, and is absent from Scotland and Ireland. Another member of the family, the fat dormouse, *Glis glis*, was introduced at Tring in Hertfordshire in 1902, and has since persisted and spread over a small area of the Chiltern Hills. It closely resembles a small grey squirrel, but has dark rings round the eyes. It inhabits woods, orchards and gardens, and, like the common dormouse, it hibernates, often in the roofs of houses.

Family Hystricidae

The large South American coypu, *Myocastor coypus*, which produces the fur known commercially as 'nutria', escaped from fur farms in the early 1930s and established feral populations in several places, mainly in East Anglia. It is a large aquatic rodent reaching a length of a yard from nose to tail, looking like an enormous brown rat with webbed hind feet, blunt nose, small eyes and ears, and orange coloured enamel on the front of the incisor teeth. In East Anglia the population increased enormously in spite of heavy mortality in severe winters, so that the animals became a pest to agriculture and a threat to the stability of river banks. Since the early 1960s official control measures have greatly reduced its numbers.

ORDER CETACEA

Although seventeen species of whales and dolphins have been recorded as British, mainly because they have been found stranded on our coasts from time to time, they cannot be regarded as part of the British fauna as dealt with here – the wreck of a foreign ship on our coasts does not give its crew British nationality or make it part of the native population.

ORDER CARNIVORA

Of the ten indigenous species of beasts of prey two have been extinct for centuries; the remaining eight have been joined by a recent introduction derived from animals escaped from fur farms.

Family Canidae

The wolf, *Canis lupus*, was exterminated some 500 years ago in England and Wales, but survived in remote parts of Scotland and Ireland for another 250 years. Its descendent, perhaps with an admixture of other 'blood', the domestic dog, has some effect upon the country's ecology, killing according to one authority[146] some 6,000 sheep a year – in 1978 4,639 were killed and 3,833 injured – and every day depositing 500 tons of dung and a million gallons of urine 'on Britain's pavements and parks', equal to the sewage from four million people.

On the other hand the fox, *Vulpes vulpes*, is found everywhere in Great Britain and Ireland and in some of the islands. Its abundance is due to its adaptability to various habitats and foods, to its nocturnal and crepuscular habits, and to its tolerance of the near neighbourhood of man as shown by its recent extension of habitat into the suburbs of towns.

Family Ursidae

The brown bear, *Ursus arctos*, has been extinct in the British Isles for a thousand years; its natural distribution covers all of northern Europe, Asia and America. It varies greatly in size, from the comparatively small European race to the enormous 'grizzlies' of Kodiak Island off the Alaskan coast, as large as the 'Cave bear' that lived in the British Isles before the last glaciation of the Pleistocene epoch.

Family Mustelidae

The family consists of small to medium-sized carnivores, the British species characterised by long bodies and short legs. The pine marten, *Martes martes*, as large as a rabbit, with deep brown fur, a yellow patch on the throat, and long bushy tail, is an inhabitant of woodlands, where it feeds mainly on small birds and rodents. It is an agile climber. It was formerly found throughout the British Isles but has long been extinct except in northern Scotland, the Lake District, north Wales and Ireland.

Although the pine marten has been successfully destroyed as vermin in most of Great Britain, two other species, the stoat and the weasel, both subjected to similar persecution, have been able to remain plentiful. The larger of the two, the stoat, *Mustela erminea*, with head and body length of about a foot in males but some two inches shorter in females, is brown above, off-white below, and has a black tip to the tail. In the northern part of its range the winter coat is white with black tail tip; but in the southern part it resembles that of the summer; partly white examples occur in winter between the extremes of its range. Stoats are found throughout the British Isles and on some of the off-lying islands; those in Ireland, being smaller and having less white below, are recognised as a separate subspecies *M.e.hibernica*.

The weasel, *M. nivalis*, about four inches shorter than the stoat in both sexes, is similar in colour but does not have a black tail tip. The winter coat is not white in British weasels, though further north on the continent it is. Weasels feed mainly on voles and mice, whereas stoats take larger prey as well, especially rabbits. They are found throughout the mainland of Great Britain and some of the islands, but not in Ireland.

The polecat, *M. putorius*, is larger than the stoat but similar in build; the fur is brown with a white patch on the face between eyes and ears, the two often joining to form a bar. There is a white patch under the chin extending up onto the muzzle, and the edges of the ears are white. The ferret is a domesticated form of the polecat, perhaps with some hybridisation with the Steppe polecat of eastern Europe which may be specifically different; as it breeds successfully with the polecat, and some specimens cannot be distinguished either by colour or skull structure, the specific name, *M. furo*, for it seems superfluous. Albino ferrets are popular with the breeders and users of these animals. The polecat is an unselective carnivore; it was exterminated as vermin over most of Great Britain by the beginning of the twentieth century, but remains common in the greater part of Wales and the Welsh Marches.

The mink, *M. vison*, a native of North America, escaped from fur farms and became established as a feral member of our fauna in the 1950s; it is now widespread in Great Britain and common in many places – it is also present less widely in Ireland. The mink, about the size of a polecat, with a rather bushier tail, has very dark brown fur with white spots on the chin and throat. It is an unselective carnivore, and the effect of its activities on the native fauna has yet to be assessed – it may not be as destructive as some people have feared.

The well-known badger, *Meles meles*, grey above and black below, with a fore-and-aft black streak over eye and ear on each side of the white head, is found throughout the mainland of the British Isles and on some of the islands, and is common in many parts. It is a comparatively large animal – weights of over 35 pounds have been recorded – and is so widely spread because it is adaptable to many different habitats, has discreetly retiring habits, and is omnivorous, eating anything from earthworms to rabbits and from fruit, bulbs, and nuts to corn and grass. It comes out to forage at night, remaining underground in its set by day.

The otter, *Lutra lutra*, on the other hand is restricted in habitat to the neighbourhood of water, and, though formerly found throughout the British Isles and the off-lying islands, is consequently much less common than the badger; since about 1950 it has declined greatly in numbers over most of mainland Great Britain, but it is still plentiful in western Scotland, Ireland, much of Wales and south west England. The aquatic habit of the otter is shown by its webbed feet and broad snout with long tactile whiskers. The fur is brown all over, lighter on the throat, and the tail is long and tapering. The diet of the otter consists mainly of fish, freshwater or marine, for in the west of Scotland it is as much an inhabitant of the sea shore as of fresh waters.

Family Felidae

The wild cat, *Felis silvestris*, somewhat larger than most domestic cats, is a tabby with dark cross stripes on a grey background, and bushy tail ending in a rounded, not pointed, black tip. It has long been extinct in most of Great Britain and is now found mainly in the highlands of Scotland where it is extending into its former range; it was never native to Ireland. Its food includes rabbits, hares, rodents, and birds. It has hybridised much with feral domestic cats – domestic cats both feral and tame are probably the most destructive of all predators to the small mammals and birds of our fauna.

ORDER PINNIPEDIA

The seals are only marginally part of our fauna, for they are confined to the waters off the coast and to the sea shore from which they come a short way onto land only in remote undisturbed islands. They are, however, animals of particular interest to zoologists, and of unusual endearment to the public in general. Two species live and breed on British coasts; five others are merely accidental vagrants from northern seas, and thus form no regular part of our fauna.

Family Phocidae

The common seal, *Phoca vitulina*, and the grey seal, *Halichoerus grypus*, are not easy to tell apart when in the water, unless very close to the viewer. The coat colour of both species varies greatly; the basic pattern is of dark spots on a grey background, the spots tending to be smaller in the common seal, but no two individuals are exactly alike. Bull common seals reach a length of two metres overall, cows about 20 cm less, whereas bull grey seals reach three metres but the cows some 45 cm to 60 cm less. The snout of the common seal is comparatively short, giving the head a rounded appearance and a 'dished' profile; in the grey seal it is long and high, giving a convex profile to the head. Both species can be found on many parts of our coasts, but concentrate in special places to form breeding colonies. The common seal is least likely to be met with on the southern and western coasts of

England and Wales; it breeds at several places on the east coast, especially in the Wash, in Orkney and Shetland, on the west of Scotland and the islands, and the east of northern Ireland. On the east coast of England the main breeding colony of the grey seal is at the Farne islands; in Scotland it abounds in Orkney and Shetland and many islands of the west. There are also breeding colonies on the coasts of Wales, Cornwall, and much of Ireland. The common seal prefers shallow waters with sand and mudbanks and is often found in estuaries, whereas the grey seal lives in deeper waters off rocky coasts. Both species come ashore to give birth, the young of the grey seal remaining on or above the beach for about their first three weeks, but those of the common seal, born on sand or mudbanks covered at high tide, swim with their mothers from the first.

ORDER PERISSODACTYLA

Family Equidae

Wild horses have been extinct in the British Isles for about 10,000 years, but half-wild breeds derived from introduced domestic horses exist in several districts of extensive unenclosed land.

ORDER ARTIODACTYLA

Family Suidae

The wild boar, *Sus scrofa*, has been extinct in Great Britain for some 300 years. Although its domesticated descendants have played an important part in the rural economy of Ireland it was never indigenous there.

Family Cervidae

Stags of the largest of our two native species of deer, the red deer *Cervus elaphus*, stand up to about four feet at the withers, hinds about six inches less. The coat colour varies greatly; in general it is red-brown in summer, grey-brown in winter, with a white patch on the rump. Calves at birth are reddish-brown with white spots, but lose the spots at their first moult at the age of about two months. Horns, now generally called antlers, a term originally meaning the branches or tines, are carried only by stags. They are dropped from the pedicles, from which they grow on the forehead, in spring or summer, whereupon new ones at once start growing and are complete by the autumn. The red deer, formerly present throughout the British Isles, remains as a truly wild animal only in Scotland, the Lake district, on Exmoor and the Quantock Hills, and in south-west Ireland; elsewhere feral deer, often derived from escaped park animals, are present in many places. In Scotland the deer are animals of the hill, but in lowland England they are more generally inhabitants of woodland where they reach greater size and the stags bear larger antlers.

The sika deer, *C. nippon*, smaller than the red deer but similar in build, was introduced from the Far East in the second half of the nineteenth century, and feral populations have become established in a number of places in the British Isles. The coat is red with light spots in summer, darker and unspotted in winter; the rump patch and tail are white except for a narrow black line on the latter. The antlers of the stags are smaller and have fewer tines than those of the red deer, and lack a bez tine between the brow and trez tines. Sika deer inhabit woodlands from which they come out to graze from dusk to dawn. They hybridize freely with red deer where the ranges of the two species overlap.

The fallow deer, *Dama dama*, is another introduced species, but has been adopted into our fauna for a much longer time – probably almost a thousand years. It has for long been a favourite ornament in parks from which it has escaped so that feral populations are widespread in England, Wales and Ireland, and are found in some parts of Scotland; those in Epping and the New Forests probably represent the early stock. Bucks stand about three feet high at the withers, does a few inches less; the antlers of the bucks are usually handsomely palmated. The colour varies greatly but is light with spots in summer, much darker and generally without spots in the winter. The border of the white rump patch is black, as is the upper surface of the tail.

The roe deer, *Capreolus capreolus*, is a true native of Great Britain but not of Ireland. It is plentiful in Scotland and northern England, but has been introduced into southern England, and into East Anglia where it was exterminated some two hundred years ago. It is a small deer, barely two feet six inches at the withers, with no visible tail. The colour is tawny red, the muzzle black and the chin white; in the darker brown winter coat two white patches appear on the throat. The antlers of the buck are short spikes each with one forwardly directed tine at the base and a backwardly directed one at the top. Roe live in woodlands, which they leave to browse on bushes at dawn and dusk.

Two other small species of introduced deer are at large in parts of England, descended from animals that escaped from captivity during the present century. The muntjac, *Muntiacus reevesi*, is widespread through much of south, central and eastern England, and is still increasing its range. It is not more than eighteen inches high at the withers; the coat is deep chestnut in colour, lighter below. The antlers are short spikes carried on long hair-covered pedicles prolonged forward as ribs on the face. Muntjac live in dense cover where they are more easily heard than seen, for they utter a short sharp bark repeated many times when disturbed. The Chinese water deer, *Hydropotes inermis*, is slightly larger, reddish to greyish brown, and with large ears; the bucks do not have antlers but long upper canine teeth that project from the mouth as tusks nearly three inches in length. Water deer live among long dense herbage on which they graze – they are less widespread than the muntjac, being feral but numerous in parts of Bedfordshire, Northamptonshire, Buckinghamshire, and Huntingdonshire.

Family Bovidae

Cattle, sheep and goats do not exist in the wild in the British Isles. Wild cattle, from which domestic cattle are descended, have been extinct in Great Britain for some three thousand years – the 'wild' white cattle preserved in several parks are derived from domestic animals. A primitive breed of sheep, the Soay breed, has long been present on the island of the St. Kilda group to which it gives its name meaning 'Sheep island'; it is derived from domestic stock. The 'wild' goats that are feral on mountains or islands in various parts of the British Isles are derived from domestic animals, for the species has never been indigenous. The domestic sheep, however, has played an important part in shaping the ecological background of the British fauna, much of our so-called man-made landscape being in fact a sheep-moulded landscape.

In the chapters that follow we consider the biology of this mammalian fauna, enquire into its origin and present distribution, and investigate the way of life of its various members, and how it shares the approximately 75 million acres of its homeland with over fifty million human beings.

CHAPTER 2

ICE AGES

THE small number of mammalian species now living in the British Isles is sometimes spoken of as an impoverished fauna. This is not strictly correct; it is a small fauna compared with those of some other lands, but of the forty-six indigenous species only five have been exterminated in historic times, whereas fourteen that are not indigenous have been introduced and now permanently enrich it. The causes of the present composition and distribution of our indigenous mammalian fauna must be sought in the geological history of the islands.

The basic geological structure of the country has evolved through enormous periods of time during which the rocks were laid down as deposits on the floors of successive seas, or extruded through the earth's crust by volcanic activity. If we could see from a satellite the events forming the present topography of the earth as in a time-lapse film, so that many millions of years were concentrated into an hour, the tortured crust would appear to be in constant movement, writhing and squirming as immense forces distorted it. The tectonic plates jostling each other or drawing apart to form the oceans, pushed asunder by the material rising between them from below, were sometimes sunk far beneath the sea from which they received deposits of enormous thickness, or thrust up into mountains and lands from which erosion carried their substance back to the oceans – everything was, and still is, in constant flux. During all these upheavals plants and animals were evolving ever since life first appeared on the earth some time in the Precambrian epoch, perhaps as much as three thousand million years ago.

The successive epochs into which palaeontologists divide geological history each had their characteristic faunas and floras which left their remains as fossils in the rocks, representing a biomass, or aggregate of living matter, so great that it is almost beyond comprehension to the human mind. Among this teeming swarm the mammal-like creatures first appeared in the Triassic epoch, which began some 225 million years ago; but ten million years were to pass before the Eutheria, the placental mammals, evolved towards the end of the Cretaceous epoch. In the succeeding Eocene epoch, which began about seventy million years ago, the orders of mammals that we know as living animals were already differentiated together with others that are now extinct.

During the following epochs, the Oligocene and the Miocene, in which great crustal disturbance took place, including the upraising of the great mountain ranges, the evolution of the mammals produced a vast variety of forms which reached a peak in numbers before the end of the Miocene some twelve million years ago. In the succeeding Pliocene, which lasted about ten million years, the land masses gradually took on their present shapes, and mammalian species began to decline in number, a decline that continues to the present day. Throughout these epochs the climate varied from time to time, sometimes temperate, at others cool and wet, or warm and arid, but it was not until the Pleistocene that the greatest climatic change in later geological history took place.

The Pleistocene epoch was comparatively short; it has been deeply studied using modern techniques during the last fifty years so that our knowledge of it increases every day. It was formerly thought to have lasted about a million years, but is now known to have been probably twice as long – some authorities consider it to have lasted as much as three million years. It is popularly called the 'Ice Age', a name that over-simplifies the matter, for the ice ebbed and flowed so that mild periods of sometimes almost tropical warmth, separated successive glaciations. At its height ice sheets covered most of Europe, North America and northern Asia, while another covered Antarctica, as it still does.

It was in 1837 that Louis Agassiz, the Swiss and later American geologist and zoologist, first drew attention to the evidence that glaciers had once covered much of the land, evidence which he had discovered in 1836 on his field excursions in search of fossil fishes.[4] His views were adopted by the Reverend Dr William Buckland F.R.S., Canon of Christ Church and Professor of Geology at Oxford, later Dean of Westminster, the English pioneer geologist and palaeontologist. He found similar evidence in the British Isles, especially the grooves and scratches scored in rock surfaces of the north, over which glacial ice had flowed engraving the substrate with the burins of its entrapped stones.[28]

Buckland was the first President of the British Association for the

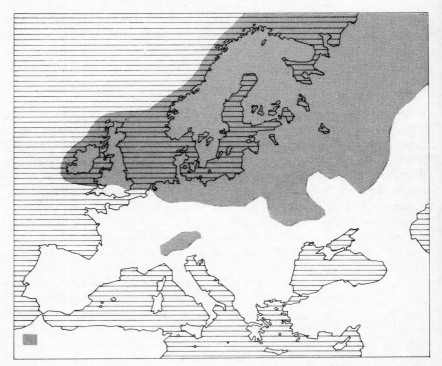

Fig. 2. Position of the ice edge at maximum cover of Eurasian glaciation during the Anglian glaciation of the British Isles.

Advancement of Science, and when he addressed the 'British Ass' on the subject of glaciation one of his waggish friends drew a caricature of the great man standing on a surface covered with glacial scoriations while at his feet lay two pebbles, one of them labelled 'specimen no. 1, scratched by a glacier thirty-three thousand three hundred and thirty-three years before the creation'; the other, 'no. 2, scratched by a cart wheel on Waterloo bridge the day before yesterday.'

As with all new theories before they become accepted as established truth, the glacial theory at first met with much opposition as well as ridicule – indeed Buckland himself at first strongly disagreed, and it was only during a tour of Scotland in company with Agassiz in 1840 that he was convinced. Thereafter he has strongly supported the theory and, through the evidence of glacial action on polished and scoriated rocks and the presence of morraines, most of the leading geologists of the day agreed with him. He was also the first to suggest that the famous parallel roads of Glenroy in Scotland were the former shore lines of a glacial lake formed by the damming of Glen Spean by two glaciers coming down the north and east sides of Ben Nevis.

The knowledge that the country, and later that all countries on both sides of the north Atlantic, had once been in the grip of an Ice Age stimulated geologists to more detailed research, and it soon became apparent that there had been not one Ice Age but several. The difficulties of identifying and dating them were enormous, because younger glaciations are bound to disturb, distort, and confuse the traces of older ones, as are denudation, erosion, and changes of sea level in the often long intervals between them. Local variations in the extent and intensity of glaciation further complicate the problem.

The basic pattern of the successive glaciations in Europe was appropriately worked out by investigating the glaciations of the Alps, where Agassiz had first discovered evidence of the 'Ice Age'. About the beginning of this century Penck & Brückner[122], after prolonged study of the gravel terraces laid down by rivers rushing forth from beneath the melting glaciers, concluded that there had been four main ice ages separated by long interglacial periods when the land was free from ice-cover and the climate was comparatively warm. They named the four glaciations after rivers flowing down from the Austrian alps to southern Germany, in the valleys of which they examined the fluvioglacial gravels and moraines; the oldest they named Günz, and the succeeding ones Mindel, Riss and Würm.

The last glaciation, the Würm, reached its peak about 20,000 years ago, but it was not so severe or long-lasting as some preceeding ones. During the Mindel glaciation the ice sheets reached their greatest size and covered an enormous area of Europe, much more extensive than that covered in the later Riss and Würm stages. The interglacial stage between the decline of the Mindel and the onset of the Riss lasted nearly a quarter of a million years, during which a contemporary intelligence might have thought that ice ages had gone never to return. Although the Günz was designated the oldest or first glaciation, there are now known to be indications of numerous glaciations older still, hence the differences of opinion between authorities on the probable length of the Pleistocene epoch. There cannot, in any case, have been any sharply defined boundary between the Pliocene and the Pleistocene, for the whole of geological and biological evolution is a continuous process. The boundaries between all the geological epochs are arbitrary, and are used merely as a convenience with the tacit admission that they cannot represent any specific moment in time.

The history of the Pleistocene is, however, by no means the simple and clear cut sequence as might appear from the basic pattern. During glaciations the edges of the ice sheets advance and retreat to different extents and in different places, and during interglacial periods they re-advance from place to place and retire again in an unending chain of fluctuations that bring variations in topography, climate, flora and fauna. Furthermore, the sequence worked out for the glaciations of the Alps may not correspond exactly with those found elsewhere.

Geologists of many lands studying the glaciations and alternating interglacial periods of the Pleistocene in their own countries have gone deeply into the problems of correlating their local findings with the basic alpine pattern. A general measure of success has been achieved in this though much detail remains obscure, and the sequences in Scandinavia and northern Europe and in North America are found to correspond reasonably closely. They are, as well, found to correspond with the pluvial sequences found in land further south which, though never covered with ice sheets, experienced periods of high rainfall when the ice held more northern latitudes in its grip.

Although the pattern of successive glaciations in the Alps corresponds roughly with that of other parts of Europe and elsewhere, it is in some ways a special case. Even at the maximum of glaciation when a continuous sheet of ice blanketed northern Europe and Asia and covered the British Isles and the site of the North Sea, the ice cap over the Alps was separate and not continuous with the great ice sheet. The causes of the glaciations were similar for both regions but the effects were subject to local variations; consequently the nomenclature for the Alpine glaciations is now applied less uniformly to those of regions further north, including the British Isles.

The difficulty of making exact correlations between Pleistocene events in different places has been resolved by classifying them according to local stratigraphy. Pleistocene deposits, both those of glacial and interglacial stages, are not continuous, and the geologists have to put together the history of the epoch from the examination of scattered and limited samples from many different places. The glacial and interglacial stages are named after the places where well-known deposits of each stage have been studied, and consequently the nomenclature for north western Europe differs from that for the Alps, and from that for the British Isles. Thus the last or Würm glaciation of the Alps corresponds to the Weichselian glaciation of north-western Europe, and the Devensian of the British Isles.

In the British Isles many of the typical pleistocene sites are found in East Anglia and take their names from nearby towns and villages of Norfolk, Suffolk and Essex. The last glaciation however takes its name from the Devenses, the ancient British tribe that lived over 50,000 years later in the area including Four Ashes in Staffordshire, the typical site.[128] The succession of deposits is not complete, so that information is lacking about the earliest Pleistocene, and for a period of about a million years in the middle Pleistocene. In spite of these gaps the deposits indicate alternating colder and warmer phases but give no unequivocal evidence of glaciation, with ice sheets covering much of the country, until comparatively late in the epoch when ice cover reached its maximum during the Anglian glaciation, corresponding with the Elster glaciation of northwest Europe and the Mindel of the Alps.

Conditions immediately after the end of the Pliocene, some two to two-and-a-half million years ago, are imperfectly known but there appears to have been a cold stage at first, represented by the Nodule Bed at the base of the Red Crag deposits of East Anglia. A gap in the record of nearly half a million years is then followed by an alternation of two warm and two cold stages represented by pre-glacial deposits of the lower Pleistocene. These are the Ludhamian (Ludham, near Norwich) warm, Thurnian (river Thurn, Norfolk), cold, Antian (river Ant, Norfolk) warm, and Baventian (Easton Bavents, near Southwold, Suffolk) cold. At the end of the Baventian stage another gap in the record lasting about a million years is followed by the warm Pastonian stage (Paston, near Cromer, Norfolk), the first stage of the middle Pleistocene, about half a million years ago.

The following Beestonian (Beeston, near Dereham, Norfolk) was the first cold stage of the middle Pleistocene and was succeeded by a warm stage, the Cromerian (Cromer, Norfolk), which lasted until the onset of the great glaciation over 450,000 years ago. This, the Anglian glacial stage (East Anglia), lasted between fifty and sixty thousand years and covered the whole of the British Isles as far south as the

Thames with a sheet of ice that produced the greatest glaciation in the whole of the Pleistocene. When the Anglian stage came to an end the land was free of ice for about 185,000 years during the temperate Hoxnian stage (Hoxne, on the Suffolk–Norfolk border near Eye and Diss); in this stage the temperature was at times higher than that of the present day.

The next glaciation, the Wolstonian (Wolston, near Coventry, Warwickshire) lasted some 60,000 years from about 240,000 to 180,000 B.P. The ice cover did not extend as far south as in the Anglian stage; the ice edge ran south from northern Norfolk and then west across the midlands to the mid Welsh border, thence turning south to reach and follow the north coasts of Somerset, Devon and Cornwall. The succeeding Ipswichian (Ipswich, Suffolk) temperate stage lasted about 60,000 years until about 120,000 B.P. when the cold returned with the onset of the last, Devensian, glacial stage in which the ice covered Scotland, northern England, Wales, and most

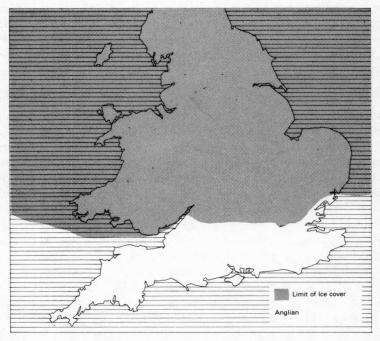

Limit of Ice cover

Anglian

Fig. 3. Limit of ice covering during (a) the Anglian, (b) the Wolstonian and (c) the Devensian glaciations.

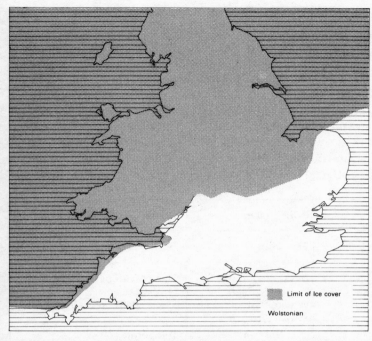

Limit of Ice cover

Wolstonian

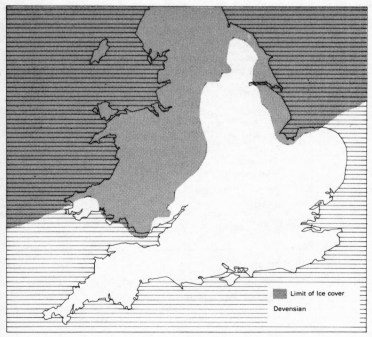

Limit of Ice cover

Devensian

of Ireland. A large area of the midlands and east Yorkshire was thus free from ice cover, though the ice covering the North Sea encroached on the east coast as far south as Norfolk. The ice of the Devensian stage melted comparatively quickly some twelve thousand years ago so that before 10,000 B.P. the post glacial or Flandrian temperate stage was established, which extends to the present day; it takes its name from the transgression of the North Sea over the former dry land bordered by England and Flanders, when the sea level rose as the water from the ice returned to the sea.

In all the glacial stages there were at least two maxima of cold

Epoch	British Isles	Climate
Holocene	Flandrian	Temperate
Upper Pleistocene	Devensian Ipswichian Wolstonian	Glacial with permafrost Temperate Glacial with permafrost
Middle Pleistocene	Hoxnian Anglian Cromerian Beestonian Pastonian	Temperate Glacial with permafrost Temperate Cold with permafrost Warm
Lower Pleistocene	(Gap) (ca. 1 M. years) - - - - - - - - - - - Baventian Antian Thurnian Ludhamian - - - - - - - - - - - (Gap) (ca. ½ M. years)	 Cold with permafrost Temperate Cold Temperate
Pliocene	Waltonian	

Fig. 4. Stages of the Pleistocene in the British Isles.

separated by less cold interstadial intervals, and similarly in the interglacial stages the climate fluctuated between cold, temperate, and warm. The beginnings and ends of the glacial stages were gradual, so that as the ice retreated after a glaciation the land was at first polar desert becoming steppe or tundra as the temperature rose; it was then invaded by open boreal forest with birch and pine dominant, which in turn was replaced by dense deciduous forest with alder, oak, ash and other broad-leaved trees. As a glacial stage approached the succession was reversed.

Apart from the climatic changes correlated with the glaciations and producing their advances and retreats, there were during the Pleistocene great changes in the level of the sea in relation to the land. The enormous masses of water withdrawn from circulation and locked up in the form of ice caused a fall in sea level of many hundreds of feet – indeed, it is reckoned that if all the ice even now in the form of glaciers and ice-caps were to melt the level of the sea would rise about three hundred feet.[155] On the other hand the land is depressed towards sea level during glaciation by the sheer weight of ice resting upon it. At the same time there has been throughout the Pleistocene from time to time a slow upraising or lowering of the land, the eustatic movements of the tectonic plates.

An important consequence of these changes in sea level, whether caused by withdrawal of liquid water or by movement of the land, was that the British Isles were periodically part of the continent of Europe so that they shared its fauna and flora. Thus the bed of the southern part of the North Sea has for long periods been dry land, and the final opening of the Straits of Dover did not come about until some seven thousand years ago. One cannot help wondering whether this was a sudden dramatic happening in some furious equinoctial gale when low atmospheric pressure and a high spring tide combined with a surge such as those that have brought disastrous floods to East Anglia in recent times, broke the crumbling barrier and sent the waters of the North Sea pouring over into the English Channel – or whether an unusually high tide crept over a low dune between the salt marshes on each side so that the waters met and mixed with so little fuss that no one would have noticed.

The connection with the continent facilitated the return of the flora and fauna after it had been exterminated by each glaciation. At the time of the greatest glaciation some 450,000 years ago an unbroken sheet of ice covered the whole of northern Europe, including the

British Isles, except southern England south of a line joining the Thames to the mouth of the Severn.[61] The part left free of ice was deeply covered with winter snow, and the sea was full of floating ice. It is doubtful if any of the flora or fauna was able to live there; certainly no mammals could survive, and consequently our present fauna must have arrived after the ice of the great glaciation retreated.

Subsequent glaciations were less extensive so that the midlands as far north as York and the southern part of Ireland were free of ice and provided a possible habitat for those species that could withstand the arctic or subarctic conditions. The changes in flora and fauna are sometimes spoken of as retreats to more congenial climates in the south during the glaciations – the distribution of the plants and animals retreated, but there was no physical movement of individuals, they were merely killed. The return during interglacials was different; the flora gradually spread in by the usual manner of seed dispersal, but the animals and especially the mammals did move in 'on the hoof', not as mass migrations but in the course of populations extending their ranges under pressure of numbers as new habitats became available.

The amount of extermination among the mammalian species even in the last glaciation, which did not blanket the whole of the British Isles and ended some twelve to ten thousand years ago, is shown by comparing the 167 species of land mammal now living in western Europe with the 41 of Great Britain and the 21 of Ireland.[151] Our fauna is not so much 'impoverished' as incomplete; there was not a long enough period of time before the breaching of the Straits of Dover for more species to extend their range into the islands. As H. W. Bates, the naturalist of the Amazon and later for many years secretary of the Royal Geographical Society, said in 1878, the British Isles are 'a half starved fragment of the Palaearctic'.[18]

Many methods are now used for dating the events of the Pleistocene: geological methods such as the study of varves, the annual variation in the composition of deposits giving laminated sediments in freshwater lakes; investigation of the palaeomagnetism of rocks; and chemical methods such as radio-carbon dating of organic material derived from living organisms, and potassium-argon dating for older rocks. But in tracing the changes in the composition of the flora and fauna the discovery and study of the fossil or subfossil remains of the plants and animals themselves provides the most important evidence. If the horizons in which mammalian remains are recovered are accurately recorded it is possible to know the composition of the fauna from time to time, and to infer much about the conditions of the environment – when, for example, hippopotamuses lived in the Thames before the Devensian glaciation the climate was, presumably, much warmer than at present.

On the other hand the presence of various species of elephant need not of necessity imply that the climate was warm; the order Proboscidea, now reduced to only two species facing extermination in the not too distant future, was once numerous in species some of which were no doubt able to live in temperate or even cold climates provided there was sufficient vegetation for their food – it does not follow that all were warm climate creatures because their living relatives are. Indeed the mammoth, which was clothed in a warm coat of shaggy hair, was an inhabitant of cold regions. Similarly the woolly rhinoceros, which also had long hair, was present with the mammoth in the last cold interstadial of the Devensian glaciation.[155] But hair on rhinoceroses does not imply that the animals live in cold climates for the hairiest of the living species, the Asiatic two-horned rhinoceros, lives in tropical south east Asia.

The hair sticking to the frozen remains of mammoths found in Siberia is red, but may have been darker or brown in life, for the pigments in long-preserved hair, especially when buried, undergo a change towards an auburn red – the hair of Egyptian mummies often has this tinge. The hair of Ben Jonson, who died in 1637, was found to be red when his skull with hair still attached was exposed in 1859 during the reburial in Westminster Abbey of the remains of John Hunter, the surgeon and anatomist.[26] When the skull of Sir Thomas Browne, who died in 1682, was exhumed in 1840 the hair associated with it was 'of a fine auburn colour'; before it was re-interred in the chancel of St Peter Mancroft, Norwich, in 1927 it was examined at the Royal College of Surgeons by H.L. Tildesley,[144] who remarked that 'hair of persons long buried is commonly found to have acquired a reddish tinge, whatever the original shade.'

Our most detailed knowledge of the composition of the flora and the nature of the climate, at different times during the Pleistocene is, however, derived from the study of fossil pollen, a technique now known as palynology. In addition, a study of peat, freshwater and marine molluscan shells, and of insects, especially the wing covers of beetles, has thrown much light on the changes in climate.

The outer layers of a pollen grain are made of the substance *sporopollenin* which, unlike the inner cellulose layers, is extremely resistant to the action of chemical changes so that pollen grains are almost indestructible by natural agencies. Vast quantities of pollen released by plants, and especially those species that are wind-pollenated, became mixed with the soil and waters and included in the deposits and sediments. The surface of pollen grains is thrown into a great range of shapes and patterns that are characteristic of, and identify, the different species; the presence and relative quantities of pollen in any sample of Pleistocene deposit therefore show the presence and relative abundance of the plants from which they were derived. So, for example, a predominance of conifer pollen indicates a cool climate, and a preponderance of oak pollen points to a milder climate. There are, naturally, difficulties in using pollen analysis; pollen can be carried great distances by the wind, and the indestructible nature of the pollen coat itself allows pollen from old deposits to be washed out and included in younger ones. Palynology has nevertheless proved to be one of the most valuable tools in reaching an understanding of the changes during the Pleistocene.

Palynology was born in Denmark and was developed with great success in the British Isles by Sir Harry Godwin and his pupils at Cambridge so that the history of the British flora, and with it that of the environmental ecology, is now better known than that of any other area of similar size.[67] The earlier work of Zeuner[155] on the climate, chronology, and faunal successions of the Pleistocene, not only in the British Isles but throughout the world, was extended in great detail by Charlesworth twelve years later.[33] This immense work summarises and reviews world-wide research on the Pleistocene up to 1956, and discusses all the different theories that have been put forward to explain its occurrence and the fluctuations that took place during it.

Charlesworth points out that terrestrial causes such as deformations of the crust of the earth are not sufficient to have brought about glaciations. He favours the theory that long-term variations in the amount of solar radiation reaching the earth were the probable cause, though it may not be possible to prove their occurrence by direct observation. This hypothesis was first made by Simpson,[130] who suggested that an increase in solar radiation by raising the world temperature intensified the atmospheric circulation, and brought about glaciation by augmenting the amount of cloud and precipi-

tation. Charlesworth points out that glaciation was probably produced by a number of factors, of which variation in solar radiation
was only one, and that meteorological, geological, and astronomical
changes 'all interacting and so delicately balanced that a slight
change, such as would be undetected by less than a century of acute
observation, might induce great effects.'

As an outcome of recent studies it is now widely accepted[87] that
major glaciations are due primarily to the positions of the continents
resulting from continental drift and the movements of the tectonic
plates. Ice ages can only occur when there are land masses in high
latitudes on which ice and snow can accumulate – the condition of the
earth today, with an Antarctic continent and an Arctic sea surrounded by land. With the continents in these positions the
'Milankovitch effect' comes into operation, and small regular
changes in the earth's orbit and orientation towards the sun cause the
rhythmic alternation of glaciations and mild interglacial stages
through the changes in the amount of heat received by high latitudes.
The 'wobbles' in the earth's movements are astronomically predictable, and consequently the sequence of ice ages can be shown to
have occurred many times, probably twenty or more, during the
Pleistocene.[19] Predictions warn that our present interglacial may not
last more than another thousand years until it begins to decline into
the next glaciation, which, at its peak after some 20,000 years will be
more severe than the Devensian.

'Little ice ages', such as the cold period that lasted from about 1650
to 1850, occur at more frequent intervals. They are caused by a
temporary decline in sunspot activity combined with an increase in
terrestrial volcanic activity, which produces a veil of dust in the
atmosphere that reduces the solar heat reaching the earth. Major
glaciations, however, only occur when the earth periodically 'wobbles' to produce the Milankovitch effect.

Whatever the causes of glaciation may be, we may take it as certain
that the present mammalian fauna of the British Isles originated after
the end of the great Anglian glaciation nearly half a million years ago.
Furthermore it seems probable that few species of mammal survived
the Devensian glaciation, during which ice covered the northern part
of the islands, and the southern parts were subjected to a severe
periglacial climate with permafrost producing frost-tundra having
little plant cover. At the end of the Devensian the succeeding

Flandrian post-glacial stage saw the establishment of the mammalian fauna as we see it today, although it is now reduced by the loss of several species that have been exterminated by man.

During the last hundred and fifty years a host of geologists and palaeontologists, amateur and professional, has collected great quantities of mammalian fossils from the Pleistocene deposits, and has worked on the difficult problems of deducing the composition of the faunas of the various stages. The earlier workers did not appreciate the importance of recording the exact horizons at which they found the fossils, and consequently their specimens give less information than those collected by later workers who adopted a stricter discipline. In addition, much material collected on sea beaches came from strata exposed in the cliffs above, and cannot be accurately assigned to the horizon from which it is derived. Similarly fossil and subfossil bones found in caves have frequently been excavated without recording the precise horizon from which they came. The stratigraphy of cave deposits is complicated by the way in which the fossils were included. The remains from which the fossils are derived were often washed in by floods, or carried in by predators, so that specimens of different provenance are confusingly mixed.

The researches of many workers nevertheless combine to give a picture of the succession of faunas that can be accepted with confidence as reasonably accurate. The results are widely scattered throughout a vast literature, but the Monographs of the Palaeontographical Society[120] in which large numbers of mammalian fossils from the Pleistocene have been described and illustrated during the last hundred and thirty years, deserve special notice. Many authorities, too, have gathered the available information together to give an account of the Pleistocene faunas, one of the earliest being Buckland's 'Reliquiae Diluvianae'[27] published in 1823, which described fossils from caves and 'diluvial gravel' as evidence of 'the action of a Universal Deluge'. A later classic is Owen's 'History of British Fossil Mammals and Birds' published in 1846,[118] and from the nature of the material available necessarily dealing mainly with Pleistocene faunas. In contrast a modern synthesis based on the results of researches supported by the latest technologies such as Stuart's review,[136] shows the complexity of the succession of faunas, and the differences in fauna with the alternation of cold and warm, glacial and interglacial stages. The following summary of events is based in part on this important work.

The deposits of the lower Pleistocene are the strata of the Red Crag, with the Norwich Crag lying above them, that cover much of East Anglia. The oldest part of the Red Crag is the Nodule Bed found at its base in several places. All are marine deposits laid down when the sea level was considerably higher than at present, sometimes as much as forty feet. The fossil bones of land mammals found in them must therefore represent animal carcases that were washed into the sea, especially by rivers in flood, and consequently may not be a fair sample of the contemporary fauna. The Red Crag Nodule Bed, however, is derived partly from the breakdown of older rocks and contains the remains of their fossils in addition to its own contemporary ones; some are derived from Pliocene or older formations and are much worn and polished by wave action.

The alternating temperate and cold stages of the pre-glacial Lower Pleistocene occupied about the first three-quarters of the epoch, some one and a half million years, leaving only half or at most three quarters of a million years for the more spectacular events of the Middle and Upper Pleistocene. The flora of the different stages, and consequently the nature of the contemporary climate, are inferred from a study of pollen analyses and the invertebrate and vertebrate faunas. Throughout this immense period of time the fauna appears to have changed little in composition. The mammalian fossils known from the deposits laid down in the British Isles during the Lower Pleistocene include giant beavers, voles, bears, a panda, hyaenas, sabre-toothed and other cats, elephants and mastodons, horses and zebras, a tapir, rhinoceros, deer and oxen, all of extinct species, together with the still existing beaver and red fox.

This list does not represent a large fauna for so long a period of time but when we remember that, with the exception of a few species known from the cave deposits in Dove Holes, Derbyshire, all are from marine deposits, it is not surprising that it is short. The carcases of animals washed into the sea soon decay and disintegrate so that the bones are scattered and the most durable parts, the teeth, are those more likely to be preserved in marine deposits. The Nodule Bed of the Red Crag, as mentioned above, contains a mixture of fossils. We can well imagine the sea eroding the cliffs of Pliocene or earlier epochs, and then rolling and polishing the released fossils on the beach until they were again buried in new deposits, just as today the fossils of the Crag can be found lying loose on the beach. Some of the fossils thus represent animals that were not members of the Lower Pleistocene fauna, for example the tapir, three-toed horse, and the panda.

The Middle Pleistocene began with a temperate stage, the Pastonian, which was followed by a cold subarctic stage, the Beestonian; this gave way to another temperate stage, the Cromerian, which preceeded the onset of widespread glaciation. The deposits of the Pastonian are marine sands and gravels known as the Weybourne Crag, the lower part of which was laid down in the Baventian stage of the Lower Pleistocene. The stages that follow are represented by the Cromer Forest Bed series which includes both marine and freshwater sediments and contains many mammalian fossils. A comparatively large mammalian fauna has been recorded from these beds; some species can be assigned to the cooler or to the temperate stages, but the exact position of many remains doubtful.

The fauna of the temperate Pastonian stage included extinct species of ground squirrel, beaver, voles, mammoth, horse, rhinoceros, deer and bison, as well as the still existing wolf, otter, wild boar and hippopotamus. Some of these species may belong to the succeeding cold Beestonian stage when the ground was frozen with permafrost in places, but it has not been possible to reconstruct the mammalian fauna of the stage; it was probably reduced in variety and confined to arctic species.

The rich fauna of the temperate Cromerian stage has yielded a great quantity of fossils that have been collected and studied for nearly two hundred years. Many of them, however, cannot be assigned to the various zones into which modern research has divided the stage because, as already mentioned, the early collectors did not appreciate the importance of recording the exact horizons from which they took their specimens. The mammals living during this stage included a monkey, many different species of rodent large and small, many carnivores from wolf and red fox to hyaenas, lion and sabre-tooth. The 'big game' were well represented with elephants and mammoth, horses and zebras, rhinoceros, wild boar and hippopotamus, giant and smaller deer, bison, aurochs, musk ox and sheep.

Some of the species of this extensive list are typical of colder climates such as the ground squirrel, pine vole, glutton, and musk ox; and others of warmer ones such as the monkey, spotted hyaena and hippopotamus. The majority, on the other hand, are species that might live under a temperate climate like that of the present day in the British Isles. When the Cromerian stage drew towards its end the climate became cooler, and mixed oak forest was replaced by boreal forest with pines and birch, and with open heaths, until the Anglian glacial stage wiped out most of the flora and probably all of the mammalian fauna. The history of the present mammalian fauna of the British Isles must therefore start at the end of the Anglian glaciation, which wiped the slate clean for a new start, leaving us only a few tons of fossil bones from which to infer what had gone before.

It is not surprising that hardly any mammalian fossils are known from the Anglian glaciation, for at its severest the southern part of the country, the only part that was not covered by the deep ice sheet, was an arctic desert. The few that have been found are assigned to the early or late parts of the stage when glaciation was developing or retreating – a ground squirrel to the former and the red deer to the latter. As, furthermore, no vertebrate fossils of other classes are known from the Anglian the conclusion that the glaciation exterminated the entire mammalian fauna is inescapable. The deposits of the Anglian stage are a complicated series of tills, including the Boulder Clay, produced by the ice moving in different directions at different times as the glaciation proceeded.

When the ice at last retreated the temperate flora and fauna of the Hoxnian stage gradually moved in from the continent as the desert gave way to tundra, then to boreal forest followed by mixed oak forest. The fossils of this interglacial stage are preserved mainly in freshwater deposits, though some marine and estuarine deposits exist from its later part. It was during this stage, too, that man first made his way into the British Isles, for his palaeolithic flint artifacts have been found in several places. The former claim that man had been present at a much earlier time is now discredited – the 'eoliths' from the Crag that were supposed to be primitive tools are no more than fortuitously broken stones. The only skeletal remains of alleged palaeolithic man living in the Hoxnian stage that have been found in the British Isles are some fragments of a skull from the Thames terrace gravel at Swanscombe, Kent. One bit of the skull was found in 1935, another in 1936, and a third in 1955. Although Oakley in 1969[116] tabulated the Swanscombe skull, among the 'early Neanderthaloids' dating from about a quarter of a million years ago, the fragments, the occipital and two parietal bones, are indistinguishable from those of modern man. Since then there has been some controversy about the dating of the Hoxnian interglacial[119, 127]; but a dating of material from 'a few centimetres below' the horizon of the Swanscombe skull gave ages of up to more than 272,000 years.[139] This, unfortunately, does not give irrefutable proof of the age of the skull, and still leaves open the possibility advocated by some that the skull fragments may have become included in the gravel as intrusions at a later date. With the possible exception of the Swanscombe skull, the earliest remains of man in the British Isles, apart from his artifacts, date from the middle of the Devensian glaciation, at least some two hundred thousand years later.

The Hoxnian mammalian fauna that moved in from the continent differed from that of the Cromerian, although many species were the same, or similar, such as the beaver, some voles, the wolf, marten, lion, boar, the straight-tusked elephant *Palaeoloxodon antiquus*, and the red, fallow, and roe deer. New arrivals included the arctic lemming, several voles, the cave bear, two species of rhinoceros replacing *Diceros etruscus*, *Megaceros giganteus* replacing several other species of giant deer, and the aurochs. Those that did not return, or were by then extinct, included the vole genus *Mimomys*, the sabre-tooth, the southern elephant, etruscan rhinoceros, hippopotamus, zebrine horses, several species of deer, giant deer, and elks, the bison and musk ox.

When the climate became colder with the onset of the Wolstonian glaciation which reached its peak about 140,000 years ago, the fauna became more typically arctic, and those parts of the country not covered with ice were inhabited by hamsters, the arctic, Norway and steppe lemmings, the woolly mammoth, *Mammuthus primigeneus*, the woolly rhinoceros, *Coelodonta antiquitatis*, and the reindeer *Rangifer tarandus*.

At the end of the Wolstonian stage, about 120,000 years ago, the temperate Ipswichian interglacial stage began and lasted about 50,000 years. The climate and flora followed the usual sequence of an interglacial stage, the temperature reaching a peak higher, however, than that of the present day, and the flora progressing from arctic tundra to boreal forest, mixed oak forest and then regressing by similar steps to the onset of the next glaciation. Mammalian remains of the Ipswichian occur in river and lake gravels, muds, and brick earths, and in the deposits of some caves. Many of the mammals are species that form part of our present day fauna, and include the bank, water and field voles, the wood mouse, the red fox, badger, and wild cat, the red, fallow and roe deer; and some extinct only in historic times such as the beaver, wolf, brown bear, wild boar and aurochs.

The cooler parts of the stage were also marked by the presence of ground squirrels, the woolly mammoth and the musk ox, whereas the warmer parts supported the spotted hyaena, the lion, the straight-tusked elephant, two kinds of rhinoceros, the giant deer, and the hippopotamus, the last indicating a comparatively high temperature as does the presence of the European pond-tortoise *Emys orbicularis*. Palaeolithic man, as shown solely by his artifacts, was present throughout the stage.

The following Devensian glaciation began about 70,000 years ago and lasted nearly sixty thousand years until it came to an end rather quickly about 10,000 years ago. It was the least severe of the three great glaciations as it left southern England and the midlands free of ice and thus a possible habitat for many species that can withstand a cold climate. During this stage the sea fell some three hundred feet below its present level so that England was widely connected with the continent over the site of the southern part of the North Sea, and northern Ireland was narrowly connected with southern Scotland. Stuart[136] remarks that the vast majority of Pleistocene vertebrate remains found in the British Isles, excluding post-glacial material, is probably of Devensian age. Most of the remains are found in river gravels and caves, some of the later ones in lake sediments. The flora of the ice-free regions was mostly tundra or open grassland, with some patches of boreal forest during short interstadial recessions of glaciation.

The fauna is typical of cold regions, though it includes some species of our present fauna such as the common shrew, the bank, water and field voles, the mountain hare, the fox, stoat, polecat, and red deer. Some of the species are not now associated with severely cold climates but nevertheless can withstand more cold than might be supposed; these are the leopard, lion, and spotted hyaena. On the other hand there are many species typical of colder habitats: a pika *Ochotona*, ground squirrel, the arctic lemming, several voles including the northern and tundra voles *Microtus oeconomus* and *M. gregalis*, the arctic fox *Alopex*, polar bear, glutton, woolly mammoth which became extinct at the peak of the glaciation about 18,000 years ago, woolly rhinoceros, reindeer, and musk ox. Several other large mammals left abundant remains in gravel and cave deposits; they include the wolf, the brown and cave bears *Ursus arctos* and *U. spelaeus*, a sabre-tooth *Homotherium*, the horse, giant deer, elk, a bison *Bison priscus*, and the aurochs.

Man returned after the peak of the Devensian glaciation as shown by his artifacts and by a few skeletal remains.[30] Some human teeth of middle Devensian age from Picken's Hole cave in Somerset are the earliest human remains known in the British Isles apart from the Swanscombe skull whose alleged age has been challenged by some people. The largest find of palaeolithic man belongs to the late Devensian deposits of Aveline's Hole in the Mendip Hills of Somerset, where bones representing thirty-one skeletons were excavated.

As the ice melted during the late glacial stage of the Devensian the climate became milder and reached a peak after about a thousand years in the Allerød interstadial or 'amelioration' as it is sometimes called, though amelioration could have a different meaning for a reindeer than for a red deer. Thereafter the climate again became colder until about 10,000 years ago when the ice finally disappeared inaugurating the Flandrian interglacial which has lasted until the present. By the end of the late glacial many of the large mammals had become extinct, although there appears to be no reason why they should not have survived into the Flandrian. Perhaps the change of climate and the resulting changes in vegetation deprived them of their ecological niches, but it is also possible that improved hunting skills of upper palaeolithic man may have overcropped and thus exterminated them. The few species not part of our present mammalian fauna that survived from the late glacial disappeared in the early part of the Flandrian, which is discussed in the next chapter.

CHAPTER 3

THE EVOLUTION OF THE ENVIRONMENT

AT the beginning of the Flandrian stage, when the glaciation started to recede, the climate became warmer and thereafter varied between warmer and cooler so that it is convenient to subdivide the stage according to the prevailing climate of the time. In the first, Pre-boreal, phase the frost tundra of the country south of the ice began to be covered with growths of the dwarf or arctic birch, a shrub with stems and branches generally spreading over the ground and making a bush only a couple of feet or so high in sheltered places; it is a characteristic plant of the arctic and high mountains. It was followed by the tree birches spreading to make a forest so that in the following Boreal phase, when they were joined by pine and hazel, the forest cover was complete. During the Boreal phase the melting of the ice brought a rapid rise in the level of the sea which finally cut through the Strait of Dover about 7,000 years ago, whereas the southern part of the North Sea and eastern end of the English Channel had been dry at the beginning of the Pre-boreal. At the same time the climate became several degrees warmer than at present, producing the Atlantic phase, during which the forest cover was enriched by the addition of oak, and alder. Thereafter the climate became cooler about 4,500 years ago, introducing the Sub-boreal phase, and the forest was further enriched by ash, elm and lime. A minor rise in sea level marked the end of the Sub-boreal phase about 2,250 years ago, and the climate entered the Sub-atlantic phase that we endure at the present day.

At about the end of the Devensian glaciation the upper palaeolithic culture that man had evolved through many grades during the middle Pleistocene, was succeeded by the mesolithic culture charac-terised by the small flint artifacts called 'microliths'. Of the several known mesolithic occupational sites, that at Starr Carr near Scar-borough in Yorkshire has been meticulously excavated by Professor J. Clark and his colleagues, who have been able to draw a picture of the life of the inhabitants, and of the fauna and flora.[35] The site was

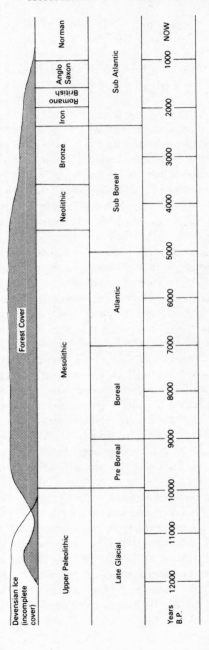

Fig. 5. The Flandrian succession in the British Isles after the ice of the Devensian glaciation melted.

occupied about 9,500 years ago as a winter hunting camp by three or four families of nomadic people; the settlement lay at the edge of a lake in the Vale of Pickering, with closed birch forest on the hill rising behind and willows along the reedy shore. The people lived on a platform of birch brushwood and were occupied not only in hunting and gathering roots of reeds and bog-bean, but also in knapping flint to make tools, some of which were used for making barbed spearheads from slivers cut from the antlers of red deer. The bones and antlers they left on the site show that they lived mostly on the flesh of red deer, but that they also killed roe deer, elk, aurochs and wild boar in lesser numbers. They had no domestic animals, and did not cultivate any crops. The remains of other mammals show that the fauna included the pine marten, fox, wolf, badger, hedgehog, hare and beaver.

This late Pre-boreal fauna shows that forest animals, the deer and aurochs, had replaced the tundra-living mammals such as the reindeer, bison and wild horse while the birch forest increased with the rise in temperature. Until the rise in sea level at the end of the Pre-boreal phase, although Ireland had long been separated from Great Britain, the site of the southern part of the North Sea was dry land with the coast line extending from Flamborough Head to Jutland with a northern loop including the Dogger Bank. At the same time the English Channel extended no further east than Beachy Head.

The mesolithic people remained in occupation for over five thousand years, during which the sea level rose and cut off the British Isles from the continent. About 4,500 years ago the neolithic people arrived, migrating across the sea from the east, and soon completely replaced the mesolithic culture with their own. Throughout the many hundreds of thousands of years of the preceding part of the Pleistocene the palaeolithic and later the mesolithic people were no more than part of the fauna, and produced no appreciable alteration in the environment. They were plant gatherers and hunters and, though they may have contributed towards the extinction of some of the large mammals such as the mammoth, their influence on the composition of the fauna was in general negligible. They probably had to work hard to earn their living in the British Isles, but further south on the continent, where the climate was milder and food abundant, they appear to have satisfied their wants more easily so that they had enough leisure to make paintings on the walls of caves, to make sculptures and carvings, and to engrave stones and bone artifacts with abstract and representational designs.

The neolithic people were altogether different. They were farmers, and brought with them the arts of agriculture and animal husbandry. They found a land covered with forest which had to be cleared to make way for their crops of cereals and flax. Their enterprise began the process of transforming a natural environment to a man-made one, a process which continues to the present day. They made their clearings by burning the forest, and as the population grew the scale of clearing increased with it, and continued to increase throughout the ensuing bronze age that replaced the neolithic culture about four thousand years ago, and lasted about 1,500 years. This must have been a period of peace and prosperity, for it was then that the numerous hill-top settlements were set up, culminating in such stupendous constructions as Maiden Castle in Dorset, and religious or cultural centres as Stonehenge, Avebury, Silbury Hill, and many more. The hill-top settlements or 'camps' were probably not built for warlike purposes in the first place but rather as agricultural cities, in which the inhabitants corralled their flocks and herds so that they should not stray over an unenclosed countryside, and in which they stored their harvested crops. The labour needed to build such enormous structures must have been immense and could not have been devoted to such work unless the country enjoyed a state of settled peace. The skill in design, and in the logistics of maintaining so large a labour force, indicate a high degree of prosperity if so many mouths could be fed while so many hands were diverted from the production of food. Conditions probably differed when the spectacular military ramparts of the Iron age were later added to such camps as Maiden Castle.

All through this time, when the climate was in the Sub-boreal phase, the clearing of forest went on, and gradually the upland areas became covered with a thick mantle of blanket bog in place of trees.[112] The blanket bog resulted in the formation of peat dominated by heather over large areas, from much of which it has since been removed by man for use as fuel. With the coming of the iron age about 2,500 years ago, when the climate entered the Sub-atlantic phase, there was a sharp increase in the rate of forest clearance, not only for agriculture but also to provide charcoal for the smelting of iron ore. The clearances thus extended into the valleys from the uplands that had been permanently cleared in neolithic times – the southern downs, the wolds, Salisbury Plain, the Cotswolds, Mendips and the breck district of East Anglia. The growing of cereals, mainly emmer wheat and barley, and the browsing of stock had prevented the regeneration of forest, and produced the cover of upland blanket bogs.

In the Sub-Atlantic period the climate became moister, with lower summer and higher winter temperatures, so that the former dry heaths became waterlogged, and bogs of sphagnum peat developed. The forest cover of oak, alder, birch, elm, beech and lime which replaced the pine forests of the Boreal stage, was progressively destroyed by the action of man so that few if any fragments of it now exist. A few species of plants typical of the arctic, however, survived from the Ipswichian, the last interglacial stage, on refuges that were not covered by ice during the Devensian, and some are said to survive on certain mountain tops to the present day.

While the different types of forest cover crept over the land in response to the changing climatic conditions they were accompanied by a host of herbage and shrub-layer plants that showed similar successions, providing diverse habitats for the different species of mammals. It is doubtful whether any of the indigenous mammals modified these habitats to any great extent. It was man and his domestic animals, with the non-indigenous species that he introduced, that changed the whole appearance of the countryside in the most drastic manner. The changes are, however, comparatively recent and took place mainly in the last two thousand years, from the iron age onwards, though their beginnings were evident nearly two thousand years before in neolithic times.

The evolution of the environment under the influence of man continued with ever increasing speed in the following Romano-British, Anglo-Saxon, and Norman cultural phases. In iron age and particularly Romano–British times there was a great increase in sheep grazing on the cleared uplands, whereas previously the important domestic animals were cattle and swine, both species characteristic of woodlands. The sheep flocks increased in subsequent periods until wool became England's staple trade in mediaeval times; as a consequence the character of the vegetation of much of the country was determined by sheep, together with the rabbit which is believed to have been introduced in Norman times. Both species graze herbage close to the ground and both prevent the regeneration of woodland cover by destroying tree seedlings.

Romano-British times saw the beginning of the draining of the marshy and swampy lowlands, not, however, for agricultural but for military purposes. The draining of the fens and meres for agriculture and the building of sea-defences, with the reclamation of coastal lowlands, came later and culminated in the great drainage works of the seventeenth century, which have continued to the present. One of the largest man-made changes in the environment was caused by the extensive extraction of peat in East Anglia during mediaeval times, which resulted in the formation of the broads of Norfolk and Suffolk.

The enclosure of fields with hedges or dry walls began on a small scale at an early date, as shown by the still recognisable 'celtic' lynchets, and was more commonly practiced in the east than the west, but over much of the country the open field system of agriculture persisted until the great enclosures of the second half of the eighteenth century and the beginning of the nineteenth. Before the enclosure acts were passed wide areas of heath or waste, over which commoners held grazing and turbary rights, existed alongside the open fields divided into strips only by the plough.

The great improvement in roads that came with the introduction of the turnpike system and the innovations of John McAdam was contemporary with the enclosures, as was the building of the great network of canals that was soon to be made obsolete by the invention of railways with steam traction. All these alterations of the environment modified existing habitats or provided new ones; far from reducing wild animal populations they often produced conditions favourable to their growth and extension.

Man and his domestic animals by shaping the environment have thus produced a great variety of habitats, making a system much more complex than that existing naturally before the interference began. The forest cover, broken by swamps and fens in low-lying areas, has been replaced by open agricultural land with woods and copses scattered through it in much of England, whereas formerly the extensive general forest was interrupted only by scattered grassy glades in which wild cattle, and later domestic cattle, grazed. The hills of Wales, the north, and of Scotland, now covered by rough grazing, heather moors, and peat, were also formerly densely forested, as is shown by the stumps and roots of pine trees still exposed in many places where the surface soil is eroded. Although the character of the environment is man-made it cannot be correct to regard it as unnatural, for man is surely as much a part of nature as any other member of the fauna. We do not, for example, think of the changes made in plant cover beneath the trees of a heronry or roost of starlings as unnatural – nor the destruction or distortion of tree growth by deer using young trees as fraying stocks for their antlers – the changes made by man may be larger and more far-reaching but they are not unnatural although they are artificial.

The great diversity of habitats makes a formidable problem for the ecologist trying to define the relationships of animals to their environment – how is he to understand the implications for the fauna of such habitats as bare hill and mountain, conifer and deciduous forest or woodland, meadow, pasture and arable land, hedgerows and plantations, still and running freshwaters, and the sea-shore? Similar problems face the botanists, who were the first to make an

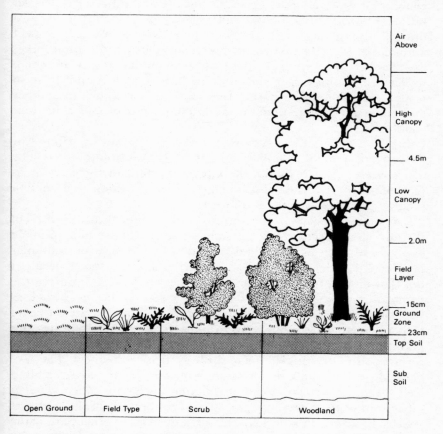

Fig. 6. The classification of the Terrestrial System (modified from P.N. Ferns).

attempt at arranging plant communities in systematic order; the classic study being the comprehensive volume written by A.G. Tansley in 1939.[140] The work by C. Elton, of equal value on the ecology of animals, appeared in 1966, embodying the experience and considered opinions of a lifetime of study, bringing an ordered arrangement to the immense complexity of eco-systems.[58] It has been well summarised for the study of mammals by P.N. Ferns.[60]

The appearance of the countryside is determined by its topography, the nature of the underlying geological formations, and the character of the plant cover which is itself governed by these basic factors. The different kinds of habitat can therefore be mapped geographically, and that generally means according to the vegetation. Elton divided habitats into seven main systems, each subdivided into smaller categories, so that the habitat of any species of animal can be referred to with precision. This classification serves excellently when we are dealing with small animals, especially small invertebrates, but larger and more mobile animals do not fit in so neatly because by their nature they can move from one to another and make use of more than one at different times or under different conditions.

Elton's seven habitat systems are the Subterranean, High Air, Terrestrial, General, Domestic, Aquatic and Transition systems. The Terrestrial system is by far the most important of them as far as mammals are concerned, though none of them is without mammalian inhabitants at some time or another.

The Subterranean system consists of all habitats below the level of the subsoil; in practice they are mainly natural caves and man-made excavations such as mines, adits, and wells. No British mammals permanently inhabit the Subterranean system, but those species of bat that hibernate in caves are temporary residents in it during the winter months. Some individuals of some species, however, such as the whiskered and pipistrelle bats use the less deep parts of caves rather irregularly throughout the year. Many invertebrates are permanent inhabitants of this system, and a few live far below the surface as an interstitial fauna in the interstices of the rocks. They are generally minute aquatic forms; an interesting example is the blind well-shrimp *Niphargus aquilex*, that often comes to notice when it moves out of the interstices into the waters of wells in the southern parts of England, and the 'lavants' of Hampshire. In other parts of the world the Subterranean system is used for dens by larger animals such as hyaenas and wintering bears.

No animal permanently inhabits the High Air system which is used during the migration of some flying animals, from bats and birds down to the minute insects and other arthropods sometimes called the aerial plankton. The High Air is also used by vultures and storks when soaring while searching the ground for food. The lower air immediately above the other systems is not included in the High Air system.

The General system contains a number of special, usually small habitats, most of which can also be classified in one of the other systems. They are for the greater part inhabited by small invertebrates but are not thereby irrelevant to mammals because some species form part of the food of small mammals. Nearly all habitats of the General system are those of decay and biodegradation, the final stages of the recycling of energy universal in the living world. Such habitats are dead wood and other rotting plant materials, the faeces of larger animals, the dead bodies of animals, the fruiting bodies of the larger fungi, and the debris in the nests and burrows of all kinds of animals. Perhaps the smallest of such habitats is a small animal itself which forms the habitat for its load of external and internal parasites.

The Domestic system consists of habitats produced by man for his own direct use, such as houses and other buildings, sewers, and cultivated gardens. In the British Isles, as we have seen, nearly the whole of the country has been transformed from its pristine condition by man, so that it is often difficult to define the bounds of the Domestic system – even such typical features of the countryside as hedgerows are human artifacts. It is necessary therefore to restrict the Domestic system to urban areas and the immediate surroundings of buildings. The mammals that inhabit this system are the commensals and domestic pests of man, the most closely restricted to it being the house mouse and the brown and black rats of the towns; in rural areas the first two species are more loosely associated with this system, for in summer both house mice and brown rats often live away from man's buildings. On the other hand such typically outside species as the wood and yellow-necked mice come into buildings in search of food and shelter at some times of the year. Some bats, too, are permanent inhabitants of the Domestic system, when they are not in flight hunting for their food; the pipistrelle and whiskered bats may have permanent homes in crevices in roof spaces or the masonry of buildings. Although this is true of some individuals it does not hold for the species as a whole because others may inhabit the subterranean and terrestrial systems, thus showing that the larger or more mobile an animal is the better it is able to adapt to different habitats.

A similar qualification applies to the mammals that inhabit the Aquatic system, which includes all bodies of water, fresh, salt, or brackish, flowing or still. The mammals that inhabit this sytem are those that find their food in it, for all of them except the cetacea and sirenia come onto land for breeding and resting – the whales, dolphins, and the sea-cows are the only mammals that spend their whole life in the Aquatic system. In the British Isles most of the mammals inhabiting this system live in the freshwater formation, only the grey and common seals, and sometimes the otter, living in the sea. Although the freshwater species find some or much of their food in the water they are by no means closely confined to the Aquatic system for all of them breed in the Terrestrial system, and some of them are commonly to be found far from water. Even such a typically aquatic animal as the water shrew has been trapped constantly in hedgerows hundreds of yards from the nearest pond or ditch, and the introduced coypu has become an agricultural pest in East Anglia by devouring crops of sugar beet and brassicas well away from its aquatic habitat. Similarly the water vole feeds much on land, grazing the grass at the sides of rivers and ditches, in the banks of which it makes its burrows.

All these animals spend much of their lives in the Transition system, the zone between the water and the dry land, consisting of the shore and beach, both covered by water at times of flood or flood tide. Swamps and salt marshes also belong to this system, and are equally liable to periodic alternating inundation and desiccation. Many animals, particularly among the invertebrates, are confined to habitats in the Aquatic or Transition systems, but all our freshwater aquatic mammals are highly mobile and can move into or out of them or the adjoining Terrestrial system whenever they choose – or, more strictly, whenever they are stimulated to do so by changing conditions either in their surroundings or within their own bodies.

The Terrestrial system is by far the most important one for mammals in the British Isles; most of the mammals live in dry-land habitats, and even the aquatic ones, as we have seen, spend much of their lives in it. All the habitat systems are subdivided to enable the habitat of any particular species to be exactly defined. The subdivisions of the systems considered above have not been discussed because most of our mammalian fauna inhabits the Terrestrial system, and although those subdivisions are important in relation to other animals they are of little concern to most of our mammals.

The Terrestrial system is divided into four Formation types which are distributed geographically or horizontally. Open ground consists of those areas bare of vegetation or with scanty or scattered plant cover less than 15 centimetres (6 inches) in height. It occurs on some mountain tops and similar places with harsh conditions, and is typical of much of the land of the high Arctic. The Field type of formation consists of all arable land, grassland and heath – the greater part of the lowlands of the British Isles, and much of the hill country as well. It is defined as carrying plant cover of herbage not exceeding two metres (six feet) in height, though it may have taller scattered shrubs. The Scrub formation is dominated by the presence of small trees and shrubs not exceeding 4.5 metres (fifteen feet) in height. The scrub cover may or may not be continuous, and where it is not the spaces are occupied by herbage that may be anything up to two metres (six feet) or more in height. The Woodland formation consists of trees the tops of which form a high canopy that may be open or closed depending on how closely the trees are spaced. The high canopy contains everything above 4.5 metres (fifteen feet) from the ground, and may extend up to twenty metres (sixty feet) and more. Where the high canopy is open there is often below it a low canopy of younger trees and shrubs from six to fifteen feet in height, or where this is absent, herbage up to six feet high.

The four formation types divide the Terrestrial system horizontally but in a three-dimensional world, they must be further subdivided vertically. Starting at the bottom, the Subsoil extends from the underlying rocks of the Subterranean system to about 23 centimetres (nine inches) below the surface of the ground. The roots of trees and of herbaceous plants with tap-roots penetrate this zone but otherwise it is comparatively sterile. It is used by the larger burrowing mammals such as the rabbit and fox whose burrows extend into it, but the deepest digger is the badger which excavates extensive sets far below the surface, and often throws out surprisingly large quantities of spoil. The Topsoil, some 23 centimetres (nine inches) thick, overlies the Subsoil and, from the high proportion of humus that it contains, is the fertile layer; its quality determines the productivity of the plant cover rooted in it. Thus old arable and garden land that has been manured and tilled for centuries has a high content of humus which gives the crumbly structure known as 'good tilth', thus providing a suitable seed bed and growing medium for man's crops. On low lying ground the old but now less common practice of flooding watermeadows in the winter left a deposit of fertilising silt that produced a lush crop of hay or grazing in the summer.

Another important matter affecting the soil layers of the Field type of formation in the British Isles is the artificial drainage imposed by man. In crude form this has been provided by ditches for many centuries, but the necessity for adequate drainage to prevent water-logging and consequent exclusion of air was widely recognised only in the first half of the nineteenth century. The extensive drainage operations undertaken in the 1830s and 1840s brought great areas of unthrifty land into production; a perusal of Hoskyns' anonymously published 'Talpa, or the Chronicles of a Clay Farm' brings out the importance that land drainage then attained.[84] Thorough drainage incurred the laying of unglazed earthenware pipes about a metre (yard) beneath the surface in the subsoil – less permanent drains were made with brushwood, and the modern mole-drain which cuts an unlined hole at a similar depth achieves the same end. This unseen system of drainage channels has a widespread and profound effect on the ecology of much of the countryside, and in particular the Field type of formation. The larger mammals whose burrows extend into the subsoil naturally have to pass through the topsoil to reach it, but the smaller burrowers are confined to the topsoil. The smaller rodents, the mice, rats, and voles, seldom penetrate the base of the topsoil, and the mole lives in it permanently. The mole too, gains from man's drainage works, for it cannot dig its system of deeper burrows in permanently waterlogged soil.

Above the surface of the soil the first 15 centimetres (six inches) of space, generally covered with low herbage or litter, forms the Ground zone in which the great majority of our mammals spend most of their lives, some of the smaller ones being almost confined to it and seldom leaving it. The Ground zone gives varied habitats, for the cover of low herbage may lie below higher growths, and in the scrub and woodland types of formation much of it is covered with debris derived from the shrubs and trees. The litter layer of dead leaves makes a habitat where insectivores and small rodents find much of their food. Although the Ground zone provides the main habitat for most British species of mammal, some of them make excursions into the layers above. The first of these, the Field layer, extends upwards for two metres (six feet), its upper limit thus coinciding with the top of the tallest herbage in the Field, Scrub, and Woodland systems. Some of the small rodents such as the wood mouse, the dormouse, and the bank vole spend much of their time in this layer, and the harvest mouse makes it its main habitat during the summer.

Above the Field layer the low canopy extends from two to 4.5 metres (six to fifteen feet) above the ground surface, reaching the top of the shrubs forming the Scrub formation and the top of the smaller trees and shrubs in the Woodland formation. The bank vole, the dormouse, and the edible dormouse commonly extend their activities into this layer. The High canopy, extending 4.5 metres (fifteen feet) upwards to the tops of the tallest trees, is inhabited by fewer species of mammal, chiefly by the red and grey squirrels. Some of the carnivorous mammals also commonly enter and seek their prey in the low and even high canopy layers; the pine marten is a most agile climber and sometimes makes its breeding nest in disused dreys of squirrels or nests of large birds, and the stoat, an equally adept climber, often has its breeding nest high above the ground in a hollow tree trunk or among the heavy growth of ivy clinging to it. The Air Above the canopy is that close to it, used by some species of bat in foraging, and lying below the indefinite lower boundary of the High Air system.

Elton uses certain qualifiers to define habitats more precisely within the systems and formation types described above. In the Terrestrial system the formations are generally not sharply de-markated from each other, but gradually merge together. Thus the qualifying label 'edge' is used for the transition zones between woodland and scrub, scrub and field, and field and open ground. It is the equivalent on a smaller scale within the Terrestrial system of the Transition system between Terrestrial and Aquatic systems. Hed-gerows, which form a characteristic and important subdivision of the Terrestrial system are designated as such for convenience, though Elton regards them fundamentally as Scrub-edge between the Scrub and Field formations.

Additional qualifiers applied to Woodland and Scrub formations denote the dominant kinds of trees or shrubs – Deciduous, Conifer, or Mixed. For Open ground and Field formations qualifiers denote the nature of the soil and underlying rock, Acid for the grass and heathlands on acid soils, and Non-acid for the grasslands over basic and neutral rocks such as clays, chalk, or limestone. Coastal areas of these formations that are or have been affected by the sea are qualified as Maritime, such as cliff-tops where the vegetation is modified as a result of blown spray, and so on. The application of the qualifier Arable is obvious, but it also includes leys of grassland that are sown crops and not permanent pasture.

The classification of habitats not only gives a convenient way for recording observations but gives the possibility of treating the information gathered statistically, though attempts at forcing an essentially inexact science such as biology into a mathematical straight-jacket do not always provide results as satisfactory as might be desired. The smaller animals, especially many invertebrates, do fit neatly into one of the defined habitats, but the larger and more mobile higher vertebrates such as birds and mammals which are versatile and adaptable are not so closely confined. Although many of our mammals have preferred or characteristic habitats, few are entirely restricted to any one.

Two British species that inhabit highly specialised habitats are, nevertheless, almost universally distributed – the mole and the field vole. A glance at the distribution maps for these species shows that they are found throughout the mainland of Great Britain and some of the western isles of Scotland, but not in Ireland or the Isle of Man. Their absence from parts of the British Isles is due to prehistoric causes, for those parts were separated from the mainland of Great Britain during the Pleistocene before the species arrived after the penultimate glaciation. The habitat of the mole is confined almost entirely to the topsoil, and that of the Field vole to the soil surface of the Ground zone, yet they are both found throughout all the formation types of the Terrestrial system. The mole lives almost its entire life in burrows in the topsoil, even its deeper runs seldom extending far into the subsoil, and its excursions onto the surface, though frequent, are brief. The Field vole lives in runs on the ground surface beneath dense matted vegetation of rough grassland, hedgerows, scrub and woodland. It constructs nests of frayed-out grass leaves either on the surface or in shallow burrows an inch or so below the surface of the topsoil. Its food consists almost entirely of grass stems, so its habitat, although restricted, provides it with food and shelter within a small compass, like a grub in a nut. The habitats of both the mole and the field vole are found throughout all the formation types of the Terrestrial system, hence the ubiquitous distribution of both species.

On the other hand the restricted distribution of some species is not due to lack of suitable habitats but to interference by man. This applies particularly to some carnivores which have traditionally been regarded as vermin detrimental to the interests of man; such are the wild cat and the polecat, now geographically confined to parts of Scotland and of Wales respectively, but found widely throughout Great Britain in historic times. Their decrease in distribution is due less to destruction of habitat than to direct extermination by trap, poison, and gun.

For the smaller rodents and insectivores the layer of litter formed of fallen leaves and other vegetable material in the Ground zone of Scrub and Woodland formations, is an important habitat. The litter layer is the starting point of the recycling of energy received from the sun and fixed by the photosynthesis of plants. Here the process of decay and biodegradation begins through the agency of bacteria, fungi, and innumerable kinds of invertebrates, which form a food chain of organisms feeding on the material of the litter and on each other. The mammals that live among the components of this layer are far up in the food chain, and lie at the end of it until an owl swoops down or a weasel breaks in and takes their place. Until they are thus moved along the food chain they are themselves continually adding to the cycle, for their droppings provide material for the start of further chains, as do their dead bodies if not removed by predators.

The litter layer is a good example of the immense complexity of eco-systems, especially of micro-flora and micro-fauna, all impinging on each other and interacting at different points. Elton likens them to the links of chain mail, giving a pattern of activities linking communities of separate but adjoining micro-habitats. Such a chain-mail link is well shown in the example discussed in the last paragraph. The owl swooping from the High canopy to snatch a mouse from the litter of the Ground zone and the weasel that belongs to the Ground zone and Field layer of several formation types link their several habitats when they enter the field vole habitat to seize their prey.

The small rodents and voles in the litter layer individually have small habitats, much smaller than those of the owl and the weasel, but much larger than those of the invertebrates of the litter on which they feed wholly or in part. There is thus an inverted pyramid of habitats in which the animals of the lower levels individually eat less than their predators in succeeding levels above them. As a consequence there are fewer large invertebrates than small, fewer insectivores and rodents than large invertebrates, and fewer owls and weasels than shrews, mice and voles. In the inverted pyramid of habitats, therefore, the higher the consumer level at any stage, the fewer and larger are the animals inhabiting it, and the greater is the range of habitats to which they can adapt.

As the number of smaller animals – the invertebrates – feeding directly on the plant debris in the litter layer is greater than that of the larger ones, extending up to the vertebrates, that feed upon them, there is thus also a pyramid of numbers which decrease from below upwards. Elton points out that this is really a pyramid of consumer layers, and that it is matched by the inverse pyramid of habitats. The original pattern of herbivorous animals confined to specific plants or groups of plants tends to be obscured by the inverse pyramid of habitats as the links in the food chain proceed, although it is not entirely lost.

Just as the geographical distribution of the formations of the Terrestrial system is discontinuous, so the distribution of mammals within them is uneven. Although the density of a population is often given in terms of so many per acre (or hectare) this is merely an average, and does not necessarily represent the true distribution of a species through its habitat. The quality of a habitat varies from place to place, and the animals living in it tend to concentrate in the most desirable parts. Those parts may be determined by physical features such as the suitability of the substrate for burrowing, the local availability of food, or by the social habits of the animals themselves.

The Terrestrial and Transition systems thus offer a great number of different habitats, from bare mountain tops, through the heaths and close-cropped grasslands of the hills, the arboreal and litter-layer habitats of woodlands, the meadow, pasture and arable habitats of the lowlands, the hedgerows and field banks, to the still and running freshwaters and the sea shore. All these are but major divisions, and each can be subdivided into many minor types of habitat, all interlinked like Elton's coat of chain mail.

The present diversity of habitats may be contrasted with the limited number available when more uniform types of environment succeeded each other while tundra gave way to birch forest, followed by pine and then deciduous forest, as the land became exposed when freed from its ice-cover at the end of the glaciations. It was not until neolithic man began deforestation about four thousand years ago that the process of unwittingly providing the great variety of habitats now available began. As we have seen, this process has continued ever since, and has gained speed in the last thousand years, culminating in the profound changes of the last two hundred. But when the process began it was too late for fresh species of mammals to immigrate and take advantage of the new habitats, for the connection of the British Isles with the continent had been cut some three thousand years before, when the Straits of Dover were finally opened.

We can infer, therefore, that had the opportunity for immigration been there, our mammalian fauna could have been richer in species than it is – many habitats have been provided that would have suited some of the species that inhabit the continent opposite our shores. There were 'ecological niches' that could have been filled by species that were unable to reach them.

Our fauna, not impoverished but incomplete, as pointed out in chapter 2, could have been considerably more varied. This is shown by the way in which certain species artificially introduced by man have flourished and become established as permanent members of our fauna. Apart from the house mouse, which is closely dependent upon the dwellings of man for its habitat – though there are at least temporarily 'outdoor' populations – and which is our most ancient introduction, having arrived during the pre-Roman iron age, the rabbit is the outstanding example. It has been with us for nearly a thousand years and has occupied the whole of the country; even the pandemic of deadly myxomatosis has failed to eradicate it. Yet, as far as we know, the rabbit has not displaced any native species, and has indeed provided an abundant source of food for some of them. The later introduction of the black rat, followed after some centuries by the brown, resembles the circumstances of the establishment of the house mouse.

Although we had two species of native deer, the red deer and the roe, the introduction of the fallow deer in early historic times provided another permanent member of the fauna, and here again, as far as we know, it has not competed with the native species but has flourished alongside them. Even species from the other side of the world, such as the grey squirrel, mink, and coypu from America have readily become established in spite of strenuous efforts by man to exterminate them. From Asia we have the sika deer and muntjac, and from Australia a wallaby though its hold is as yet tenuous, but none of them appear to have competed seriously with our native species to their detriment – not even the grey squirrel which has merely occupied a habitat left vacant by the decrease in numbers of the native red squirrel.

These successful introductions, together with a few others of less importance, show that the great variety of habitats provided by human activity might well have been occupied by the natural immigration of species from continental Europe had they had the opportunity. Thus although the character of the environment in the British Isles is entirely man-made, directly or indirectly, the diversity of habitats thereby made available has not been left unfilled. Some of our guests may be unwelcome, but they certainly appreciate the hospitality afforded them by the works of man.

CHAPTER 4

DISTRIBUTION AND HABITATS

WE have now to consider how our mammalian fauna is distributed through the mosaic of differing environments and potential habitats, bearing in mind that the mosaic is largely made by man and differs widely from the more uniform environments that evolved before his activities impinged so drastically upon them. Most mammals are adaptable to variations in their environment, and consequently it is not surprising that many of our species are widely distributed throughout the British Isles because, although environments may differ, suitable habitats can be found within them.

About two dozen species are universally distributed throughout most of Great Britain, though they are not necessarily equally common everywhere. They include the hedgehog, mole and the three red-toothed shrews, several bats particularly the Daubenton's, pipistrelle, and common long-eared bats, the rabbit and brown hare, the three native voles, the wood and house mice, and common rat, and of the carnivores the fox, stoat, weasel, badger, and otter. It may be inferred that these species were early arrivals from the continent after the great Anglian or a later glaciation, and were able to extend their ranges northwards after the retreat of the Devensian glaciation. This is no doubt true for some of them but several are absent from Ireland, which was separated from Great Britain long before the onset of the Devensian glaciation. Thus the mole, the common and water shrews, several bats, the brown hare, the voles, and the weasel failed to make the crossing. The others were probably in Ireland before the Devensian glaciation, and survived in the south and other parts of the island that remained free of ice-cover.

An even longer list is filled by species absent from the Isle of Man, though they are present either throughout the mainland or on the neighbouring regions of Great Britain. In addition to those species absent from Ireland the Isle of Man lacks several other species of bat, the fox, pine marten, badger, and all the native deer. The Isle of Man, like Ireland, was cut off from the mainland of Great Britain long before the Devensian glaciation, and was completely ice-covered

77

during at least part of it. The previously existing mammalian fauna must therefore have been totally exterminated during the Devensian; and the species now found there must have arrived after the melting of the Devensian ice some 10,000 years ago. Only one species, the otter, has any capability as a long distance swimmer so that it can be considered as perhaps having reached the island by its own efforts; all the others, with the exception of the bats, must have arrived by assisted passages. It is of course possible that some may have travelled on driftwood, though the mathematical odds against such an occurrence must be enormous; by far the most probable explanation of their presence is that they were introduced either deliberately or unintentionally by man, who has enjoyed the attractions of the island from neolithic times to the present day.

A similar reason may account for the presence of some of the species in the Irish fauna which may well have been introduced as a result of human activity. We know that this is the reason for the presence of the latest newcomer to the fauna, the bank vole; it has now spread over several counties of the south-west from a centre probably in County Cork where it was first found in 1964.[59] It is indeed surprising that other species common in Great Britain have not been similarly introduced into Ireland.

A past generation of naturalists, some of whom had little or no scientific training, appears to have been obsessed with a mania for finding small differences between animals collected in different places and describing them as distinct subspecies. This pastime resulted in an accumulation of subspecific names that obscured the true state of affairs instead of illuminating it, though doubtless it gave much comfort to the participants in the game. The players seem to have been unable to understand that they were quite out of touch with reality, and that the schemes of classification that they devised were fantasies of their imaginations. They were not describing nature, but setting forth systems of taxonomy of things as they thought they ought to be, but not as they were in fact. Apart from their determination to create subspecies whereby to inflate their self esteem and to impress their colleagues, they were led astray by examining far too few specimens and jumping to conclusions on inadequate evidence – put plainly, by their ignorance and arrogance.

Modern research has demolished most of this unnecessary edifice raised on insecure foundations, and has revealed a very different and far more interesting picture of the interrelations between the animals found in the different parts of the British Isles. There are indeed a few subspecific differences between British and continental species, and between populations in different parts of the country; in addition some species show geographical clines, and others genetically determined biochemical differences, differences undreamt of by the earlier seekers for subspecies.

Most of the British species formerly thought to be sub-specifically different from those found in Europe are now known to show no such difference. The common shrew of Great Britain was accepted as the subspecies *Sorex araneus castaneus*, by Miller[107] on the grounds that it is slightly lighter in colour and smaller in size. This and a number of alleged subspecies from different parts of the continent are now discredited. Similarly the British water shrew is indistinguishable from that of the continent; the supposed lighter colour of the under parts is not a constant feature and consequently *Neomys fodiens bicolor* is invalid. Of the British bats only two species have been squeezed into the straight-jacket of subspecific nomenclature, the greater and lesser horseshoe bats which were supposed to be smaller than their continental relatives; *Rhinolophus ferrum-equinum insulanus* and *Rhinolophus hipposuderos minutus* are not valid subspecies. Miller thought the British brown hare, though closely related to the continental form, is 'readily distinguishable by its darker, browner, general colour'. But introductions from the continent have interbred so much with our natives that if any distinction ever existed it is now swamped. Thus *Lepus europeaus (= capensis) occidentalis* has been discarded.

The mainland form of the bank vole, once thought to be smaller and less intense in colour than that of the continent, and named *Evotomys (= Clethrionomys) glareolus britannicus* has been shown by Corbet[38] to be indistinguishable. Similarly, the supposed southern British and Scotch forms of the field vole, *Microtus agrestis hirtus* and *M.a. neglectus* are not now recognised as different from those of the continent. The water vole has been subjected to even greater surgery. It was formerly regarded as a distinct species, *Arvicola amphibius*, peculiar to Great Britain, but was later found to be indistinguishable from the continental *Arvicola terrestris*, though because of the slightly larger size of some specimens it was made the subspecies *A.t. amphibius*, now itself obsolete. The black form, once labelled *A.a. reta*, is discussed below in the paragraphs dealing with subspeciation within the British Isles, as are the alleged subspecies of the wood mouse. The British form of the yellow-necked mouse is not separable from those of the continent, and consequently the subspecies *Apodemus flavicollis wintoni* is not valid. Miller[107] showed that the supposed British subspecies of dormouse *Muscardinus avellanarius anglicus* is not distinguishable from dormice taken in Switzerland and Italy.

Among the carnivores the distinction of the British stoat as *Mustela erminea stabilis* on the grounds of alleged possession of larger teeth is no longer upheld, though the Irish stoat, *M.e. hibernica*, is generally regarded as a good subspecies. The attempt to differentiate the British polecat as *Mustela putorius anglius*[124] by the character of the pattern of facial markings is now known to be erroneous.[125] Similarly the alleged British badger *Meles meles britannicus* has no existence outside the realms of fancy. The separation of the Scottish wild cat as a subspecies, *Felis silvestris grampia*, is based on characters that are so variable throughout the range of the species that it cannot be upheld; furthermore there has been much interbreeding between truly wild and domestic cats so that specific characters, let alone subspecific ones, are often confused. In addition the domestic cat is itself considered to be derived from the north African subspecies of *F. silvestris, F.s. libyca*.[74]

The differences between the red deer of Scotland and those of selectively bred park origin appear to be due to differences in nutrition and bleakness of habitat rather than to genetic factors; *Cervus elaphus scoticus* appears therefore to be no more valid than many of the subspecific races described from the continent. None of the four subspecies of roe deer enumerated by Miller, including the alleged British subspecies *Capreolus capreolus thotti*, are now considered to have more than doubtful validity, and are better disregarded.

In addition to the now unaccepted taxonomy that tries to establish British species as distinct subspecies peculiar to the British Isles, a host of subspecific names has been bestowed on different populations of some species within them. They have been applied particularly to the populations of small mammals found on various off-lying islands, generally of small size. About the beginning of the century certain naturalists recognised that the mice and voles from some islands are recognisably different from those found on the mainland; in particular Robert Drane, the veteran naturalist of South Wales, in 1897 noticed that the bank voles on the island of Skomer off the coast of Pembrokeshire differed from those of the mainland, though it was not until 1903 that a sub-specific name was given to them.[14] In 1898 Millais obtained specimens of voles from Orkney that differed from

PLATE I. *Above*, a hedgehog in its nest among scrub. The photographer found the nest by hearing the inmate snoring. *Below*, a young hedgehog from the nest anointing its spines with saliva. Hedgehogs often do this if stimulated by a strong or unusual scent.

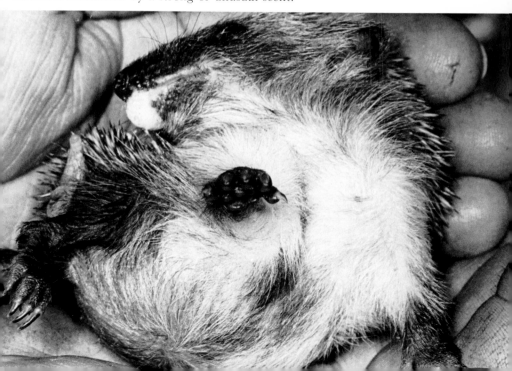

PLATE 2. *Left*, common shrew. *Centre*, pygmy shrew. *Below*, lesser white-toothed shrew. The ears of the first two are barely visible, but those of the third are conspicuous.

PLATE 3. *Above*, a water shrew leaving the pool. The ear is marked by the white patch. Though there are drops of water on the surface the fur is not wetted. *Below*, a noctule bat putting its tongue out. The tragus is the small lobe at the entrance of the ear.

PLATE 4. *Above,* a roost of greater horseshoe bats in a cave. Horseshoe bats hang freely from the roof but most other species creep into crevices or cling to the side. *Right,* the rare mouse-eared bat in flight. Its open mouth is sending out echo location pulses and its ears are turned forward to receive the echoes.

PLATE 5. *Right*, a water vole. *Centre*, a bank vole. *Below*, a field vole's nest of shredded grass which has been torn open to show the vole and her young.

PLATE 6. *Left*, a yellow-necked mouse. The large eye and ear are characteristic of the yellow-necked and the wood mouse. *Centre*, the surface entrance of the wood mouse burrow. *Below*, harvest mouse and summer nest among wheat stems.

PLATE 7. *Above*, a common dormouse.   *Below*, the introduced edible or fat dormouse, larger and with a much bushier tail.

PLATE 8. *Right*, a well trodden runway of the common rat. *Centre*, common rat feeding. *Below*, the introduced coypu is an agricultural pest in East Anglia, and is controlled by trapping in large cage-traps.

those of the mainland, and in 1904 he named them as a new species, *Microtus orcadensis*.[106] In 1895 de Winton described the field (wood) mice he had collected the year before in the island of Lewis, Outer Hebrides, as a new species, *Mus (= Apodemus) hebridensis*,[53] and in 1899 Barrett-Hamilton named the field (wood) mouse from St Kilda *Mus (= Apodemus) hirtensis*.[12] Apart from these island forms de Winton in 1894 drew attention to the presence of the yellow-necked mouse in Herefordshire, and in 1900 Barrett-Hamilton[13] gave it the subspecific name *Mus (= Apodemus) sylvaticus wintoni*, later regarded as a different species, *Apodemus flavicollis wintoni* by Miller in 1912.[107]

In the early 1900s several other island forms were named as subspecies, and then in 1912 and 1913 the Scotch naturalist Ogilvie-Grant organised an investigation of the small mammal populations of the western islands of Scotland, during which nearly 300 mice, voles, and shrews were collected. They were examined and described in 1913 by Barrett-Hamilton and Hinton who made from them several new species and subspecies.[16, 17] The 1914–18 war then put a stop to further exploration until in the early 1920s a group of Cambridge undergraduates took up the hunt in their vacations, and added a new cluster of subspecies from the islands not visited by the pre-war investigators. They appear to have been determined to find a new subspecies in each island on which they set foot – and they succeeded to their satisfaction.[108] Seeking new worlds to conquer some of them went to the Channel Islands and manufactured a new subspecies of the greater white-toothed shrew of Guernsey, *Crocidura russula peta*.[109] Thereafter the enthusiasm for subspecies-hunting seems happily to have waned so that only a few casual additions have been made up to the present, such as *Apodemus hebridensis nesiticus* from Mingulay in the Outer Hebrides in 1940.[149]

The result of all this enterprise left us with a list of native rodents that made a formidable array. Of wood mice, *Apodemus sylvestris* we had seventeen forms, of field voles *Microtus agrestis*, seven; of Orkney voles *M. arvalis*. six; and of bank voles *Clethrionomys glareolus*, five. Readers curious to see the list should turn to the Appendix, p. 197.

With over thirty species and subspecies of mice and voles before them our predecessors tried to find a credible reason for their presence and distribution. The explanations they proposed depended upon the supposed immigration of the fauna from the continent after the Pleistocene glaciations, though the information available about the glaciations was far less complete than that of the present day. We would agree with their suggestion that the animals entered in the south and spread northwards as the glaciation retreated. They, however, carried their theorising too far, for they thought that when the species arrived in Scotland they were able to pass into land that later became cut off as the Inner and Outer Hebrides, Orkney and Shetland. Thus the wood mouse, *Apodemus*, was supposed to have evolved into a new species, the Hebridean mouse, *A. hebridensis*, which gave rise to separate island subspecies when they were cut off from each other. In the most distant island, St Kilda, another species, *A. hirtensis*, had evolved, as had another on Fair Isle which gave rise to subspecies on different islands of Shetland. All this is a fallacy because the islands were separated from the mainland long before the Devensian glaciation, so that when the mice arrived in the north after the land became ice-free they would have been faced with a breadth of stormy sea barring their way to the islands.

The theory put forward to explain the distribution of voles was even more complicated. It was supposed that *Microtus arvalis*, the common vole of the continent, arrived in southern England by way of the Channel Islands in the late Pleistocene, and steadily spread northwards until it reached Orkney. This ignores the fact that there was then no land connection between the Channel Islands and England. Then *Microtus agrestis* arrived from the continent at a later date and drove out or replaced *M. arvalis*, moving relentlessly to the north of Scotland but not crossing to Orkney where *M. arvalis* was now isolated. *M. agrestis*, however, did advance into many of the Inner and Outer Hebrides and diverged into various species or subspecies when the islands were separated from the mainland. As a further complication *M. agrestis* was supposed to be represented by two species *M. neglectus* which came first, and *M. hirtus* which followed and drove the other north so that *neglectus* is the Scotch species and *hirtus* the English.

A similar argument was applied to the bank vole; one larger species was believed to have arrived first and to have been replaced by a smaller species except on some of the Hebrides, Skomer, and Jersey which were separate from the mainland when the second species arrived.

It is surprising that these conclusions were reached by zoologists who specialised in the study of Pleistocene rodents. Today it is hard to understand how they could believe that the islands were accessible by land connections after the ice of the Devensian glaciation had melted;

now that the much earlier separation of the islands is established, their whole scheme falls to the ground. The fallacy arose largely as a result of studying minute differences in skeletal structure and assessing the value of the differences subjectively. The many publications of M.A.C. Hinton described the remains of fossil pleistocene voles and mice often solely from their minute teeth; for example, many of the *Microtus* species he described are now considered to have been merely one, *M. oeconomus*, now extinct in the British Isles, but living in continental Europe. When discussing the alleged species and subspecies of the wood mouse, *Apodemus*, he wrote that the precise identification of them 'is a matter of considerable difficulty, calling for great patience, skill, and accuracy of skull measurement and calculation, which in most cases will probably be beyond the powers of an ordinary field naturalist'.[15] He also said in conversation with the present writer that it was impossible to state exactly the features of the fossil teeth of voles that led him to attribute them to one species or another, but that through long study the expert 'got his eye in' and knew the different species without being able to say precisely how he knew them. This was surely subjective judgement running wild – having a "hunch" is little or no better than guesswork.

An interesting discovery in 1924 added a species of a genus new to the British mammalian fauna, for in that year Hinton[83] described the lesser white-toothed shrew from the Scilly islands as the Scilly shrew, *Crocidura cassiteridum*, which he fancied to differ slightly from *C. suavolens* of the continent and some of the Channel Islands. It was suggested that this species might have migrated from the Channel Islands or Brittany when there was still a land connection, a proposition much more difficult to accept than that of the immigration of other species further to the east before the Straits of Dover were opened.

The complicated network of species and subspecies of small mammals lasted until 1961 when Dr Corbet of the British Museum (Natural History), wielding Occam's razor like a hero of old slaying a mythical monster, slashed through the tangle and revealed the truth that should have been apparent long before had not the experts been enmeshed in their own web.[37] The only reasonable explanation for the presence of the small mammals on the islands was that they had been carried there by man, either deliberately or unintentionally, probably the latter.

The islands have been visited or inhabited by man for many

thousands of years, starting soon after they became accessible with the melting of the Devensian ice, and inevitably the small mammals would have occasionally come with him as free-loaders. Very few animals would be enough to start the colonisation of an island, even a single pregnant female could suffice, and a population once established would inevitably develop some differences from a large mainland population owing to the limited gene pool of the founder stock. The argument is so convincing, even obvious, that it is a wonder that it was not put forward long ago.

Thus the presence of *Microtus arvalis* as a subspecies on Orkney, and as another on Guernsey is no longer a puzzle, nor is the fact that the Orkney voles of Sanday and Westray differ slightly from those on the other islands inhabited by the species, especially as subfossil remains show that they have been there for at least 4,000 years.[39] Similarly, the island races of the bank vole must have arisen from animals introduced by man; and their evolution into recognisable subspecies on Skomer, Jersey, Mull, and Raasay, may indicate that their rate of change has been higher than that of other small mammals. Not one of the many slightly differing island forms of the wood mouse can be clearly distinguished from all the others, a fact that could be accounted for by a slower rate of change, or by repeated introductions bringing different genes into the founder stock.

Changes leading towards subspeciation can occur in a comparatively short time. The house mouse of St Kilda, which must have arrived with man, as the species is his commensal, was sufficiently distinct to be regarded as a subspecies – even as a full species – when first described;[12] its dependence upon man was shown by its rapid extinction after the island was deserted by its human population in 1930. We do not know when it first came to the island, but the date may have been comparatively recent, because the subspecies of the Faroes has arisen in less than a thousand years, for the species is known to have been introduced there not less than 250, and not more than a thousand years ago.

The irregular distribution of the shrews on some of the islands is reasonably explicable only on the assumption that they were introduced by man. Thus the greater white-toothed shrew, *Crocidura russula*, is found only on Alderney, Guernsey and Herm; the lesser white-toothed shrew, *C. suaveolens*, only on Jersey, Sark, and most of the Scilly islands. The common shrew is found on most of the Inner Hebrides, but not the Outer Hebrides, Orkney, Shetland, the Scilly

Islands, or the Channel Islands except only Jersey; the water shrew only on some of the Inner Hebrides, but the pygmy shrew, our smallest terrestrial mammal, is ubiquitous and absent only from Shetland, the Scilly and Channel Islands. These uneven distributions are undoubtedly the result of man's traffic.

The true nature of the relationships between the slightly differing island populations was revealed when they were studied by statistical methods. Delany[50, 51] and Delany and Healy[52] using large numbers of specimens, investigated the characters of different populations of wood mouse (*Apodemus sylvaticus*) by multivariate analysis, using both factorial analysis and discriminant function analysis. The analysis of ten measurements such as the length of skull and various bones, and of weight, colour and tooth size showed that much of the variation between island populations is due to general size and life history – that is, the rate and amount of growth, which depends on the availability of food and other environmental influences. There is some indication that the island populations are distinct, but there is so much overlap among them, and between them and the mainland forms, that it is impossible to find criteria for distinguishing them as subspecies. This result is consistent with the suggestion that the island populations arose from small founder stocks unintentionally introduced by man, with possibly further casual introductions from time to time. This is precisely what would be expected to arise from the given premises.

A similar argument applies to the differing populations of the bank and field voles, with the exception of the four named island subspecies of the former which owe their distinctness only to their isolation, for they are all capable of breeding with each other and with the mainland form. Neither species, however, is uniform throughout the British Isles, for they both show an increase in size from south to north, accompanied by a slight increase of complexity in the pattern of the molar teeth. There is no break between the different forms; the change is gradual, forming a cline in which the individuals at the ends of the distribution differ from each other but are connected by an indefinite number of intermediate forms without any discontinuity, so that the extremes gradually merge one into the other.

A cline in the opposite direction is shown by the water vole, in which the animals from the north of Scotland are slightly smaller than those living further south, though the cline is less extensive than in the two smaller species. The water vole however shows another well marked local difference in populations, the cause of which is genetic.

In the north of Scotland and in two districts of East Anglia all the water voles are black, in strong contrast to the normal uniform brown colour, lighter on the belly. There appears to be no information about the boundary between the black and normally coloured animals but occasional black specimens turn up in areas populated by the brown ones. Similarly nothing is known of the ecological or other influences that keep the two forms apart.

Although a great number of alleged subspecies of British mammals have now been discarded as invalid, there remain some that are acceptable to modern standards of taxonomy. Of these some are animals that differ subspecifically from their continental counterparts, but others are based on subspecific differences between different populations within the British Isles. Four species are subspecifically peculiar to the British Isles, the mountain hare, the red squirrel, the Irish stoat, and the Orkney/Guernsey vole. The mountain hare of Scotland *Lepus timidus scoticus*, is smaller than that of the continent, and *L. timidus hibernicus*, the Irish hare, is larger, redder in colour, and does not become completely white in winter. The British red squirrel *Sciurus vulgaris leucourus*, is distinguished by the ear-tufts and tail fading from dark brown to white by the time of the autumn moult. The Irish stoat, *Mustela erminea hibernica*, is smaller than that of Great Britain, and the white of the underside is comparatively greatly reduced. The characters of the Orkney and Guernsey voles, *Microtus arvalis orcadensis* and *M. arvalis sarnia*, have already been mentioned. The bank vole, *Clethrionomys glareolus* is the only species that is indistinguishable from the continental form, yet has recognisable subspecies within the British Isles, the four island subspecies already discussed.

Most of the mammals of the British Isles are confined to the ground zone of the Terrestrial system defined in chapter 3, and, as there pointed out, although some are almost universally distributed throughout the country others are restricted, apart from the island forms which are necessarily confined to their particular terrains. Even the universally distributed species are seldom evenly distributed, for their abundance or scarcity is governed by the distribution of suitable habitats; the mole and the field vole have already been mentioned as examples in chapter 3.

The hedgehog is essentially an inhabitant of the ground zone of the Scrub or Woodland edge formation, using the cover as shelter, and foraging by night for its food consisting of beetles, caterpillars, earthworms and other invertebrates, on the grasslands of the adjacent Field formation. As this kind of habitat includes hedgerows the hedgehog occurs throughout the British Isles with the exception of some of the Scotch islands and the hilltops above the tree line. The similar habitats provided in the suburbs of towns, and the food supply provided by human untidiness, support an abundant population of the animals in the Domestic formation. On the other hand the common and pygmy shrews are abundant in the Field, Scrub, and Woodland types of formation wherever there is plenty of low vegetation to provide cover, the numbers of the former exceeding those of the latter. Although the water shrew often occurs far from water it is mainly aquatic, feeding in streams, ponds, and ditches and burrowing in the Transition system of the banks. Thus its distribution, though covering most of Great Britain, is concentrated round the Aquatic system.

Three species of bat are widely distributed, Daubenton's which is absent only from the highlands and islands of Scotland, and the Isle of Man, the pipistrelle absent only from Shetland, and the common long-eared bat absent only from northern Scotland and most of the islands. All of them roost in buildings so they are found wherever man provides shelter. In addition Daubenton's and the long-eared bats roost in trees in the summer, and all three often inhabit caves in the winter. The first two prefer open country with trees and woods, whereas the pipistrelle adapts to all sorts of habitat and is frequently seen even in urban areas flying above the city streets. Their habitats are therefore partly in the Domestic and the Woodland formation types, and unlike the terrestrial mammals, the bats extend into the third dimension of the Air above when they are feeding; their distribution is largely a reflection of the distribution of man-made habitats.

The universal distribution of the rabbit is due to its introduction by man, for it is not a native, but the wide distribution of the brown hare throughout the whole of Great Britain, except the north west of Scotland, is probably natural. Its presence on some of the Hebrides and Orkney, north-west Ireland, Man, Anglesey and Wight is due to introduction by man. The main habitat of the brown hare is open agricultural land, meadow and pasture, beyond which it does not extend far onto moorlands. Before the clearance of the earlier Flandrian forest cover by man from the iron-age onwards, the brown hare must have been much less widely distributed, for it is essentially an inhabitant of open steppe and savanna country, though it does also enter open deciduous woodland. On the other hand, as remains of the brown hare have not been recorded from any pleistocene deposit, and dense forest still covered the land when Great Britain was isolated from the continent by the opening of the Straits of Dover, it seems possible that the brown hare may have been introduced by man after he had produced extensive areas of suitable habitat for it. It is even possible that man brought the brown hare as a house pet, for hares are easily tamed and domesticated.[42]

The British red squirrel is one of our few arboreal mammals, which is consequently limited in its distribution by the distribution of woodlands. It is particularly an inhabitant of coniferous woods where its main diet consists of shoots and the seeds in pine-cones, but it also lives in deciduous woodlands when its numbers are high. Less than a hundred years ago it was universally distributed throughout the British Isles except the Hebrides, northern isles, and the Isle of Man, and was common in woods everywhere. After the beginning of the twentieth century, however, it has become extinct in most of England, and locally in Scotland and Ireland. This contrasts with its history in the eighteenth century when it became extinct in Scotland and Ireland, which were re-stocked by introductions from England. The causes of these fluctuations in numbers are not known, but they were not due to competition from the grey squirrel which did not spread far from its centres of introduction until the 1920s.

Of the universally distributed rodents we have already discussed the distribution of the bank, field, and water voles, and the wood mouse, in considering their subspecific variation. It need only be added that although their preferred habitats are widely spread the animals are separated by the discontinuous nature of them. The bank vole, unlike the field vole discussed in chapter 3, inhabits the Woodland and Scrub edge types of formation, including hedgerows, and is partly arboreal, being an agile climber, in the field layer and low canopy of scrub and hedges. Its habitat, less uniform than that of the field vole, provides a much more varied diet, from seeds and fruits to leaves and invertebrates. The water vole, like the water shrew, is aquatic, though only in the British Isles, for it is terrestrial on the continent. It seeks its food not only in the water but also in the Transition system, grazing the grass on the banks, in which it digs its burrows. Within its wide distribution it is thus restricted to habitats near water, which have been much extended by man-made ponds and ditches. The wood mouse, sometimes said to be the most numerous mammal in Great Britain, is adaptable to so many different habitats that its occurrence as well as its distribution is practically universal. Although it is called wood mouse it needs only low ground cover of vegetation to find almost any habitat acceptable, including arable fields without hedges, and even entering closely built-up urban areas along scrub-covered railway embankments.[154]

The house mouse and the common rat owe their universal distribution to their commensalism with man; they are primarily inhabitants of the Domestic system from which they extend into the ground zone of all formations of the Terrestrial system except Open ground. This extension is greater with the common rat, which also inhabits the river banks and sea-shore of the Transition system.

Five species of carnivore enjoy almost universal distribution, and of them the fox is the most nearly ubiquitous, being absent only from the Isle of Man, the northern islands and the Hebrides except Skye. It needs the cover of scrub or woodland, or the shelter of rocks where other cover is not available, but it is highly adaptable to a great variety of conditions, so that there is not only a suburban but an urban population in many towns and cities, where it lives largely by scavenging human garbage. Away from towns it is a carrion eater and predator on anything from field voles to rabbits and ground nesting birds, and is a pest to gamekeepers and poultry farmers.

The stoat and weasel, very similar in appearance except for size, are universally distributed throughout Great Britain apart from most of the Hebrides and the northern islands; the stoat also inhabits Ireland and the Isle of Man from both of which the weasel is absent. Both need the shelter of some sort of cover, either woodland, scrub, hedgerows, dry walls, tall herbage, rocks and so forth, one or another of which can be found almost anywhere. The main prey of the stoat was the rabbit and still is in many places – one may speculate about its food before the Norman Conquest. After the pandemic of myxomatosis in 1954 eliminated its main food item its numbers fell dramatically in some places and only slowly recovered when it had to make do with birds and small rodents, as presumably it did before the introduction of the rabbit. The weasel, on the other hand specialises in voles and wood mice, and is small enough to follow them into their burrows. The distribution of both species is controlled by the occurrence of their food, and as rabbits and voles and wood mice are nearly ubiquitous so are their predators.

The badger is universally distributed throughout the British Isles except the northern islands, the Hebrides and the Isle of Man. It lives in deep and often highly complex systems of burrows known as 'sets', from which it emerges by night to forage on a great variety of foods, for it is omnivorous. Earthworms form an important part of its diet and when feeding on them it slurps them down 'like eating spaghetti'.[115] Its distribution, however, is governed not by the availability of its food, but by that of suitable geological formations for digging sets. Badgers especially prefer a sloping site where they can dig their burrows between strata of differing quality, particularly where they can dig into a comparatively soft stratum below a harder one which is strong enough to prevent the roof collapsing. They also prefer to have some cover so that a sloping deciduous woodland, scrubland, or old hedgerow on a bank is a favourite place.

The otter is, or was until recently, almost universally distributed throughout Great Britain and Ireland and all the islands with the exception of some heavily industrialised areas. It is more closely tied to the Aquatic system than any other British mammal except the seals. It lives in streams, rivers and lakes, and on the west coast, especially of Scotland, often lives on the sea shore and feeds on marine fish and crustacea. It lies up by day, and breeds, in 'holts' usually underground but sometimes on the surface, in the Transition system. As geology in general governs the distribution of the badger, so hydrology governs that of the otter.

Turning now to the mammals that have only a restricted distribution in the British Isles we find among the insectivores only the white-toothed shrews, confined to their islands into which they were introduced. Of the seventeen species of bat only the three mentioned above have universal or nearly universal distribution in the British Isles. Of the remaining fourteen, five are vagrant or extremely scarce species; the particoloured bat has occurred a few times as a vagrant, Nathusius' pipistrelle has been found once, Bechstein's bat rarely, and small colonies of the mouse-eared and of the grey long-eared bats have recently been found in the extreme south of England, but none of them can be considered as more than marginally part of our mammalian fauna.

Natterer's and the whiskered bats are the most widely spread of the remaining nine species. They are both found throughout England, Wales, and Ireland, but the former extends further into Scotland than the latter. Both roost in buildings as well as trees, and in caves in winter. Brandt's bat, too, has a fairly wide distribution in England and Wales but its difference from the whiskered bat has only recently been recognised, so it may prove to be much more widespread. Leisler's bat inhabits the whole of Ireland and most of England and Wales as far north as Yorkshire; the allied noctule is absent from Ireland but extends north into southern Scotland. The barbastelle similarly is absent from Ireland but is found in England and Wales extending north to Lancashire and Yorkshire.

The remaining three species have much narrower distributions; the serotine only south of the line from the Wash to the Severn but not Devon and Cornwall, the greater horseshoe bat inhabits south-west England and south Wales, as does the lesser horseshoe bat which also extends into the whole of Wales and part of western Ireland.

Of the nine species of limited distribution the horseshoe bats roost in caves during winter and in the roof-spaces of houses in summer; the remainder live in trees or houses or both, and sometimes caves, so their distribution cannot be restricted by lack of suitable habitats, nor by lack of food, for they are all insectivorous. Their limited foothold in the British Isles appears to represent the most northerly or westerly extremes of their ranges, for they are all widespread throughout much or all of the Palaearctic region, but the limiting causes, whether climate, temperature, or other, are unknown. The disturbance caused by people visiting caves has sometimes driven away the roosting bats, and in particular seems to have caused a recent large diminution in the numbers and distribution of the greater horseshoe bat.

The mountain hare inhabits the ground zone of the Field formation type at heights above about 800 feet, that is the heather-covered hills of the Highlands of Scotland, but it has been introduced into many of the islands, southern Scotland, the Peak district, and north Wales. The Irish subspecies inhabits lower ground; this is said to be because there are no brown hares to compete with it, but there appears to be no proof of the assertion. The natural distribution, restricted to the Highlands of Scotland, appears to be determined by the occurrence of suitable habitat, but the successful introduction of the species into the Lowlands, and the habitat used by the Irish subspecies shows that it can adapt to other habitats. The reasons for its natural restriction therefore remain obscure, unless it is indeed true that it cannot compete with the brown hare.

Three species of rodents have only limited distributions in the

British Isles. The yellow-necked mouse is restricted to the southern and eastern parts of England and to Wales and is absent from much of the area; it shares the habitat of the wood mouse, but appears to prefer low-lying woodlands interspersed among arable fields.[40] The conditions that govern its distribution are not precisely known – indeed some heretics doubt whether it is really a distinct species. The harvest mouse is known from most of England, parts of Wales and of southern Scotland. It inhabits the ground zone and field layer of the Field and Scrub formation types, and is said to have declined in numbers during the present century owing to changed agricultural methods. There is growing evidence, however, that it is more numerous and widespread than was generally supposed.[77] As it is distributed through the Palaearctic region from England to Japan its limited range in the British Isles is unexplained, though its absence from Ireland must be because man has not carried it there. The dormouse is absent from Ireland for the same reason, but its distribution, confined to the southern parts of England and Wales, is not understood – it cannot be due to lower temperatures in the north because the dormouse is one of the few British mammals, apart from the bats, that hibernate and can thus survive rigorous winter temperatures, as it does on the continent. It is an inhabitant of the ground zone, field, and low canopy layers of the Scrub and Woodland formation types, a habitat that is widely available.

Three carnivores owe their restricted distribution to persecution by man; all were widespread throughout Great Britain within historic times but, as they are vermin, the poultry keepers and particularly the gamekeepers have banished them to comparatively small areas.[97] All, pine marten, polecat, and wild cat, are inhabitants of woodland, the polecat being the most adaptable to other habitats as well. The pine marten, but neither of the others, is also a native of Ireland, where it is widely but thinly spread. In Great Britain it occurs mainly in the Highlands of Scotland, with small populations in the Lake District, North Wales, and a few other places. The wild cat is at present spreading in northern Scotland from the Highlands where until recent years it was confined. The polecat has survived in Wales and is now spreading into the Marches. The former distribution of these species shows that there was no natural constraint upon their distribution, and their restriction is solely due to human destruction.

The grey seal inhabits the waters off all our coasts except the eastern part of the English Channel; the common seal is less frequent on English coasts from Dover to Land's End and thence north to the Solway, but occurs on all others. The distribution of both species when they come ashore is controlled entirely by the position of suitable breeding beaches, the most important condition being freedom from human disturbance.

Both our native deer, the red and the roe, though widespread in early Flandrian times, were driven into Scotland and northern England by human population pressure before the end of the eighteenth century. The red deer was formerly kept in many parks throughout the country; the park breeds are noticeably bigger and bear larger antlers than the native wild animals. Feral populations derived from the park animals are now present in many wooded areas or hill moorlands from Devon to East Anglia and from Hampshire to Yorkshire. A few small populations exist in Ireland, that of the south-west perhaps being truly wild, for the species was indigenous to the country. The roe deer has never been part of the Irish fauna, but is common in Scotland and northern England. It is also feral in much of southern England and in East Anglia, having been introduced into both places during the nineteenth century.

The fallow deer is not a native to the British Isles, though it was present before the Devensian glaciation. It was introduced in mediaeval times, and descendants still live wild in Epping and the New Forests, and in Staffordshire. The fallow deer has traditionally been kept as an ornament to gentlemen's parks from which they have escaped and become feral, especially during the disorder brought by two major wars. They are now widely distributed wherever there is sufficient woodland cover throughout most of England, much of Wales and Ireland, but only in a few districts of Scotland. They do much damage to agriculture, horticulture and forestry but manage to survive plentifully in spite of the onslaughts of poachers and hooligans. It is surprising that animals as large as fallow deer can be plentiful in agricultural districts, and yet remain inconspicuous so that they are seen by few people, and then usually only at night.

Of the recently introduced mammals two species, both from America, have become widespread members of our fauna. The grey squirrel was liberated at some thirty places in England and Wales, several in Scotland, and one in Ireland up to 1920, by people of whom it is charitable to say that they were misguided. In the light of present knowledge it seems incredible that well-meaning persons should so arrogantly commit such vandalism by releasing this universal pest.

The animals are now firmly established over most of England and Wales, with separate populations in central Scotland and eastern Ireland. The grey squirrel is an inhabitant of the low and high canopy layers of the Scrub and Woodland formations so that it occurs wherever there are trees. There are, however, other conditions controlling its distribution, for it is absent from parts of East Anglia, and from the Lake District and Northumberland. In parts of Suffolk every autumn grey squirrels can be seen invading from west to east, but for some unknown reason they do not become established in the eastern and northern parts of East Anglia.

The mink, introduced from America for fur-farming, established a feral population by escapes from fur-farms, and since 1960 has spread with astonishing speed, so that it is now universally distributed throughout Great Britain, and has several large populations in Ireland. Its habitat is in the Aquatic and Intermediate systems, and centres upon streams and rivers. It has defeated all efforts to check its spread, and must now be accepted as a member of the fauna. Some people think that because it is a predator it is a threat to the wellbeing of our wildlife, from fishes and amphibians to birds and mammals, as also to domestic poultry. Up to the present it seems to have had less devastating effects than was feared.[98, 101]

The fat dormouse has spread to only a small area near Tring in Hertfordshire where it was released over seventy years ago. It is arboreal in habitat, and does some damage in orchards, but it cannot be considered as an important part of the fauna. The coypu has also become established in only a limited, though larger, area. It is the 'nutria' of the furriers, and escaped from fur farms in several parts of the country, but is now confined to East Anglia, where it inhabits the Aquatic system but feeds extensively in the Field formation of the Terrestrial system. It is thus a pest to agriculture and a menace to waterways, in the banks of which it burrows. It built up to a large local population approaching a quarter of a million, but fortunately great numbers were killed by severe winters such as those of 1946–7 and 1962–3; an intense trapping campaign maintained by the Ministry of Agriculture, Fisheries and Food has got its numbers down to a few thousand.

Of the introduced deer only the muntjac seems likely to become a widespread member of the fauna. It is a native of China and has spread from Woburn Park in Bedfordshire over a large part of southern England. It lives in dense cover in the Woodland and Scrub formation types. The Sika deer, from east Asia, is established in small areas in south and north England, Scotland and Ireland. The Chinese water deer, also an escape from Woburn Park, is thinly spread but locally numerous in parts of Bedfordshire, Huntingdon-shire and East Anglia. Although they are interesting additions to the fauna none of these species as yet forms an important part of it.

CHAPTER 5

RANGES, TERRITORIES AND POPULATIONS

ONE might well think that wild mammals, like the wind which bloweth where it listeth, are free to come and go wherever they choose, and are circumscribed only by the type of habitat that they prefer. No so: lions do not roam the vast plains of Africa at random, but each frequents its own home range covering some ten to twenty square miles and, although there may be no physical barrier to wandering beyond, stays at home. Even the great whales, that apparently could go anywhere in the limitless oceans, do not normally venture beyond the invisible bounds of certain areas which, though enormous in comparison with the home ranges of land mammals, are nevertheless well defined. Every kind of terrestrial mammal lives within a home range, which for many is centred upon a nest, burrow, lair, or other place where it rests and sleeps, and which often serves as a cradle and nursery for its young. The immediate surroundings of the centre frequently form a territory from which other animals of the same kind are excluded, and is thus the private property of the occupier, at least for the time being, and is indeed the only sort of personal property that can be held by any animal apart from man.

The phenomenon of holding territory was first discovered by the ornithologists who observed that during the breeding season most birds occupy an exclusive area surrounding the nest and drive away all intruders of the same species, often advertising their ownership and warning off others by their song. Zoologists later recognised that the holding of territory is common among animals, both the invertebrates and the vertebrates. With the mammals, however, the matter is not quite so clear-cut as in the breeding territories of birds, and it was not until 1943 that the American zoologist W.H. Burt proposed and defined the difference between territory and home range in mammals.[29] 'Home range is the area, usually round a home site, over which the animal normally travels in search of food. Territory is the protected part of the home range, be it entire home range or only the nest. Every kind of mammal may be said to have a home range, stationary or shifting. Only those that protect some part of the home range, by fighting or aggressive gestures, from others of their kind, during some phase of their lives, may be said to have territories.' These concepts, sometimes modified in various directions, in general still hold good.

Burt regarded the home range as the area traversed by a mammal in its normal activities of finding food, a mate, and caring for its young, and considered that occasional excursions beyond its borders, whether exploratory or otherwise, do not extend it. Mammals may not occupy one home range for the whole of their lives, but may abandon an old one and establish a new one elsewhere, and migratory mammals have two home ranges one at each end of the migratory route which itself need not form part of the home range. The size of the home range naturally corresponds roughly with the size of the animal occupying it; the home range of a pygmy shrew is measured in square yards, the range of a wood mouse may extend to five acres at most and is generally much less, whereas that of a fox may be two thousand acres or about three square miles.

The size of the home range also varies according to the sex and age of the animal occupying it, and also with the season of the year. Furthermore the home range of neighbouring animals may overlap to some extent, the overlap forming a neutral ground on which the tenants may meet without hostility though more generally each enters the overlap only when the other is elsewhere. Weasels, for example, have ranges that vary in size and exclusiveness according to the numbers and concentration of their prey.[93, 102] There is considerable overlap of ranges but marking the boundaries by scent keeps the common owners apart so that neighbours avoid each other and do not meet. A similar mutual avoidance between neighbours using overlapping ranges is shown by the domestic cat. On the other hand, the ranges of dominant male field voles do not overlap, as is shown by careful tracking of individual animals.[90] Among gregarious animals a number of them share the same home range. The size of the home range is also affected by the density of the population, the greater the density the smaller the home ranges, which in extreme cases may be no more than the defended territory of each individual.

One must be careful not to think of each species in isolation with all its individual animals living snugly each in its home range centred on its private bit of territory. Even in the British Isles with only a small number of species in its mammalian fauna we have some twenty-five different kinds that are widely distributed; if the home ranges of all the individuals of one species were mapped we should have an entirely different picture from the corresponding map for another species. So although an animal may have a home range that appears to be its private property held against intrusion by other members of its species, it is in fact sharing it with the home ranges of several other individuals of other species. Thus the home range of a weasel might cover the home ranges of hundreds of field voles, and that of a fox might cover those of a dozen weasels and of thousands of field voles. Home ranges therefore separate the individuals within a species but do not separate those of different species. The overlap may sometimes have little or no effect on the different species – a group of grazing deer, for example, are indifferent to the voles scuttling among the grass roots beneath them or the mole in its burrow below, and vice versa. But a fox or stoat hunting through its home range has an obvious effect on the voles and other small rodents whose home ranges lie within the larger home range of the predator.

As we have seen, the home range of an animal is the area over which it normally travels in carrying out its routine activities. It follows that this area must be of a size large enough to produce the food to meet the energy requirements of the individual, and hence the population density of the species is an important factor in determining whether the sizes of home ranges are adequate. The dire effects of population density that reaches a level high enough to restrict home ranges seriously are discussed below.

It might appear that the productivity of a home range would be at least partly controlled by the requirements of other species with ranges that are superimposed, but this is largely offset by the different species living on slightly differing diets or inhabiting slightly different micro-habitats within the main habitat. Thus wood mice tend to occupy areas with less dense ground cover than do bank voles, and eat more invertebrates and less foliage of woody plants, so that there is some separation between them by micro-habitats and diet; and the shrews with ranges superimposed on theirs feed wholly on invertebrates, especially earthworms, beetles, and woodlice, so that they are separated from the others by diet. Although the two species of shrew are sympatric, that is they both occupy one and the same habitat, they are partly separated by their behaviour, the common shrew being more active underground and the pygmy shrew on the surface. This relationship is not produced by the two species being sympatric, for the pygmy shrew shows a similar preference for activity on the surface in Ireland from which the common shrew is absent.[57] These are but simple examples of the extreme complexity of the inter-relations between the different components of the huge biomass of living creatures in any environment. The species mentioned influence the plant composition of their environment by feeding upon it or upon the invertebrates which themselves affect it in different ways. The web woven by the food chains is so complicated by interactions and feedbacks that it is impossible to unravel it completely by existing techniques.

The predators which have superimposed home ranges on those of smaller animals, such as the mice and voles, also alter the distribution of the ranges of the latter whenever they are successful in their hunting. As soon as they have removed an individual from the population the vacant home range is filled either by the arrival of a young animal that has not yet established a home range, or by the neighbours extending their ranges into the vacant range and partitioning it among themselves. On the other hand, the abundance and availability of the prey species affects the size of the home ranges of the predators, for no animal other than man works harder than is necessary to satisfy the basic needs of obtaining its energy requirements, and securing a mate.

No small mammal can survive unless it has a home to give it shelter from the weather and predators, and a home range in which it can find enough food. As a consequence the most dangerous time in the life of a small mammal is when it reaches adolescence and has to leave the nest where it was born and reared, and find a new home of its own. If it is unusually fortunate it may find a range from which the owner has recently been removed by a predator or by death in some other form, but if it is not it must try to establish itself within a home range that is already occupied. It may be able to do so in part of the home range of its parent, but its range will be small, and it will be restricted to the immediate surroundings of the burrow or nest where it has established itself; not until the animal has asserted its rights to the territory round its home will it be able to extend its home range.

As the young mammal grows up it makes short exploratory sorties in its parent's home range and gradually extends it with familiarity, and thus learns the topography of its immediate environment. This exploration and learning are of vital importance. Small mammals do not wander at random over their home ranges, but adopt regular routes from point to point within them along which they go and return. Hence arises the system of runways above ground and of burrows below, marked by the wear of frequent passage and the body scent of the animal. As a result the animal becomes so familiar with its range that if it is disturbed or alarmed it can make a quick dash for home almost automatically by rushing back along the well known trail. The runs of small rodents and shrews are not generally conspicuous or even visible to a human observer because they are hidden below the herbage or litter, but those of some medium-sized mammals are obvious.

Badgers, for example, wear conspicuous paths through their home ranges, so denuded of vegetation that people sometimes mistake them for human footpaths and, as Neal says, only discover their mistake when the path disappears beneath a low bush. The paths radiate from the badgers' set – the home territory – and are marked by the animals' scent, so that in following the course of one a badger is guided by its nose rather than by its eyes. Badgers are so habituated to using the well-known paths that if frightened when away from home they dash back to their set along the path, even though they could get there more quickly by leaving the trail to take a short cut. Rabbits also use well defined paths and are even more conservative in their use of them; if one looks closely at the run it is apparent that the vegetation is more worn down at short intervals, the worn patches being the places where the rabbit puts its feet as it lopes along treading in the same footsteps every time it passes. The use of familiar paths enables the animals to get home in a hurry without 'thinking', just as a human motor-car commuter can arrive home and muse 'Well, I must have passed through such-and-such a place because here I am at home, but for the life of me I can't remember seeing it or passing through it!'

The use of tracks or runs generally lead the animals to centres of activity, places where food is abundant or where cover makes foraging comparatively safe from predators. The tracks are not used solely for foraging but also for patrolling the home range and marking it with the owner's scent which is set in several ways, using urine, faeces, or the secretion of special scent glands – some would call them stink glands. The frequent patrolling keeps the owner familiar with its escape routes and allows it to chase away any trespassing intruder.

The home range, as just mentioned, is marked at intervals by the animal's scent, but scent setting is much more intense if there is a defended territory at the focus of the home range. Badgers set scent from their subcaudal and anal scent glands by rubbing their anal region on trees, the stems of bushes, stones, the ground at the entrance of the set, and other objects. They also mark their territories by defaecating in dung pits which they dig in the neighbourhood of the set and use daily until so full that a new one has to be dug – the countryman's explanation of the dung pits used to be that the badger's faeces are so overpoweringly foul that even the badger cannot tolerate the stink and so used a latrine. Similarly the smaller carnivores such as the stoat and weasel mark their ranges and territories with urine, scent from special glands, and faeces, though they do not dig dung pits.

Scents of one sort or another for marking territories and home ranges play a large part in the life of mammals, and form the chief method of communication among many species. Scent marking is, in a way, the earliest form of writing, for one animal leaves a message that can be understood by another in the absence of the first. The message may contain more information than merely 'another animal has been here', and can identify which animal, its sex and age, because each individual has its own scent by which it can be identified. This individual variation of the scent common to all animals of a species must be due to subtle chemical differences in the composition of the secretions of each, and is evidently unmistakable. A flock of sheep or a rookery of seals has a strong and generally unpleasant smell to human nostrils, which however are acute enough to discriminate between the two. The animals have a much greater power of discrimination, for a ewe recognises her own lamb by its scent and rejects a stranger, and a cow seal similarly knows her own pup. Scents evidently form a medium of communication that can convey much more information to animals than we can appreciate.

In some mammals the mother appears to recognise her young by her own scent imposed upon it, rather than by the intrinsic scent of the young. Experiments with goats[72] have shown that if a kid is removed from its mother within five minutes of its birth it is not recognised when later allowed to approach her. On the other hand if the newborn kid is left in the company of its mother for not more than eight hours, during which she licks and suckles it, it is thereafter recognised and accepted. It is likewise recognised and rejected by other mothers who will, however, accept a strange kid that has been taken from its mother within five minutes of its birth. It is thus evident that during the early hours of contact the mother labels the kid by licking and suckling it. Labelling the young by the mother may occur in other species, just as the badgers of a family label each other by deliberately setting scent on their siblings, as described below.

It may seem peculiar that the most frequent medium of scent communication is provided by the metabolic excretions of the animal. The excretions, however, inevitably leave an unmistakable sign of the presence of an animal, and so the mammals have made a virtue of necessity and re-inforced the information content of their messages by adding the secretions of special glands. The glands are therefore of necessity developed in the excretory regions of the body, and thus we find anal, subcaudal, perineal, and preputial glands sited so that they add their secretions to the excretions. With the further evolution of behaviour the glands have often been given an independent function so that the animal may use them alone for setting scent, apart from the generally associated excretions. Badgers, for example, set scent from the subcaudal gland to mark their territory and foraging trails; furthermore they set scent on each other so that all the members of a family living in a set carry the mixed signatures, enabling them instantly to recognise each other 'as family' or to warn off a stranger. The anal glands on the other hand appear to be used solely for flavouring the faeces, and are not used separately in setting scent, apart from excretion.

Many small mammals that live in burrows have special scent glands under the skin of the flanks so that they automatically mark their burrows as they run through them. These glands are generally the equivalent of highly developed sebaceous glands, the glands which secrete an oily substance that acts as a hair-dressing for the fur, and gives a characteristic odour to the animal. The specialised flank glands produce a scent that not only marks the animals' burrows, but makes shrews and moles distasteful to most predators. Domestic cats and wild foxes often catch and kill shrews, and sometimes moles, but seldom care to eat them; the unpleasant scent from the flank glands appears to be the deterrent. On the other hand owls, which like most birds, have a poor sense of smell, are the main predators on shrews. The function of the flank glands is undoubtedly to produce a secretion to mark the burrows and not to be a defence from predators – it is little use to make a predator turn up its nose if it has already killed you. Tawny owls also eat many moles, especially sub-adults dispersing from their nurseries in early summer.

Bats are well endowed with skin glands, generally on their faces, but often elsewhere as well, particularly in some exotic species. There appears to be no information about territory marking in bats, though hollow trees and other places used as roosting or breeding dens by some of our British species such as the noctule may stink dreadfully, but this could be due to lack of sanitation rather than deliberate marking. Whether deliberate or not the dens are certainly marked unmistakably. The nursing females of an American species of *Myotis*, however, have been found marking a tree about halfway between the roost and the feeding ground some 200 metres distant. It was thought that this marking may have served as an orientation post to the young in their early foraging flights.[25] With some tropical species that roost in caves in vast numbers, literally hundreds of thousands, the urine-soaked deposit of bat guano on the floor sometimes gives off such volumes of ammoniacal vapour that the fur of the bats is bleached, and a human visitor to the cave is in danger of asphyxiation.

The small rodents, the mice and voles, generally use faeces and urine, re-inforced with the secretions of the anal and preputial glands, for territorial marking; but the water vole has a flank gland and transfers the secretion from it to its feet by scratching the fur surrounding it, so that it lays a trail as it goes.

The rabbit marks its territory with urine and faeces re-inforced by the secretions of the anal and preputial glands, and uses landmarks such as ant heaps and stumps as defecating places to mark territorial bounds. The marked places retain their scent for long periods; after myxomatosis has wiped out a local population, and rabbits are absent for months or years, the newcomers that later repopulate the area use the same traditional marking places formerly used by their pre-decessors. In addition, rabbits have a special scent marking gland under the chin, and a careful observer can see them deliberately setting scent from this gland by rubbing the chin on herbage and the stems of shrubs.

To human noses the carnivores are pungent scent-setters; we have already noticed the habits of the badger, but the fox is equally easily recognised by the scent of its urine and products of the anal glands. The strong scent makes the fox an ideal creature for hunting with hounds; that, and its fleetness of foot which gives a good run once he is found and hounds set on. The smaller carnivores, such as the stoat and weasel, mark their territories and ranges with urine and faeces reinforced with the secretion of the anal glands. In the polecat the anal glands are comparatively large and open on the perineum; their secretion is used in setting scent to mark territory, and is also discharged if the animal is frightened. The last use seems to be a protective function, for the secretion is so strong and foul-smelling that the polecat's vernacular name 'foumart' means 'foul marten'.

The otter, which generally occupies an extensive home range up to a dozen kilometres in diameter, marks with the faeces – called 'spraints' by otter hunters – scented by the anal glands. It deposits them in habitual sprainting places, often on a stone in a stream or some landmark on the bank. The wild cat marks with faeces and particularly with urine; the sight of a domestic tom walking round the garden and marking the plants by raising his tail and giving a backwardly directed squirt of pungent urine is familiar to everyone.

In the deer further glands are developed which serve for marking territory and for keeping the members of a group of these gregarious animals together. They have an interdigital gland that opens between the toes and so automatically lays a trail wherever an animal goes. This marks the deer paths that extend throughout the home range, and so keep the herd together as it feeds over its habitual grazing lot. For most of the year the sexes live separately, the adult males remaining apart from the females and young animals of both sexes, but in the breeding season, or rut, the males take up territories of comparatively small size. They mark their territories in various ways; the red and fallow deer mark with urine scented from the preputial glands, scrape the ground bare in places with their feet, and fray the vegetation or bushes with their antlers thereby spreading the secretion from the glands on the face just below the eyes. They also mark themselves by wallowing in wet places so that they become plastered with urine-soaked mud. The facial gland between the antlers and the eyes of the roebuck swells up and secretes under the influence of the sex hormones during the rut but then regresses, unlike the interdigital glands and those in the skin at the hocks which are active throughout the year.[1]

As well as marking, the deer advertise their possession of territory by their voices, the red stag by roaring, and the fallow buck by making a loud groaning noise. The roe buck has a similar territorial behaviour, but does not roar or groan, giving only an occasional bark. In addition, he makes 'rings', more or less circular paths trodden out around a bush, tree or other landmark around which not only the buck but also the does and fawns run during the rut; the precise function of the rings remains obscure. The males of all three species defend their territories during the rut, chasing away any other that challenges him, with much sparring and fighting and shoving contests with heads lowered. Though one sometimes is killed the contests usually end with the challenger retreating, for the occupier, even if not greatly stronger, has the great 'psychological' advantage over an aggressor of being in possession.

Nearly all the special scent glands in the mammals are modifications or super-developments of the sebaceous glands which produce the oily secretion that protects the skin and pelage. If our sebaceous glands get stopped up with dirt they form 'blackheads', and if they become infected with bacteria they produce acne. The oily secretion, or sebum, sometimes mixed with the watery product of the sweat glands, has a characteristic scent derived from the mixture of various fatty substances in it, which are further modified by the degradation products resulting from the action of bacteria. It is peculiar that these scents are generally nauseous stinks to the human sense of smell, but when they are greatly diluted they may sometimes be sweet and pleasant. Rarely the raw scent may be pleasing, as that from the perineal glands of the civet or the preputial glands of the musk deer, both of which are valued commercially – fortunately for the British mammals none of them produces anything desired by the perfumer.

The home ranges and territories of ground living mammals can be mapped in two dimensions, but those of a few species that live in trees and can go up and down, as well as to and fro, are three-dimensional and more difficult to determine. The red and grey squirrels are the main examples in the British Isles, with the harvest mouse, dormouse, pine marten, stoat, and bank vole occupying three dimensions to a lesser extent. None of them is confined to the arboreal habitat. The squirrels make their homes in the trees, building large dreys or nests of sticks lined with finer materials among the branches, or denning in holes. As the home range of these species extends to many trees the animals often descend to the ground when passing from one to another, although when trees are closely spaced they are most agile in jumping from branch to branch. The ground area covered by the home range seldom exceeds some 500 yards in diameter and is generally much smaller. The territory of squirrels surrounding the drey is defended against intrusion by others of the same species, but there seems to be little information about the marking of territories and ranges. From what we know of the importance of scent marking to mammals it is probable that red squirrels mark their territories and ranges at least on the trees that contain or are close to their home territories, and the most probable medium for doing so is their urine. Grey squirrels mark their territory in this way[141]; they also gnaw patches of bark on tree trunks and branches and mark the bare places with urine.

The harvest mouse occupies three dimensional space on a more modest scale as befits its diminutive size, for it seldom climbs more than six feet above the ground. It is an agile climber that works more carefully than the squirrels – whereas a squirrel runs along branches with apparent wild abandon, even out to the furthest twigs, the harvest mouse climbs the stems of tall grasses and herbage grasping not only with its feet and hands but also with its prehensile tail wrapped round the support. The harvest mouse, too, lives in burrows during the winter, but in summer makes its breeding nest of shredded grass blades suspended from the stems and twigs of herbage a foot or so above the ground, weaving a globular structure with a small entrance hole. The nest is the centre of the female's territory and is kept as private property, but the home ranges of neighbours appear to overlap considerably so that defended territory seems to be limited.

The dormouse, like the harvest mouse, builds its summer nest above ground, and winter nest below. Much of its activity is three dimensional, because it forages among the branches and twigs of the field layer and into the low canopy. The home range is comparatively small, but whether the dormouse defends or marks the territory around the nest appears to be unknown. The summer nest is generally within a few feet of the ground, and the winter nest in which the dormouse hibernates is on or below ground; it is made of grasses and leaves and particularly of the shredded bark of the honeysuckle which readily peels away from the stem.

The pine marten is as much terrestrial as arboreal, but is nevertheless extremely agile as a climber – the flying leaps from tree to tree made by the semi-tame martens filmed by H.G. Hurrell, the Devonshire naturalist, made one wonder why birds had bothered to evolve wings. The marten maintains several dens in its extensive home range, and scent marks both its territory and landmarks outside it in the home range not only with faeces scented with the secretion of the anal glands but also with that from a separate scent gland on the belly. A marking gland in this position is highly appropriate for an arboreal mammal, for it marks its trail as it climbs on tree trunks and branches in much the same way as the flank gland of shrews marks the burrows that the animal traverses.

The stoat, though primarily terrestrial, is also a good climber and ascends into the third dimension in search of prey, and often makes its nest at some distance above ground in hollows among thick ivy clinging to a tree trunk. Such territory is marked and defended in a similar way to territory on the ground or below it.

The bank vole, too, though a burrower that nests underground, includes the upper part of the field layer in its home range and even extends into the low canopy; its defended territory, however, is below ground and its above-ground home range is probably not exclusive to individuals.

The scent marking of territories and ranges maps out the countryside for wild mammals as definitely as the hedgerows, fields, footpaths, lanes, roads, farmsteads and villages mark it out to show human occupation and ownership. Had we as acute a sense of smell as the other mammals the scene might appear very different from what we are accustomed to see; the universal and constantly changing scent-marked mosaic makes a pattern of which most people are totally unaware. Some countrymen and naturalists, however, know something of this, for they too can interpret some of the information given by the presence of burrows, tracks, and runways, and even scent marking points. They see that the life of the mammals is intensely individual, with each for itself, and the devil take the hindmost, in a constant struggle to preserve territories and home ranges in order to secure enough food. The only exception is the parental relationship between female, and very rarely the male, and the young. Any protection or herding given by males to females is entirely selfish, for the female is merely a sex-object to the male. The competition is bound to become more intense the higher the concentration of the individuals of a species on a given area, and hence the population density is of first importance.

The populations of mammals are not, as we have seen, scattered at random over their habitat, but confined to home ranges and territories. At each breeding season a new generation of individuals is added to the population, and must seek to establish homes and ranges of its own. At the other end of the scale natural mortality removes some of the oldest animals that have not sooner fallen victim to predators. Far more young are born than can hope to find homes, and consequently a high mortality rate eliminates many before they can become adult and themselves breed to produce yet more young. Many small mammals experience only one breeding season, after which they die. The field vole, for example, may produce several litters of young during a single summer, and die in the autumn. The over-wintering population therefore consists of immature animals that will breed the following summer. The winter population is thus able to establish home ranges and territories by the spring, using the area formerly inhabited by the parent generation of the previous summer. The animals of the overwintering population, being immature, are smaller and lighter in weight than their parents so that the diminished food supply in the winter supports a larger number of them than it could of adults. The common and pygmy shrews, also, are annuals; the adult generation that has bred during the summer dies in the autumn so that the winter population consists almost entirely of immature animals.

When home ranges are established by newly adult animals about to breed for the first time in early summer, the number of animals that a habitat can support depends upon the abundance or scarcity of food; the sizes of the home ranges and hence the density of the population are thus determined. When conditions are unfavourable the competition to establish homes is great, and the mortality among the unsuccessful is larger than in more genial seasons. The sizes of populations thus depend upon the productivity of the habitat, and will necessarily vary from season to season in step with it, apart from other fluctuations such as a reduction in numbers due to an exceptionally severe winter. The peak in numbers produced during the summer breeding season provides the raw material for the conditions of the environment to sort out onto the home ranges and territories of the following year, discarding the excess in the process.

The small and medium-sized rodents form the mainstay of the diet of the predators, which need a home range at least four times larger than that of their prey, and often much more. The density of the predator population thus depends largely on that of the prey, so that predators are forced into strong competition for ranges when the availability of prey is low. Causes similar to those governing the size of small rodent populations govern those of predators when the young annually disperse from the parental den on reaching adolescence. The young of the carnivores, however, remain dependent on the parent for comparatively much longer than do those of small rodents, so that dispersal and occupation of new ranges may be deferred until the year after their birth or even longer.

The fluctuations in population density sometimes give rise to plagues of small mammals in which the population explodes into numbers so large that eventually the habitat cannot support them, not for lack of nourishment but from lack of room. In the British Isles this phenomenon occurs most frequently among the field and bank voles; on the continent it is also found in other species, the best known being the Norway lemming, though it sometimes occurs in the dormouse and other species.

The habit of 'mast seeding' in trees is one of the things influencing the periodical growth of small mammal populations. Some kinds of tree such as the oak, beech, and ash produce great quantities of seed in certain 'good' years, but less during several intervening ones. The good years when all the trees of a species are highly productive are 'mast years', and an interesting theory has recently been proposed to explain the evolution of the masting habit.[129] The bountiful production of mast years provides food for an increasing population of small rodents and invertebrate feeders, but is so excessive that even when they have eaten to satiation all they can there are still vast numbers of seeds left to germinate. In the intervening non-mast years of meagre production the rodents are starved, or at least short of food from the species of tree concerned, and cannot survive in the numbers that build up in mast years. 'The interactions between masting trees and their invertebrate and vertebrate seed predators are strong enough to exert the kind of selection pressures necessary to accentuate environmentally induced fluctuations in crop size through evolutionary time into more pronounced, adaptive fluctuations of the kind these trees exhibit.' The rodents fare better than the invertebrates that are tied to one kind of seed for food, as they can find other sources, so a mast year is a bonus for them though a non-mast year is not necessarily a disaster.

A plague of voles builds up in the course of two or three years to a high density of animals, and the peak is followed by a swift crash in numbers that leaves only a small population of survivors. At the height of the plague the voles seem to swarm everywhere and may reduce their environment to a semi-desert with scruffy grass tufts undermined by burrows and interlaced by innumerable runs. The cause of the plague is a succession of favourable seasons, giving plenty of food, and the absence of heavy predation, but the cause of the sudden crash from the peak has for long been a puzzle to zoologists. Intense study of the phenomenon showed that it is not due to any lack of food, nor to an epidemic of disease, though the possibility of both was closely examined; at last it was established that overcrowding alone is responsible.

In an overcrowded population of voles at the summit of the peak the animals are constantly trespassing on each others' territory from which the owner tries to drive the intruders. This brings on a state of constant harrassment, with fighting and disturbance that leads to a widespread state of stress – females are unable to devote their time to looking after their young and may even destroy them. There is, however, more than mere external strife, for the state of stress brings on an internal strife. The whole metabolism of the animal is upset, especially the reproductive metabolism, so that breeding is disorganised. The disruption is due to the malfunctioning of the endocrine system, and is manifested particularly in an increased activity of the adrenal glands followed by their exhaustion, accompanied by the resorption or abortion of the developing foetuses. The basis of the process can be regarded as psychological, for the activity of the pituitary gland at the base of the brain, which produces excess of adreno-cortico-tropic hormone (ACTH) that stimulates the adrenal gland, is itself stimulated by nerve cells in the hypothalamic region of the brain.

The overcrowding and consequent stress in a population at the peak of a plague of voles thus produces conditions that make life intolerable, so that breeding stops and the animals die from internal stress caused by disorganisation of the feedback mechanisms of the endocrine system. A somewhat similar phenomenon has sometimes occurred even in human populations; some tribes of savages have dwindled and died out when their way of life has been disrupted by the arrival of Europeans who tried to impose their kind of civilisation upon them – conditions became intolerable to them and they just lost the will to live.

On a much larger scale the population of grey seals that lives on the shores of the British Isles shows the effects of a population explosion that has not yet worked through to its final solution. In the last thirty years the population has increased enormously; on the Farne Islands off the coast of Northumberland for example, the numbers of grey seals rose from a few hundred in the 1920s[82] to 8,500 in 1977.[137] Grey seals come ashore for breeding in the autumn; the bulls arrive first and are joined later by the cows. The cows give birth to their pups, come into a post-partum oestrus and are inseminated by the bulls. They suckle their pups for about three weeks and shortly afterwards part company with them for good.

As the population has built up the breeding beaches have become excessively crowded, in spite of the establishment of some new and equally rapidly expanding breeding colonies. As a result of the overcrowding there is a very high death rate among the young, ranging from about twelve per cent to fifty per cent depending on how bad the overcrowding is. The cause of the mortality is that many cows become separated from their pups in an overcrowded colony and cannot find them again, a cause that is increased by the disturbance to the colony if people visit it. The lost pups die of starvation accompanied by bacterial infections that attack when the animals become weaker, and by restless starvelings wandering to the sea and being drowned. In overcrowded colonies there is obviously a state of stress, but as far as is known it does not upset the hormonal balance of the adults, which survive to breed again.

We do not know if the natural mortality of the pups will in the end bring a reduction in population numbers; up to the present the population continues to increase in spite of this loss. In addition any effect will take some years to show itself because cow grey seals do not breed for the first time until they are at least five years old.[81] Any natural alteration in numbers has now been interfered with by man; owing to the damage grey seals inflict on the fisheries an attempt has been made at reducing the size of the seal population by killing some thousands of pups each year for over a decade.[137] The result has been disappointing, for the numbers continue to grow; this is not surprising in view of the high natural mortality of the pups – it will make no difference to the numbers if you kill pups that are going to die anyway before they can reach breeding maturity. The only way that might reduce numbers is to kill the adult cows that have survived the risks of adolescence. The first serious attempt to control the number of seals by killing some 900 cows on some Scotch islands in 1979 was frustrated, so the problem of managing the stocks of seals remains unsolved, at least for the present. The great increase in the numbers of grey seals does not appear to have been due to the protection given them by various Acts of Parliament since 1914, for the seals were not hunted or destroyed by man to an extent that might have controlled their numbers before the legislation was passed. It would have been interesting to see if the population levelled off in the end by natural means, had the process not been interfered with by attempting to control it artificially.

When young seals have been deserted by their mothers and go to sea to start their independent lives some of them wander to surprisingly long distances from the beaches where they were born. Young seals marked in west Wales have been found as far away as the coast of Spain, and the west coast of Ireland when only about three months old; others from the Farne Islands have reached the coasts of Norway at a similar age, and one from the Hebrides even reached Iceland. We do not know whether such long journeys are normal, but it is certain that the young seals are widely dispersed after they leave their natal beaches. Nor do we know whether they return to their natal beaches, or others near them, when they reach breeding age, or whether the distant wanderers are lost and never return. The seals evidently have some sort of homing instinct because the different populations breed at slightly different dates; those of west Wales for example, give birth earlier in the autumn than those of Orkney. How får the annual assembly of seals on their breeding grounds can be regarded as a true migration is still uncertain because we do not know how widely the population is dispersed at sea during the rest of the year – some seals at least appear not to go far away.

Among the land mammals of the British Isles there is none that undertakes a long seasonal migration like that of migratory birds; but, apart from the impossibility of crossing the sea, several of them do have local seasonal movements. Some of the bats occupy different homes in summer and winter, the horseshoe bats in particular use the roofs of buildings for their summer breeding colonies but hibernate in caves. Their hibernation is not continuous but is interrupted from time to time, when they sometimes move from one cave to another up to several miles away. Some of the rodents, too, have seasonal movements though they are not necessarily undertaken by all individuals. The wood mouse and yellow-necked mouse often come into houses in the autumn, and similarly outdoor populations of house mice and brown rats come into farm buildings from the hedgerows in the autumn. The well known mass movement of lemmings in Norway is not a true migration but rather a search for new homes by the excess population produced by a 'plague', and the 'mass suicides' are merely the result of accidental drownings when the animals try to cross rivers, arms of the sea, or bodies of standing water.

The red deer also shows seasonal movements, coming down from the hill tops to lower and more sheltered ground during the winter. All these seasonal movements are too limited in space and in numbers of animals affected to be termed migrations; indeed, as we have seen, most of the mammals are far too strongly attached to their home ranges and territories to leave them even temporarily.

CHAPTER 6

SOCIAL BEHAVIOUR

ALTHOUGH the species of mammal living in the British Isles have home ranges and territories they do not live in isolation from others of their kind; even those that are solitary in their habits for most of the year must come into contact with others for the sexes to meet for breeding. Some species live in 'colonies' so that the animals are constantly meeting their neighbours, as less frequently are the holders of territories and home ranges. As a consequence mammals have evolved patterns of behaviour that enable them to earn their livings without the continual distraction of each individual having to fight to hold its own against the competition of rivals. Mammals treat strangers even of their own species with suspicion that easily passes into aggression, and is allayed only by more or less stereotyped reactions enabling the confrontation to pass without strife.

An immense amount of research has been made on the subject of animal behaviour – social behaviour between animals of the same species, protective behaviour and aggression towards those of other species, and behaviour in relation to the features of the environment. Research by observing animals in the wild is the most revealing but also the most difficult, not only because it is difficult to observe wild animals in their natural habitats without disturbing them, but also because the almost infinite variations in the character of the environment introduce so many factors influencing behaviour that it is difficult to reach unequivocal conclusions. Zoologists studying animal behaviour have therefore carried out much of their work with experiments in the laboratory where conditions can be controlled, and the complications of an infinite number of uncontrollable variables avoided. The simplification thus produced allows a single aspect of behaviour to be investigated at a time, but great care is needed, in extrapolating from results derived from behaviour in a completely artificial environment, to reach valid conclusions about behaviour in the wild.

Actions that lead to the resolution of aggressive encounters between two strangers are an important and widespread form of behaviour that avoids injury or death to the participants. Among the insectivores the behaviour of the common and pygmy shrews has been studied by Dr Peter Crowcroft who succeeded in keeping the animals in good health in captivity.[43] Shrews lead solitary lives except for the short time the sexes meet during the breeding season, and are strongly territorial with each territory centring on a sleeping nest or home. Each owner of territory keeps it for exclusive use by driving away any intruder of its own species, so that the animals are spread out through the habitat and each has enough foraging room to find its food. The preservation of private territories is not, however, achieved by fierce fighting resulting in death or injury to either of the contestants; in a confrontation the quarrel is generally settled by intimidation and rarely by fatal fighting.

When two shrews approach each other the owner of the territory starts squeaking or 'screaming' at the other, which screams back at it. After a short screaming match the intruder often heeds the warning of the owner, turns tail and runs away. If it does not accept defeat the owner suddenly rears up on its hind feet, continuing to scream, whereupon the intruder generally flees, perhaps in response to this sudden apparent increase in size – or at least assertion of emphasis – of the other. If the intruder is stubborn it too may rear up and then both bite at each other though inflicting little or no apparent damage, until one breaks away and retreats. Sometimes, instead of retreating one throws itself upon its back, still screaming, at which the other runs away. Occasionally both throw themselves onto their backs and scream until they resume the contest, or they may seize each other's tails and spin round rapidly before breaking away and resuming their screaming match. There are of course minor variations in the resolution of a confrontation, but it always follows the same general pattern.

The most notable point about such encounters is that the owner appears always to be at an advantage over the intruder; its familiarity with the details of its territory and, presumably, its feeling of security through being at home on its own ground give it what may be called a psychological sense of superiority over its rival. This psychological advantage enjoyed by the owner of a territory when a stranger trespasses is not confined to shrews, but is universal among the mammals, and indeed among nearly all animals. If a shrew enters the nest of another during the owner's absence it is quickly and ignominiously ejected when the owner returns.

Dr Crowcroft discovered these interesting features of the social – or should we call it anti-social? – behaviour of shrews by watching the animals in captivity where they are necessarily confined to smaller potential territories than they are in the wild. By giving the experimental animals accommodation much larger than that of conventional cages he was able to satisfy himself that the reactions he observed were not distorted representations of those that take place in the wild, though confining the shrews in small cages does accentuate the intensity of their aggressive encounters. If two shrews in the wild meet on ground that is not near the centre of the territory of either they often turn silently and run away in diverging directions; and furthermore, unlike many mammals, the victor of an encounter does not chase the vanquished to or beyond the boundary of its territory, though it may send a few parting squeaks to speed it on its way.

The pygmy shrew, though less numerous, shares the habitat of the common shrew and consequently the two species must meet from time to time. One might expect such encounters to result in the quick defeat and perhaps death of the pygmy shrew at the teeth of the larger species, or at least a quick retreat on its part in response to the screaming of the common shrew. Nothing of the sort ever happens: the pygmy shrew is so nimble and alert that it never comes into contact with the common shrew. If foraging individuals of the two species approach each other the pygmy shrew becomes aware of the common shrew in time to turn and run silently away, so that the common shrew is totally unaware of its presence. In effect, the pygmy shrew knows all about the common shrew, but the latter is ignorant that such a creature as the pygmy shrew exists. As we noted in chapter 5 the two species, though sympatric in Great Britain, are in some measure separated by preferring slightly different ecological niches.

The solitary lives of the shrews appear to be typical of those of many insectivores that live alone except for the brief meeting of the sexes when the barrier of aggression is lowered for a short period in the breeding season. Like the shrews, the mole is a loner and a holder of territory. A mole's territory consists of a system of ramifying tunnels that may occupy an area of up to 1,000 square yards or more; it has deep permanent tunnels a foot or two below the surface, and shallow surface tunnels only a few inches down made in searching for food which consists mainly of earthworms. The animal makes its nest of dead leaves or grass in an enlarged cavity or nest chamber in one of the deeper tunnels; it does not always confine itself to one home but may have several nests scattered throughout the tunnel system. Often, especially where the deep tunnels are liable to flooding, the nest is made on the surface below a large mound of earth that has been called the 'fortress' by some naturalists, because it is much larger than the mole heaps made by pushing out the earth loosened in deep tunnelling. The breeding nest made by the female mole as a nursery for her young may be built in a fortress or in a nest chamber connected with a deep tunnel.

Each tunnel system is the private property of the mole inhabiting it, and intruders are not tolerated. Owing to the difficulty of watching the behaviour of moles in their underground tunnels we do not know if they, like shrews, drive an intruder away by displays of aggression that rarely result in a serious fight. However that may be, it is certain that encounters do sometimes lead to fighting, for moles have been seen fighting in shallow surface tunnels from which the loser escaped onto the surface. The only time when the aggressiveness of the mole falls temporarily into abeyance is when the female comes into oestrus and briefly tolerates the presence of the male.

Our largest insectivore, the hedgehog, is also entirely solitary for the greater part of its life. Each animal has a territory extending up to four or five hundred yards from the den where it lies up during the day, and whence it comes out to seek food at dusk and through the night. It is improbable that the animals preserve their territories as strictly as do the smaller insectivores, for they are not known to fight or drive away strangers by threatening displays – indeed it seems impossible for hedgehogs to fight because at any sign of aggression one or perhaps both of the contestants would presumably roll up and present an invulnerable covering of spines to the other.

The reactions of a female hedgehog when she is coming into oestrus and is approached by a male have sometimes been mistaken for a fight between rival males. Until the female is in full oestrus she will not accept the male, whose pursuit and presence probably help to stimulate its onset. At such times when the male first approaches she often erects her spines and butts at the male with those on her forehead. This repulses the male temporarily, but he persists sometimes for hours until she is finally stimulated into accepting him. This performance is not true aggressive fighting – the female is merely playing 'hard to get', a phenomenon commonly shown by the females of many mammals in the early stages of oestrus.

It is probable that the territories of individual hedgehogs often overlap and that if the animals meet they merely avoid each other. Their droppings may serve to mark their territories although they seem for the greater part to be left quite haphazardly over the foraging area; I have nevertheless seen a hedgehog night after night travelling the same route from its den to forage on a garbage heap some fifty yards away, although there were no visible signs of a path. The nearest approach that hedgehogs make to any sort of social life is in the breeding season when mating pairs may remain together for a short time.

Although the insectivores lead solitary lives and avoid any social contacts except for the brief meeting of the sexes for breeding, they all pass through a short period of social behaviour when they are young, and living in the nest where they are suckled by the mother until the dispersal of the family after weaning. The young of the insectivores, like those of most small mammals, are naked and blind at birth, but they are much slower in growing up than the young of small rodents, and consequently have a longer family life. The eyes of the red-toothed shrews and of the mole do not open until they are about three weeks old, by which age the fur is fairly well grown. Similarly, young hedgehogs are born hairless and blind and have the ears closed, but have on their backs a number of short soft precursors of spines. By the time they are a fortnight old the spines and belly fur have grown, and the eyes open shortly afterwards.

Even before their eyes open the young of these animals leave the nest, apparently in an attempt to follow and feed from their mother, who retrieves them and bundles them back into the nest. During weaning they follow the mother about as they begin to eat solid food, and she keeps her family together and rounds up any straggler. Shrews are weaned a few days after the eyes open at about the age of three weeks, but hedgehogs not until their fourth or fifth week. Shrews probably, and hedgehogs certainly, remain with the mother for some days after they are weaned, and the family breaks up when the mother drives them away and each takes up its solitary existence.

The white-toothed shrews differ in being more precocious. The fur has grown and the eyes open by the tenth day, though they are not weaned until about three weeks of age. Sometimes a few days before the eyes open, and frequently afterwards, they leave the nest in company with the mother, who leads them in line with each grasping the rump of the one in front, a habit that has been termed 'caravanning'. This has long been thought to occur only in the white-toothed shrews, but a well authenticated occurrence of it in the common shrew in 1972 is recorded.[75] A party of seven was watched for fifteen minutes caravanning along a figure-of-eight pathway between two thorn bushes about three metres apart. The habit is probably associated with the disturbance of a nest of well grown young.

The social behaviour of the insectivores thus seems to be of the simplest, as it is limited to the few weeks from birth to dispersal of the litter. Thereafter each animal keeps to itself avoiding contact with others, and has no need for a social hierarchy of dominance such as occurs in many other mammals. Their philosophy of life appears to be that of the traditional north-countryman – 'Here's a stranger; heave a brick at him'. The insectivores have aptly been described as obscure animals, living obscure lives, in obscure places.

In contrast with the behaviour of insectivores that of the small rodents, the voles and mice, is more complicated. Although basically they share the aggressiveness of the insectivores towards other animals of their own species, and each occupies its own territory, their social organisation is more complex; it permits the holding of overlapping territories and, within limits, the toleration of other individuals in close proximity. The fundamental behaviour pattern at encounters with strangers is attack followed, according to the prowess of the individual, by defence and escape, or aggression and pursuit. These reactions are modified by the establishment of social hierarchies in which the larger, older, or stronger animals become dominant over their weaker or younger conspecific sharers of the habitat. This corresponds to the 'peck order' that has been studied in much detail in the common fowl, and is also found in other domestic animals artificially forced into sharing a limited common environment. The dominant bird is given precedence by all the others, the second in order defers to the dominant but is given precedence by the remainder, and so on down the scale to the unfortunate 'omega' bird that gives way to, and may be bullied by, all those above it. A similar order of precedence is developed among domestic cattle, and among many species of gregarious animals in the wild.

A somewhat similar arrangement characterises the behaviour of the small rodents which hold individual territories but share a much larger and overlapping home range. Among wood mice the females have smaller home ranges than the males, and that of the dominant male in any colony is larger than any other.[65] The home range of the dominant male includes the home ranges of many of the subordinates; he moves over them freely so that he has access to the best feeding places and to more of the females than the others. Although he is aggressive if he encounters others, he does not seek them out for attack so that in general conflict is avoided by the subordinates keeping out of his way. This type of behaviour is modified by various biological factors, one of the most important being the density of the population; when density is low there is plenty of room for all, but when it is high aggressive assertion of the ownership of territories and home ranges is more intense.[71]

The field vole needs much less living space than the wood mouse, and can tolerate much higher population densities; consequently home ranges are smaller particularly in the autumn when the annual production of young is recruited into the population. Aggressive behaviour does not become serious unless the population reaches numbers high enough to produce a degree of overcrowding far exceeding that which would be tolerated by the field mouse. This pattern of behaviour is due mainly to the diet of the animals; they feed on the grass under the mat of which they live and make their nests, so that they have no need to go far from home to forage. It is thus possible for populations of wood mice and of field voles to occupy the same ground area without aggressive rivalry between the two species because each inhabits a different micro-habitat within it, and both largely ignore the presence of the other. They are further separated by the solely nocturnal habits of activity in the wood mouse.

The social behaviour in the family life of the small rodents fills a much shorter period of time than that of the insectivores. Mice and voles also are born blind and naked, but develop far more quickly. Their eyes open in about a fortnight, by which age the fur has grown so that weaning occurs a few days afterwards and the young, now able to fend for themselves, are driven away by the mother at an age when the young of the insectivores are still dependent upon her.

The bank vole occupies a much more varied habitat than the field vole and is more commonly found in woodland and hedgerow, although it also occurs in open fields. Unlike the field vole it is not restricted to runways under the grass mat, nor to a diet mainly of grass stems. As we have already noted, it is partly arboreal and climbs extensively in shrubs and bushes, running along branches and twigs with surprising agility and speed. Its social behaviour is thus less stereotyped, as contacts between individuals occur under more diverse conditions in a larger home range. The social relationships appear to be rather loose, with larger animals dominating the smaller ones and chasing them from food or females in oestrus. On the other hand there is some communal use of underground burrows, at least when the system of burrows lies below open ground. In a Suffolk garden sparsely covered with low herbage, and with many bare patches of earth, the entrances to the burrows were merely holes on the flat and level bare parts. There was evidently a bank vole population of some size living below because ten adult voles were caught on ten successive days in a trap placed at the mouth of one of the burrows. This implies that there is probably some sort of social hierarchy if so many were inhabiting a single system of burrows. The subspecies found on the island of Skomer showed a similar communal layout of burrows or runs under a corrugated iron roofing sheet left lying on the ground in a grassy paddock. The voles had taken advantage of the artificial cover to avoid digging, and their 'burrows' were on the surface among the dead grass. Half a dozen nests were connected by a network of criss-crossing runways some of which led to entrance holes at the edge of the sheet. There must have been frequent encounters between the owners of the different nests but, although the runways appeared to be common to all the inhabitants, the nests were no doubt defended as private property.

The social behaviour of the bank vole within the family is similar to that of other small rodents, and is of brief duration. The young, naked and blind at birth, grow fast and are weaned in less than twenty days, after which they disperse from the breeding nest, though evidently as already noted they sometimes form underground colonies with some, at least, of the burrows in common use.

Both the red and the grey squirrels show a dominance hierarchy with the larger and heavier males taking precedence and enjoying larger home ranges. As both species are diurnal their behaviour is more readily observed than that of the smaller rodents. They appear to be much more aggressive than the mice and voles and indulge in 'agonistic' behaviour throughout the year. This consists of rapid chases in three dimensions – on the ground and up and down trees – in which more than two animals may be involved, the dominants biting the tails of those they pursue and threatening with chattering noises, tail flicking and stamping of the feet. Similar chases occur during the breeding season when several males pursue a female in oestrus, the subordinate ones finally giving way to the dominant. Females become strongly territorial when they are nursing their young, driving all others away from the neighbourhood of the nest, a drey built well above the ground in a tree. The young enjoy a short family life with the mother when they are weaned and begin to leave the drey, but after a week or two they disperse to find home ranges for themselves, often at a considerable distance from their place of birth.

The squirrels, particularly the now abundant grey squirrel, are serious pests to forestry and horticulture, and consequently their behaviour and life history have been closely studied by biologists in order to devise appropriate methods of control and destruction. Similarly those other notorious pests, the house mouse, common or brown rat, and the rabbit, have been the subject of more intense study than species whose natural history may be equally or even more interesting to naturalists, but whose activities inflict less damage on human interests. House mice are highly territorial, both in outdoor populations and those commensal with man in houses and other buildings. Extensive research has been needed to gain the information required for control of commensal mice, not only because of the direct damage caused to stores but, more importantly, because house mice carry and spread the *Salmonella* bacteria which produce 'food poisoning' in people who eat food contaminated by mice. Commensal populations often build up to considerable densities in which home ranges overlap but territory is vigorously defended, and a social hierarchy of behaviour is established. The dominant male among a group is aggressive towards the subordinate members and ensures for himself priority in feeding, nest sites, and in the possession of females. The young leave their mothers almost as soon as they are weaned at about three weeks of age so that family life is extremely reduced. On the other hand female house mice commonly share a communal nest when population density is high and nest sites are limited. This is an unusual phenomenon among the mammals, and shows the adaptability of a species that is basically strongly territorial.

The common rat generally occupies a comparatively small home range, probably because being a pest of stored foods in warehouses, and a feeder on garbage in rubbish tips and sewers, it has no need for an extensive one. Where food is more widely dispersed, as for populations living in burrows at the edge of fields of cereals or root crops, home ranges are necessarily larger. Young rats reach breeding maturity at the age of rather less than three months, so that where food is plentiful a colony founded by a single female rapidly grows. All the individuals are closely related and show a considerable degree of tolerance towards each other, but strong aggression towards strangers, which are quickly driven away. They probably recognise rats of their own colony by scent, for when two meet in a narrow run they sniff noses and then one lifts a hind leg to allow the other to crawl underneath and pass on its way. As the colony increases in size and competition for food increases a social hierarchy is developed in which the larger and stronger animals become dominant and take precedence in feeding, though the home ranges of all the animals in the colony may overlap. Nestlings are born naked and blind but are weaned at about three weeks; the social structure of a growing colony of comparatively young rats is thus an extension of the family life experienced before leaving their mothers.

The social behaviour of the introduced coypu has been studied in East Anglia by Dr L.M. Gosling,[69] who found a clan structure based on a female lineage. The dominant male of a colony is subordinate to the dominant female except when she is in oestrus, and the female young after being weaned occupy home ranges partly overlapping those of the mother and of each other. Thus a growing clan expands outwards round the range of the original clan matriarch, and there appears to be little aggressive behaviour between the members, which often feed together. The dominant males have a larger home range which may overlap that of more than one clan, and they drive out the young subordinate males which must presumably either establish separate home ranges, perish, or replace the dominant male in their own or another clan. The subadult young are, however, particularly vulnerable to death by starvation in hard winters, so that some of the excess males may thus be removed from the population.

The family life of the coypu lasts much longer than that of our native rodents, for the young are not weaned until they are two months old or more. Even when they finally leave the mother the females remain part of the clan and retain a considerable degree of social contact with the parent and each other and, in due course, with their own offspring. There is no definite breeding season as pregnancy, which lasts $4\frac{1}{2}$ months, may start at any time in the year. There is, however, generally a peak in the number of births in late summer and autumn because many litters are wholly or partly lost by resorption of the embryos, or by abortion, when food is scarce or climatic conditions are unfavourable. It is unfortunate that this interesting species is a destructive pest whose numbers must be kept down by continuous trapping at great cost in money and labour – we should be better off without it.

Our knowledge of the social behaviour of the rabbit in the British Isles is based on the fundamental researches of Dr H. N. Southern who laid the foundation on which all later work is built.[132, 133] The social structure of a population of rabbits is centred on the warren, a complicated system of burrows some of which communicate but many, though closely approaching each other, do not. The feeding area round the warren may extend to several acres with the nearest part heavily grazed and the more distant part used less frequently. Although the population of the warren is subordinate to several dominant bucks, it is the does that are the most persistent holders of territory; they show quite as much aggression to their neighbours as do the bucks. Does chase other rabbits from the neighbourhood of their burrows, particularly the short burrows or 'stops' in which they make a nest of dry grasses lined with fur plucked from their own chests for rearing their litters of young. Bucks, too, chase away trespassers that come into their territory, and sometimes leap at each other in a short aggressive encounter, which ends with the retreat of the trespasser; they are, however, less actively aggressive than the does.

By far the most conspicuous social activity in a rabbit warren is sexual. The does come into oestrus early in the year and the breeding season extends to midsummer or later. They come into oestrus again shortly after giving birth to each litter so that they are pregnant with a new litter while still suckling the previous one. The bucks perform a complex display toward the does to bring them into a receptive condition. It starts with a chase in which the buck trails round after the doe on and beyond the feeding area, often in a rather half hearted way, frequently breaking off to feed. As interest increases the chase gets more persistent and the pace faster; the buck approaches the doe and circles round her with his hindquarters raised displaying the white underside of the tail which is turned up onto the back. While doing this he frequently pauses to squirt a jet of urine at the doe, or squirts her as he rushes past or leaps over her. The doe generally appears to take little or no notice of this performance, but it is evidently part of the releasing stimulus that makes her receptive; the consummation usually occurs in a burrow rather than in the open.

The doe suckles her young only once a day and closes the mouth of the stop with earth after each visit. The young come out of the stop at about eighteen days of age and are weaned about three days later;

after a few more days they leave the stop permanently. They thus have a very short family life after coming to the surface, though the doe shows some protective behaviour towards them during this brief period. Thereafter they join in the common routine of the warren, feeding at dawn and dusk, sitting out basking and grooming in sunny weather, and avoiding close contact with others, until at the age of about four months they reach sexual maturity and become increasingly involved in the sexual behaviour of the warren.

Both the brown and mountain hares live on the surface, lying up in forms among vegetation during the day and feeding by night. Mountain hares do, however, dig short burrows, but appear to make little use of them and generally sit at the entrance. The social behaviour of both species appears to consist mainly in avoiding contact with neighbours in their extensive and overlapping territories. In the breeding season they lose their solitary habit and congregate in pairs or small groups which, especially with the brown hare, show active sexual behaviour. This includes aggression between the males, with chasing and sparring, and stimulation of the females by chasing, leaping and squirting urine. In spring, before cereal crops give cover, this 'mad' behaviour of the brown hare is easily observed even by daylight.

Very little is recorded about the social behaviour of the bats found in the British Isles. They are not easy to observe when flying by night, and their day roosts are often accessible only with difficulty or not at all. When a number of bats are feeding at a preferred site, as noctules taking the insects frequenting a rubbish dump, or Daubenton's bats and pipistrelles catching insects flying over water, each appears to take no notice of the others though doubtless aware of their presence; they show no sign of any social behaviour. On the other hand there may be some social communication between bats when they are foraging on the wing. Some badminton players in Suffolk, reluctant to leave their game until dusk stopped play, noticed an early bat swooping above the court. One player hit his shuttlecock up vertically as the bat approached and was surprised to see the bat alter course and flutter round the shuttle as though inspecting it. He repeated this a dozen times or so, and then was interested to see first one, then two, and finally half a dozen others attracted to the shuttle. It could be, of course, that the others were attracted by the sound of the shuttle flying through the air, as was the first, but the episode gave the strong impression that the first was calling up the others, which may, however, have been merely attracted by the probably intense echolocation of the first as it examined the shuttle. These bats were either pipistrelles or whiskered bats, and the occasion was not unique, for bats have been attracted by a shuttle on many subsequent occasions. It has long been known that bats will swoop to examine a pebble tossed into the air, but the slower motion of a shuttlecock gives better opportunity for observation. Similarly a long flexible stick rapidly waved in the air sometimes attracts bats – mischievous boys in tropical countries use a long bamboo thus to lure bats to their deaths. Whiskered bats often fly up and down a regular beat beside a hedge or in a country lane; it may be that the beat is a form of territory or home range from which others are excluded, but there is no precise information on the point. These anecdotal observations might be made the basis of precise information by chiropterists with appropriate recording apparatus and sufficient patience.

Similarly, little is known of the social behaviour of bats in their roosts. Bats often crowd into their roosts in large numbers, perhaps because of the comparative scarcity of suitable places, and generally cluster in close contact. There may be some sort of social hierarchy in such gatherings, for those on the outside of a cluster try to worm their way towards the centre, but perhaps it is merely the strongest that get the best places. There is certainly much vocal communication at times; the chirping and twittering of a summer colony of noctules in a hollow tree, for example, can be heard at a considerable distance when the bats awake and prepare to emerge for their evening flight. It would be interesting to know what is happening within at such times. It may well be that the chorus is merely produced by many bats simultaneously emitting their usual aggressive chirps and squeaks as they jostle and disturb one another.

In the summer roosts of bats the sexes are generally separate – the pregnant females form maternity colonies to give birth to their young, though they may be accompanied by juveniles of both sexes of a previous year. The females seldom carry their young with them when they go out to feed; how they recognise their own offspring on returning, or whether the perch where it has been left has any territorial meaning, remain unknown. The winter roosts where bats hibernate are in different places from the summer colonies, and there both sexes can be found. With many species it is in the winter roosts that copulation takes place in the autumn, often during the winter, and again in spring, mating being random and promiscuous. No further precise information is available on the social behaviour of British bats at this time, but recently an American species has been found to show a definite pattern,[11] which may well be paralleled in some of our species. The males of the American little brown bat, *Myotis lucifugus*, emit a special 'copulation call' when they seize a female to mate with her. This differs from various other calls that have been identified in recorded sonagrams. The call is believed to serve as a pacification signal to the female, telling her that the male's action is sexual and not aggressive. It 'appears to be an acoustical equivalent to the many and diverse visual and tactile signals used by other animals to promote and maintain male-female contact during mating.'

Turning now to the carnivores, which are of necessity thinner on the ground than their prey and consequently often solitary for much of their lives, we find a much more varied pattern of social behaviour, particularly in family groups which remain together far longer than those of insectivores and rodents that disperse at once after being weaned. It is among the young of the carnivores that the pheno-menon called 'play' is most striking though, as Dr Loizos has pointed out,[103] because animals do not work in the sense that human beings do it is a false analogy to apply the term 'play' to any of their activities. This aspect of behaviour is discussed further below.

Among the canids the high degree of social behaviour shown by some species, notably the wolf, is not matched by that of the fox, the sole representative of the family in the British Isles. The innate adaptation to a social hierarchy in the wolf is inherited by its descendant, the domestic dog, so that dogs can accept the dominance of their human masters and become 'one of the family.' A similar social hierarchy has not been recorded as occurring among British foxes, though it has been found among some of those of North America.[148] Foxes are territorial, with the size of the home range varying greatly according to the character of the terraine; as we saw in chapter 5, they mark the boundaries of their territories with urine and secretion of the anal glands, leaving a scent so powerful that it is readily detected at a distance even by the human nose. Foxes are said to be monogamous, a statement based on behaviour observed in captivity, which may not be applicable universally to foxes in the wild, but which is given support by the habit of the dog fox sometimes bringing food to the vixen when she has young cubs.

The family life of a litter of fox cubs lasts a considerable time. The cubs, though furry, are blind at birth, and are weaned at first with food regurgitated by the vixen, and thereafter with solid food. They begin to come out of the earth in which they were born at the age of about four weeks, but do not start fending for themselves until the age of about three months, nor become fully independent until a few weeks later. There is thus a period of about two months during which the litter, which generally consists of four or five cubs, enjoys a life of social relationships in which the strongest and most active are dominant. By the time they are six months old the cubs begin to disperse and seek to establish themselves in independent territories. Though foxes are born in underground earths, and when adult often lie up by day in such retreats, they equally as often lie up in surface lairs among thick cover, especially in dense growths of gorse. Although captive foxes in fur farms are monogamous, the two sexes do not occupy the same lair in the wild though their territories may overlap so that they frequently meet, especially when the vixen is rearing her cubs.

The mustelids have a similarly long family life during which social relationships are developed. The pine marten is so rare in the British Isles that we have little information about its social behaviour in the wild. It is a slow breeder, a female producing her first litter of three or four cubs at the age of two years. They are comparatively slow in maturing and do not leave the den where they were born until they are weaned at about eight weeks, or disperse until they are about six months old.[147] In captivity the young are 'very playful', but at first seem 'terrified of heights' although when adult they are extremely agile climbers.[86] Apart from the family groups, martens are solitary and have extensive home ranges marked by secretion from the abdominal glands and by scats, but they appear to show little aggression in defending their territory.

The stoat also has a comparatively long family life; the young, born in the spring, do not disperse until they are three months or more old.[73, 74] As the family group remains together until well after the young are able to fend for themselves the sight of a large litter, which can number as many as twelve young, foraging in company has given rise to the assertion that stoats sometimes hunt in a pack of presumably unrelated adults. After dispersal of the family stoats take up individual defended territories, though when the female is rearing her young the male, like the dog-fox, sometimes brings prey to her for distribution to the young. The social behaviour of the weasel is similar, except that the male is not known to provide food for the young; the family remains as a group for a shorter period, the young dispersing by about two months of age. The weasel is more aggressive than the stoat in defending its territory, especially the den on which it is centred.[100] Little is recorded about the social behaviour of the polecat or the mink in the wild, but the litters of young remain with their mothers for some weeks after reaching adult size, and share her territory for hunting.

We have a greater knowledge of the social life of the badger, thanks to the pioneer researches of Dr Ernest Neal and those of his many followers.[115] Badgers have a much more extensive social life than most of the British carnivores, for not only do they form family groups while the young are growing up under the care of the mother, but the adults also form social groups that live together in one set. The basis of a social group is one or more females with their cubs together with one or more adult males and some of the subadult cubs of the previous breeding season. All the animals in a group know each other personally, and forage over the same home range; they may all live in one set, or if the group is large they may be divided between two nearby sets. Neal found the numbers in such a group to vary between seven and twelve. The social hierarchy appears to be rather loose, though one male is usually dominant, and of course the cubs are subordinate to their mother. The group coheres by visual, vocal and scent signals, the last being by far the most important, for the animals mark each other and their territory with the scent from their subcaudal glands, and mark their dung pits, which also form territorial boundaries, with that of the anal glands. The badgers in a social group live peacefully together, and strengthen the social bond by various activities such as 'play' and mutual grooming.

It seems probable that the more or less permanent social grouping found in the badger but not in our other carnivores is connected with the feeding habits of the animals. Unlike the others, which hunt living prey, badgers are omnivorous and take anything edible that they may find, animal or vegetable, and are particularly partial to earthworms. As Neal says, they are 'primarily foragers, not hunters', and consequently do not need to be alone when seeking food as do hunters whose prey might be frightened away by the presence of others. There is thus little rivalry in foraging so that territory can be held in common, with the advantage of extensive communal sets for permanent homes. Apart from any persecution by man the badger seems to enjoy a very comfortable bourgeois existence.

Social behaviour in the otter is mainly confined to the family group containing the mother and her cubs which remain with her for up to a year. She brings them out of the holt, or breeding den, and they start entering the water at the age of about $2\frac{1}{2}$ months, and do not disband as a group until some eight or nine months later. In the breeding season the males share territory with the females but return to the solitary way of life when the female becomes pregnant.

With the wild cat social behaviour is similarly restricted to the family, though its duration is shorter, for the young disperse before they are six months old. Apart from mothers with families wild cats are generally solitary.

Of the seals, the common seal shows little or no social behaviour even at the breeding season. When resting common seals haul out of the water on rocks or sandbanks exposed at low tide, often in some numbers, but although they lie fairly close to one another there appears to be no social organisation or hierarchy – each is in effect solitary though close to its neighbours. They thus conform to Hediger's[80] definition of the 'distant type' of social behaviour, in contrast to the 'contact type' of grey seals when they haul out together, except in the breeding season, as described below. The females give birth to a single young one and suckle it for little more than a month, after which it becomes independent. Until the young is weaned the female looks after it assiduously both on land and in the water, but the bond does not last long and is broken at weaning.

In contrast the grey seal, which has a similar life-style for most of the year, appears to have, according to Hewer,[81] a well defined social organisation during the breeding season. Hewer considered that in the autumn dominant bulls take up territory on the sea beach or further inland on islands where they are not disturbed. Shortly afterwards the cows come ashore to give birth, and enter the territories of the bulls, which cover the cows when they come into heat a fortnight to three weeks after the birth of the young. The bulls are strongly aggressive towards each other in driving intruders away, but they do not gather the cows into 'harems', merely mating with those cows that happen to give birth in their territories. The cows suckle the pups four or five times every twenty four hours and occupy a mini-territory from which neighbours are excluded while they are suckling; pups often move about between feeds and consequently the mini-territory moves with them. The pups are weaned at about the age of three weeks whereupon the mothers desert them. Grey seals also haul out to rest and sleep at other times of the year and often form sizeable herds of animals lying close together or even huddled into contact, but show no social organisation.

Recent observations[21] on the grey seals breeding on the sand dunes of Sable Island, Nova Scotia, have led to a different conclusion about the social behaviour of the species. Although the behaviour of bull grey seals on British breeding grounds is consistent with the existence of a territorial system it does not prove that there is one. On Sable Island the bulls do not defend territories nor form dominance hierarchies, but compete for a place among the females, and maintain their positions by driving away other bulls that may threaten their tenure. A re-examination of the behaviour of British grey seals tends to show that their behaviour is similar. The Canadian naturalists suggest that the behaviour of the grey seal is more characteristic of a species that breeds on floating ice floes than of one that breeds on land, and that the species originally bred entirely on pack ice, as some colonies still do in the Gulf of St Lawrence and the Baltic Sea. This hypothesis is strengthened by the fact that bull grey seals have not acquired any conspicuous signalling display to advertise the holding of territory.

If further study shows that this kind of behaviour is indeed universal in the species the social behaviour, though different from the interpretation formerly accepted is nevertheless a well-marked system. It may be that something similar, though less conspicuous, occurs with the common seal, the differences probably being due to the different habitats of the two species. The grey seal hauls out onto ice, sea beaches, or dry land where the pups remain until they are weaned, though they are able to swim if they get into the water. The common seal, in contrast, gives birth on tidal banks or rocks from which the pups are floated at flood tide so that they are forced to swim with their mothers, who can suckle them in the water. Indeed, common seal pups are sometimes actually born in the water. The common seal is thus precluded from maintaining any social relationships that last more than a few hours, apart from those of mother and young.

The social behaviour of the ungulates has been much studied since the pioneer researches of Fraser Darling on the red deer,[44] perhaps because it can be more easily observed in the wild than that of smaller animals. Our native species and the fallow deer are all gregarious for at least part of the year, and whether in small groups or large herds show well marked social relationships. In all species a young animal starts life as a member of a family party from which the young males depart when they outgrow adolescence.

In the red deer the sexes live apart except at the time of the rut. Family parties or large herds of hinds with their calves and young stags have a hierarchy or peck order and follow the dominant hind. During the rut the yearling stags, but not the yearling hinds, are driven away from their mothers so that they are forced into the company of other young males.[73] Adult stags form summer herds in which the dominance of a single beast is less pronounced, and the coherence of a group of bachelor stags is comparatively loose. In the autumn the stag herds break up and the stronger stags take up individual territories in which they herd a group of hinds and drive off rivals that seek to usurp them. They advertise their possession of territory, and attract hinds coming into heat, by roaring, and defend their territories by fighting any rival that may challenge them. The territorial fights, though sometimes ending fatally, are generally sparring matches in which after a few clashes the weaker breaks away leaving the owner in possession; it is usually only towards the end of the rut that the owner of territory, 'run out' by fasting and constant activity, is displaced by a challenger.

When red deer stags fight during the rut they roar at each other for several minutes, then approach and walk side by side separated by a short distance, sizing up each other. If the fight proceeds one stops and turns towards the other and lowers his head. The other turns quickly and also lowers his head, and the two lock antlers and push. If the contest is long they break off for a few seconds from time to time, and resume when one lowers his head again. The fight ends when one of the stags gets pushed quickly backwards, breaks contact and runs away, with the victor seldom pursuing for more than a few yards. If one slips during the pushing match the other at once tries to stab him in the flank, neck or rump, and sometimes inflicts a serious wound. Most stags suffer minor injuries from fights at some time during their reproductive lives, but injuries causing permanent effects are few.

The evolution of this type of fighting behaviour must have been due to a selective adaptation conferred by it. The costs and benefits of fighting have been assessed.[36] As successful stags may increase their harem size they fight most frequently and intensely at the time when hinds are most likely to conceive, but they tend to avoid fighting with those they are unlikely to beat. On the other hand the costs mount with the length of the contest 'with the additional possibility that a false move may lead to injury in either contestant'.

The fallow deer, introduced after the Norman conquest, has always had to cope with the presence of man and modify its behaviour accordingly. The feral population lives in small groups of does with their young of both sexes, led by a dominant doe. The bucks live apart in bachelor herds during spring and summer, but rejoin the does for the rut at the end of summer and during the autumn. At this time the bucks take up and defend territories, 'groaning' and fighting off any rivals that may challenge them. Where fallow deer are kept undisturbed in parks as ornaments to the landscape they commonly form larger herds with less pronounced segregation of the sexes, a modification of social behaviour produced by semi-domestication.

The roe deer is much less gregarious, and both sexes often lead solitary lives. When the does have young, however, they also live in small family parties of a buck and one or more does with the young of both sexes. The bucks hold and defend territories not only during the rut but throughout the summer. During the winter family groups sometimes form small herds mainly of one sex dominated by a single animal. The peculiar habit of running in a ring round some conspicuous landmark, already noticed, is indulged in by both sexes and all ages during the summer – the meaning of this part of the animals' social behaviour is obscure. A similar habit has been noticed occasionally in the fallow deer.

CHAPTER 7

BEHAVIOUR AND THE ENVIRONMENT

THE social behaviour of the British mammals shows various degrees of complexity which may well illustrate the probable course taken in the evolution of social relationships. The basic requirement of social behaviour in all animals is to bring the sexes together for breeding. Among the lower vertebrates that lay eggs this contact can be very brief and be the only social relationship that occurs in those species which abandon the eggs as soon as they are laid. Apart from the parental care that has been evolved among some species in the other classes of vertebrates – some fishes, amphibians and reptiles and almost all the birds – the evolution of suckling the young on milk secreted by the mother produces of necessity a close social relationship between parent and offspring.

In the British mammalian fauna the insectivores show the simplest form of social behaviour: the sexes meet briefly for mating and thereafter separate permanently, but the female looks after her family until it disperses after being weaned. All other social contacts are negative in that they are fortuitous, and result in the separation of individuals to lead solitary lives. Greater complexity of social behaviour occurs in those species in which many individuals live in close proximity, thereby increasing protection from danger though in an entirely passive way. There is safety in numbers because one animal alerted by danger is seen or heard by its neighbours which are thereby themselves alerted. The rabbit provides a familiar example: when a scared rabbit bolts for shelter the white underside of its tail is at once noticed by others as a signal of danger. But the rabbit has in addition evolved mutually protective behaviour from a passive to an active role. A rabbit suspicious of unidentified danger, but not frightened enough to bolt for home, thumps the ground with its hind feet, thus putting its neighbours on the alert. Nevertheless it is doubtful whether this reaction to a mild stimulus is a conscious communication to others rather than an innate response – to a human observer it seems to express impatience or even anger. The safety in numbers principle applies also to the gregarious ungulates among which, as we have seen, the social hierarchy is more complex than among our smaller mammals.

Among the carnivores, which as we have already noted are necessarily fewer than their prey and consequently more thinly dispersed, social behaviour is in some species more prominent. Young carnivores cannot immediately fend for themselves as soon as they are weaned, for catching living prey is not so easy as nibbling vegetation. The family bond between the mother and her young is thus prolonged into adolescence or beyond, as she not only protects them from danger and suckles them, but also goes hunting to catch food for them. In the smaller species the group disperses when the young are able to hunt on their own, and the individuals seek territory in which they can live alone, excluding any trespassers. But in some larger species there is a stronger and more lasting social bond. The fox is believed to pair for life, or at least for several seasons, the dog-fox and vixen inhabiting overlapping territories though not living in the same earth together. The fox earth is mainly a cradle for the cubs; the adults live as much in dense cover on the surface as underground. When the vixen has young cubs the dog fox sometimes brings food for her to give them; such paternal care for the young is extremely rare among mammals and is almost entirely confined to the canids and the primates. If indeed the dog fox is monogamous and does assist the vixen in this way the bond between the pair is much stronger than is common among mammals, and resembles the 'pair-bond' between birds in the breeding season. Although the study of animal behaviour must be objective and avoid any taint of anthropomorphism, it is hard to see the social behaviour of foxes, and especially the pair-bond, as other than based on emotion and affection.

What then of the social behaviour of the badger? We have seen that the social system of the badger is possible probably because the availability of food is such that there is no need for rivalry in foraging and the holding of private territories. The animals hold a group territory which they mark and keep exclusive, but within the group it is free for all. The basis of the group is the family, the litter of the sow, which is slow to disperse at adolescence and remains as a social group inhabiting the same set, some until they reach breeding age. There may thus be more than one breeding sow in a large set so the social group consists of several families all closely related as cousins, aunts and uncles. The identity of the group is maintained, at least in part, by the habit of the animals setting scent on each other, so that a communal group scent is produced common to all members. This kind of social grouping, maintained long after the animals become adult, and based on a combination of related families, contrasts strongly with the social grouping of gregarious animals such as deer in which the group consists of individuals that have no personal bonds after the young are weaned. There may perhaps be an emotional bond between the members of a group of badgers, but it cannot be similar to that between the dog fox and his vixen which is solely a pair-bond. It is hard to resist the temptation to see in the social system of the badger a parallel to what may well have taken place in the first stages of the evolution of human society.

We may now return to look briefly at a special form of social behaviour, namely 'play'; as already mentioned, play in animals is not the equivalent of play in human beings, which is recreation or relaxation from work, because animals, unlike some human beings, do not work. It is generally, but not always, the young of mammals that engage in play, particularly those of the carnivores. The young of most mammals have to find their food themselves as soon as they are weaned, but those of the carnivores which are not able at first to catch their prey are fed by the parent hunting for them and bringing them food. While they are thus provided for they enjoy a period of leisure in which they have nothing to do except wait for the next meal. They fill in time by exploring the immediate surroundings of the home, and giving rein to their innate aggressiveness, which is well marked from birth – one has only to watch a litter being suckled, with each animal struggling to get hold of a nipple, to see that from the first it is each for itself and the devil take the hindmost. Play thus consists basically of young animals chasing and biting at each other, but it is not carried to the length of inflicting more than trifling injury or of dispersing the family.

The innate aggression of the young animals is tempered by their immaturity and especially by their dependence upon the parent for food, and by living in a common but limited territory. Furthermore, serious aggression is returned in kind so that each quickly learns that aggression must not be carried too far. Aggression is therefore diverted into a ritualised pattern of behaviour that allows its expression without bringing dire consequences. In some species, such as the polecat,[126] play is simple and stereotyped in pattern, but in others it is more elaborate, with chasing games and 'king of the castle', as in the badger. With the badger, too, the adults sometimes engage in play, not only with the young but with each other; this takes the form of chasing and shadow fighting with pulled punches. In contrast with aggressive play the occurrence of mutual grooming, which is often prolonged, has been described as appeasement behaviour between adults as well as between young. The play of adults, however, is basically sexual and probably helps to strengthen the pair-bond.

Zoologists have put forward many explanations for the play of young animals, which has been regarded by some as an activity that has no function useful to the participants. One supposition proposes that play is training for independent adult life, but in many species there is no evidence that an animal that has not played is less successful as an adult than one that has. Other suggestions are that play works off surplus energy, or is enjoyed as a self-rewarding activity, suggestions that are now rejected by competent ethologists. Play among animals no doubt does give some satisfaction to the participants as is shown by the way ritualised invitations to play are used, often in the form of teasing the invited by the inviter. Nevertheless play is almost always the expression of aggression although it is tempered by social bonds so that it does not result in damage to the participants. Even human play is usually aggressive; all competitive games from chess to snakes-and-ladders, and from ball games to the Fastnet race, involve trying to win by beating the opponent. Man, however, carries his aggressive play far beyond that of the other animals, as when football mobs fight and even commit murder; he also invented warfare, the ultimate in rough games.

On the other hand there are occasional instances of animal play that appear to be non-aggressive and to be indulged in solely for the pleasure or satisfaction that it brings to the performer. The otter is the notable example among the British mammals; apart from the aggressive play of the young, which chase and wrestle with each other in the water, the adults use slippery surfaces such as ice or mud banks of streams as slides. The young certainly play on the mud slides and 'will follow each other in quick succession tobogganing down these slides time and time again'.[114] A light powdering of snow on the ice of a frozen lake or ditch can take tracks that show how sliding is done by adult otters. The animal runs at a gallop and then pushes off with the hind feet, holds the fore-limbs to its sides, as when swimming at speed, and slithers on its belly, sometimes as much as twenty feet, before taking another run. This behaviour is generally called 'play', but is it? It may well be that the animal is merely taking advantage of the slipperiness of the ice as an easy and labour-saving way of reaching its destination – even when it 'playfully' rolls over it may only be assuming the inverted attitude that it commonly adopts when in the water. Similarly the slides on mud banks may have nothing to do with play when used by the adults; the slide is a track regularly used for entering the water, and it is less trouble to slide down it than to walk.

There has been much speculation among students of animal behaviour about how 'play' came to be evolved. What biological advantage, if any, does it confer on the animals, or is it one of those phenomena that bring neither advantage nor disadvantage and, being consequently neutral, have not been eliminated from the genetic make-up by natural selection? Aggression towards others is innate and therefore genetically determined, but violent aggression between the members of a family would, presumably, be eliminated by natural selection, thus transforming dangerous aggression into harmless play.

A recent study of the play of young rats does, however, show that playing when young affects behaviour when the animals become adult.[56] Social rough-and-tumble play starts when the animals are about 17 days old, but declines and stops at about 50 days of age. If young rats are isolated during this play period they show severe learning difficulties as adults. Although they are very active they take a long time to get used to new objects, and are slow in learning such tasks as threading a maze correctly to obtain a reward, and are slower than normal rats in stopping or reversing a learned response when conditions change. Isolation at other ages does not have this effect on the versatility of adult behaviour and the rat's ability to learn. In contrast mice, which do not engage in play when young, suffer no disabilities in adult behaviour if they are similarly isolated. In passing we may remember the well known adverse effect of depriving young rhesus monkeys of the chance for play with others during their first year of life – they never attain normal social and sexual relationships as adults. Rhesus monkeys, however, enjoy a social system far more complex than any found among the mammals of the British Isles.

We have so far discussed the social behaviour between animals of a single species, but the behaviour shown between animals of different species can be equally important. The most obvious instance is that between predators and their prey, a matter of life and death for both. Few predators, and none among the mammals of the British Isles, are dependent upon a single prey species for a living – even the aquatic otter which is a fish-eater also takes aquatic and particularly marine, invertebrates, as well as birds and small land mammals. Predators are of necessity opportunists ready to take any manageable prey they can find; before myxomatosis nearly exterminated the rabbit foxes were thought to rely upon the rabbit for the largest part of their diet, but when rabbits practically disappeared foxes got along perfectly well with other prey, mainly small rodents.

Although the predator to prey interaction is a matter of life and death for both, in that the one must eat and the other must try to avoid being eaten, it is of greater importance to the prey than to the predator. The resulting unequal selection pressure on the prey to improve its ways of escape has been named the 'life-dinner prin-ciple',[48] for the prey is seeking to save its life but the predator is merely seeking a meal and will live even if it has to make many attempts before it succeeds. 'A fox may reproduce after losing a race against a rabbit. No rabbit has ever reproduced after losing a race against a fox.' This view of the 'arms race' tends to over-simplify the matter because when there are no rabbits foxes turn to catching other prey, in the capture of which running speed is not important but acute hearing and silent stalking are. Indeed, it is doubtful whether foxes do often run down such prey as rabbits in the open; the hunting method is that used for catching small rodents, a careful stalk ending in a final rush and grab before the prey has seen the danger. As Darwin said in 1859 the structure, and he might well have added the behaviour, of 'all organic beings is related to that of all others with which it comes into competition for food and residence, or from which it has to escape, or on which it preys'.[46]

The effects of the relations between predator and prey in the evolution of structure and behaviour are thus more complex than they appear to be at first sight, but they are simple when compared with the relations of the herbivorous mammals with their environ-ment. As we saw in chapter 3 much of the character of the English landscape has been moulded by sheep, and to a lesser extent by the introduced rabbit. Selective grazing by the rabbit turns downland, that in their absence is covered with dense herbage, into expanses of short turf with clumps of ragwort and elder bushes. But the behaviour of animals can have a much more far-reaching effect than a simple modification of the environment. Darwin's famous but incorrect story of the red clover would be a splendid example if it were true. He found that red clover is fertilised solely by the visits of humble bees, and goes on to claim that the number of humble bees in any district 'depends in a great measure upon the number of field-mice, which destroy their combs and nests. Now the number of mice is largely dependent, as everyone knows, on the number of cats; and Col. Newman says, 'Near villages and small towns I have found the nests of humble bees more numerous than elsewhere, which I attribute to the number of cats that destroy the mice'. Hence it is quite credible that the presence of a feline animal in large numbers in a district might determine, through the intervention first of mice and then of bees, the frequency of certain flowers in that district!' It is indeed quite credible, but it is an unfortunate choice of illustration by Darwin, for the 'facts' apart from the first are merely the opinions of a third party, unsupported by exact observation: it is not true.

On the other hand there is an example that would have delighted him had it been available in 1859. The large blue butterfly, *Maculinea arion*, is widely distributed in Europe but has always been scarce in the British Isles, though it has in the past been numerous from time to time in small areas, mostly in the south and southwest of England. In the British Isles it is evidently at the extreme edge of its range, and in the 1950s and 1960s it became progressively rarer, disappearing from most of its known localities so completely that it is now considered extinct; it is the only British butterfly ever to be protected by law, through the Conservation of Wild Creatures and Wild Plants Act. A committee to investigate the status of the butterfly in Devon and Cornwall was formed in 1963,[85] and in 1973 the Nature Conservancy started an extensive investigation on the biology of the species.[143] It has an unusual and complicated life history. The female butterfly lays its eggs during summer on the flowers of wild thyme, a common plant of heaths and dry grassland. The small larva feeds on the thyme flowers, and moults three times as it grows. It has a gland on the back of the tenth segment, from which it exudes a drop of secretion, said to be sweet, only when stimulated by an ant stroking it with its foot. In the autumn it stops feeding on thyme flowers and wanders about until an ant finds it, whereupon it assumes a hunched-up attitude and the ant carries it down into the ant nest.

In the ant nest the larva exacts payment for all the secretion it gives the ants when they milk it: it becomes exclusively carnivorous and feeds on the larvae of the ants. After about six weeks the larva hibernates, but on resuming activity in the spring it continues feeding on ant larvae until June, when it pupates, and after about three weeks emerges as a butterfly, makes its way to the surface, expands its wings, and is ready to breed. According to Frohawk[63] only two species of ant, of the genus *Myrmica*, will carry the larvae down into their nests and tolerate their depredations.

The ants are therefore essential for the large blue to complete its life cycle, and without them it will die. When myxomatosis almost wiped out the rabbit population in 1953 and the following year or two, the grasses which rabbits had formerly grazed down to a short turf sprang up as meadows of tall grass. The brown ant, *Myrmica sabuletti*, with which the large blue has this symbiotic relationship, does not live in areas where the grass is more than three centimetres high, and so when rabbits no longer made a short turf the ants disappeared, and with them the butterfly. The existence of the large blue thus depends upon the presence of a population of rabbits, and without them it cannot survive. Presumably, then, the large blue and the brown ant did not become part of the fauna of the British Isles until after the introduction of the rabbit about a thousand years ago, and none of the three can be a natural inhabitant of our environment, but each owes its presence to the interference of man.

In contrast to the destructive alteration to the environment caused by the feeding habits of some herbivores those of other species have a constructive effect by distributing the seeds of plants. Rabbits tend to prevent the natural regeneration of woodlands by eating young saplings and ring-barking older trees, but wood mice and squirrels, although they also damage some tree seedlings, help regeneration by their habit of hoarding or burying food when it is available in excess of immediate needs. Thus squirrels bury tree seeds from the size of walnuts downwards and fail to find many of them again, and wood mice accumulate hoards of smaller seeds from hazel nuts downwards, some of which are lost or accidentally scattered and germinate in due course. It seems doubtful whether mammals in the British Isles, unlike birds, are of much ecological importance in distributing seeds by passing them unharmed through the gut – herbivorous mammals chew their food rather than swallow it whole and thus destroy large seeds. On the other hand the carnivores which tear or cut up their food, but do not chew it, may sometimes accidentally swallow seeds which may survive in their journey through the gut. Even man can unknowingly distribute seeds in this way, as is shown by the great numbers of tomato plants that often spring up during the summer on land where sewage sludge is spread.

Although burrs, *Arctium* spp., and other seeds armed with hooks such as those of goose grass, *Galium aparine*, which cling so stubbornly to human woven garments and the fleece of domestic sheep, are dispersed through being carried by animals they cling much less tenaceously to hair and fur, in which the fibres are roughly parallel, and are consequently much more easily dislodged when carried to a distance from the parent plant. On the whole, however, mammals are of lesser importance to plants than birds for the dispersal of their seeds.

For many kinds of mammal other species of the order no less than plants form an important part of the environment. This is particularly emphasised when two closely related species inhabit a common habitat – when they are 'sympatric.' It is generally considered that they are able to be sympatric through subtle differences in the ecological niches that they occupy, with accompanying differences in diet and behaviour. We have already seen that the two species of *Apodemus*, the wood mouse and the yellow-necked mouse, tend to inhabit slightly differing habitats, but Montgomery[111] points out that separation of breeding habitats is not necessary for their co-existence, for both breed in a Gloucestershire woodland he studied, and doubtless in many another. Furthermore, the wood mouse is equally at home in wetter areas as well as being independent of deciduous woodland, and consequently lives nearly everywhere, unlike the yellow-necked mouse with its limited distribution. But he also finds[110] that the co-existence of the two where it occurs is possible because the yellow-necked mouse, with a more restricted ecological niche, is competitively superior to the wood mouse in encounters between the two. In experiments with captive mice the yellow-necked were dominant over the wood mice, and in encounters between the two there were more submissive and aggressive acts, and less introductory and amicable behaviour, than in meetings between two individuals of the same species.

In contrast the relations between the red squirrel and the introduced grey squirrel provide an example where one species is replacing the other, although at first sight they appear to be potentially sympatric. The red squirrel is typically an inhabitant of coniferous forests and the grey of deciduous woodlands. The first feeds mainly on the seeds of conifers, the second on the mast of broad-leaved trees. Yet in spite of these basic differences they are both versatile; the red squirrel has for centuries inhabited the broad-leaved woodlands of southern England, and the grey can invade conifer plantations in search of pine cones. MacKinnon[104] shows the main reason for the replacement of the red by the grey squirrel is that the habitat favours the grey squirrel, which is better adapted to competition.

The red squirrel has evolved in Europe without competition from any other species of squirrel, whereas the grey squirrel evolved in America under competition from several other species separated from it by slight ecological differences. The red squirrel, too, has suffered great variations in population numbers from time to time, apparently owing to epidemics of disease. The red squirrel breeds more slowly than the grey; consequently when the population of red squirrels in any particular region falls, the faster breeding grey squirrel moves in and occupies the habitat before the numbers of red squirrels can recuperate. Thus although it is not likely that direct aggression by the grey squirrel against the red is responsible for the disappearance, it is usurping the latter nearly everywhere, and 'over most of southern Britain the grey squirrel is here to stay and the red gone forever.'

Among the carnivores the stoat and weasel, sympatric species superficially similar in appearance and habits, have been studied by King and Moors.[94] These authors point out that the two species differ in breeding and hunting habits as well as in body size. The weasel is the more successful hunter of mice and voles because it can follow them into their burrows owing to its small size. Furthermore it can breed more rapidly and thus multiply when rodent populations reach a peak, but is liable to local extinction when the rodent population crashes. The stoat takes a wider variety of prey, and is especially a predator on rabbits, but its delayed implantation restricts it to producing only one litter of young a year, though it ensures that every young female is pregnant when the family breaks up. 'In a patchy environment of sufficient size, where local populations of prey fluctuate asynchronously, neither can eliminate the other except temporarily and locally.' They co-exist because if the habitat is diverse the weasel can avoid meeting the stoat, and the stoat does not rely upon a single species as prey. Further analysis shows that the stoat can colonise offshore islands smaller than those in which the weasel can get established. The stoat, because of its more catholic food habits, can exist on islands only 60 square kilometres in area, whereas the weasel cannot exist on islands less than some 380 square kilometres in area, as smaller islands cannot support a population of voles large enough to support a permanent population of weasels. Why then are there stoats in Ireland but no weasels?

King and Moors suggest that the weasel as well as the stoat was present in Ireland at the end of the Devensian glaciation, although there is no fossil evidence to support their plausible theory. When the ice retreated, but before the sea level rose, Ireland was connected to southern Scotland by dry land across which the weasel and two species of lemming that formed its prey migrated to colonise the Irish tundra. The field and bank voles did not arrive in the British Isles until after the connection had been submerged, so they never entered Ireland. When the lemmings became extinct as the climate softened there were no voles for the weasels to turn to for prey, and they too became extinct. The stoat, however, because it is less restricted in its choice of prey, survived and gave rise to the present Irish subspecies.

Darwin's remark that the structure of all 'organic beings' is related to that of all others with which they come into competition is illustrated by a further point, involving structure and behaviour, on which the opinions of theorists have been uncritically accepted by those who do not bother to look at what animals are doing in the wild. The coat colour of most mammals conforms to the well known principle of countershading, whereby the light-coloured belly counteracts the shadow on the underparts to destroy the appearance of solidity, but one may well question whether it is really of any importance to small mammals. It may be useful to long-legged ungulates that stand well clear of the ground, though even in them the dull 'cryptic' colour of the upper parts is probably of greater importance in rendering them inconspicuous to predators. But small mammals are so close to the ground that they are largely hidden by the cover of herbage, and even when crossing a bare patch the body is so near the substrate that the countershading effect of the light underparts may be doubted. Most of the small mammals thus rely on cover rather than countershading to remain unseen; even the rabbit, which often feeds in the open, crouches so low while it is grazing that the white underparts are out of sight and can have little if any countershading effect. If it runs for its burrow when alarmed it abandons any attempt to remain inconspicuous and relies on speed alone for safety.

Reliance on the cryptic colour of the upper parts, usually some dull shade or mixture of browns and ochres, rather than the obliteration of the appearance of solidity by countershading is well seen when a small

PLATE 9. *Above*, a mountain hare in its white winter coat after the thaw. The white coat makes it hard to see in the snow, but may be more important as a better insulator against the cold than a coloured one. *Below*, a brown hare is hard to see when it 'freezes' in its form among the grass.

PLATE 10. *Left*, the British subspecies of the red squirrel in summer coat with the ear-tufts and tail bleached white. *Centre*, a grey squirrel in its den in a hollow tree. *Below*, litter of fir-cone cores and scales left after grey squirrels have extracted the seeds.

PLATE 11. *Above*, a badger with the old bedding it has thrown out of its set. *Below*, overlapping territories: a fox and a badger meet and ignore each other.

PLATE 12. *Above*, country fox cubs at the entrance of their earth. *Below*, a town fox raiding the dustbin in a London suburb.

PLATE 13. *Above*, a hunting weasel. *Below*, the introduced mink is now a well established member of the fauna.

PLATE 14. *Above*, the tracks of an otter in snow. *Below*, a wild cat from the highlands of Scotland.

PLATE 15. *Above*, common seals on a sandbank in the Wash seen from the air. Although the seals herd together they avoid individual contact. *Below*, grey seals are alleged to damage fisheries, but the proportion of commercially valuable to useless species eaten is not known; this one surfaces with an eel.

PLATE 16. *Right*, a shoving match between two red deer stags. *Centre*, a red deer stag 'roaring'. *Below*, a stag showing the flehmen action with the upper lip drawn back over the gums.

mammal alerted to possible danger 'freezes'. By remaining absolutely still it avoids the smallest movement that might catch the eye of a predator, and crouches low so that the cryptically coloured upper parts blend into the background. This is all very well so long as an air current does not carry the animal's scent to the predator, which may pass on without finding the potential prey, but the best bet for a small mammal is to pop down a nearby burrow to safety, and freezing is only adopted in the absence of such a refuge.

Although most of the predators, too, bear patterns of countershading, they make no use of the possible concealing effect of them while hunting. A stalking fox crouches low among herbage and hides the white chin, throat and underparts by its posture and behaviour. Of the mustelids the stoat and weasel and, to a lesser extent, the pine marten appear to make no use of their countershading; they are invisible when among dense herbage but if they come into the open they make no attempt at concealing themselves, and their rapid movements make them highly conspicuous. Furthermore some predators, such as the polecat and the mink have no pattern of countershading, yet they manage to earn their livings very successfully.

The conclusion seems unavoidable that countershading is of little account to mammals under natural conditions in the wild; the cryptic colouration of the upper parts is far more important. The effect of countershading is well shown by artificial dummies, with and without light underparts, photographed against a uniform neutral-coloured background in a laboratory, but in the wild mammals do not, in the British Isles, live in habitats with such a background. Moreover, many mammals are nocturnal or crepuscular, and are active when effects of light and shade are minimal; in addition most mammals, if not colour-blind, have poor colour vision so that tone rather than hue is the effective factor in coat colouration. Countershading is doubtless useful to some mammals under certain limited conditions, but we are not justified in assuming that armchair theories are universally applicable, without testing them by looking at animals in the wild.

The white or light-coloured underparts of many mammals may have uses other than providing countershading – for example we have seen how shrews rear up and flash the light belly-colour for intimidating an adversary in an aggressive encounter. Careful study of the behaviour of wild mammals will probably find that the colour-pattern of many species plays some important part in their social behaviour rather than providing countershading. The sharp demark-ation between light and dark so often found appears to support this suggestion, for the best countershading would be provided by a gradual merging of the two. In some species it may well be that the underparts, being concealed in normal activities, do not need to be cryptically coloured and are consequently, with biological parsi-mony, left unpigmented. Or are white hairs, being filled with air, better heat-insulators than coloured ones filled with granules of pigment?

In addition to the polecat and mink the badger is an example that dispenses with countershading and actually reverses the pattern, being grey above and black below. Yet it is not particularly conspicuous by night even in full moonlight. Its colour pattern also seems likely to advertise its presence, for the head is white with two contrasting black stripes running from behind the ears through the eye to near the nose. Conspicuous patterns such as the badgers' are generally regarded as 'warning' patterns to advise a predator that it is dangerous to interfere with the bearer. The classical example is the conspicuously black-and-white skunk, which can discharge an almost asphyxiating stink that no other animal can tolerate. The badger can inflict a grievous bite, and can eject a horrid stink, though it is nothing approaching the overpowering scent of the skunk. But is the badger's pattern a warning one? There are no predators from which it needs protection – the only creature that interferes with it is man, and the badger's pattern was evolved long before man could persecute it. Dr Neal thinks that perhaps it may protect young badgers from attack by foxes, but beyond that possibility there appears to be no ground for supposing that the pattern gives protection by warning an aggressor. It cannot be of great importance in mutual recognition between badgers for that function is performed by scent, the use of which in the life and behaviour of the badger we have already seen.

The theory of warning patterns certainly fits some animals, but others with conspicuous patterns merely leave us guessing. On the other hand mammals with conspicuous patterns and unpleasant means of defence behave as though they are fully aware of their immunity from interference – skunks walk around 'as though they own the place' as, in effect, they do. Not so the badger, which is essentially shy and cautious; if this is not the result of centuries of persecution by man it throws doubt on the supposition that the conspicuous pattern is a warning to non-existent aggressors. The skunk's confidence leads to its death under the wheels of automobiles in America; and similarly the instinct of the hedgehog, which relies on the protection of its spines and rolls up when disturbed, leads to its death under the wheels of motor cars in the British Isles.

Just as the structure and colour patterns of animals are genetically determined so are their instincts or 'innate behaviour patterns'. The instructions for producing both structure and behaviour must be encoded in the genes carried in the chromosomes, but it is difficult for those who are not molecular biologists to understand how the formation of certain proteins, specified by the code, can result in the infinite complexity of the organism thereby produced. The colour patterns of mammals appear at first sight to be simple compared with those of some birds, but if not so dramatic they are equally complicated in their subtle arrangement and gradations. In the plumage of the pheasant, for example, each one of that cloud of feathers has its own pattern, yet all combine to form the more complex pattern of the plumage as a whole; it is difficult to imagine that the pattern of each individual feather is specified by the genetic code. It would be easier to think of the code as starting some sort of chain reaction which, once begun in a certain direction, follows an inevitable course, perhaps with guidance from the code on the way. Each forward step would reduce the number of possible alternative paths until the final run up the straight to produce the pre-ordained organism. But that does not take account of how behaviour patterns are transmitted – perhaps the behaviour is an essential property of the organism thus formed, just as it is a property of vinegar to be sour, sugar to be sweet, or sparks to fly upward.

CHAPTER 8

COMMUNICATION

SOCIAL behaviour among the mammals, as among all animals, needs some means of communication between individuals so that each can be aware of another's presence and actions. Hence animals possess special sense organs that can be used for recognition, though not necessarily exclusively for this purpose, and special organs that can give out signals which can stimulate the sense organs of others. Even the so-called 'simplest' of invertebrates, the protozoa, which are unicellular or acellular, react to touch, to light, to various chemical stimuli, and to acoustic and other vibrations. In the higher animals, and especially the vertebrates, the capacity to perform these reactions is concentrated into special structures, the organs of special sense subserving the functions of touch, sight, taste, smell, and hearing.

Some of the special senses are generally more important than the others to different kinds of animals; sometimes only one takes precedence. In man the senses of sight and hearing are the most important, but man and his nearer relatives of the order Primates are an exception to the ones generally found among the mammals, for in most of them the sense of smell is the one that takes precedence over the others. This does not imply that the other senses are not used – an animal living in an environment that is essentially hostile, filled with predators, elusive prey, and competitors for food or mates, needs to use to the full every means with which it is endowed to prolong the ceaseless endeavour to postpone the inevitable hour.

The senses of an animal respond to two kinds of stimuli from the environment – those that fortuitously impinge upon them and those that reach them as signals from other animals. The sense of smell or olfaction, depends especially on the latter category, and because it is of prime importance to most mammals we will examine it before the others.

The physiology of olfactory reception is imperfectly known, partly because we ourselves are not olfactory animals, and rely on vision and hearing for gathering information about our surroundings, so that we can have no subjective conception of the degree to which animals rely on smell as a source of information. Olfaction is basically the conveyance of air-borne molecules of scent to microscopic receptor organs in the lining of the nose; the receptors are stimulated by the contact to send nerve impulses to the brain where they are processed and interpreted into some kind of message. Even man with his comparatively unused olfactory equipment is able to distinguish a great variety of smells and to recognise them when he meets them again, but, as Adrian[2] says, 'we cannot analyse the sensation, presumably because for us the visual pattern is so much more worth analysing. A dog can perhaps analyse the pattern of a smell as some of us can analyse the sounds produced by a full orchestra.' He further points out that a smell that is barely perceptible to us may have the same kind of effect in a hedgehog's brain that shining a dazzling light into the eye has on the brain of a cat.

The cavity of the nose contains a number of thin plates of bone, the turbinals, each curled like a scroll and attached by one edge so that the membrane covering them presents a large area of contact to the stream of air passing over them at each breath. Most of the surface of the turbinals serves to warm and moisten the inspired air on its way to the lungs, but in the upper part of the nasal cavity the covering membrane bears the olfactory receptors. When we sniff appreciatively at a rose, or suspiciously at a curate's egg, we are drawing the air laden with scent molecules into this upper part of the cavity where the receptors lie. The microscopic structure of the receptors and of the membrane in which they lie is fairly well known, as is the anatomy of the nervous connections with the olfactory bulb of the brain. But the process by which odorous molecules impinging on the olfactory receptors cause an impulse to be sent along the olfactory nerves to the brain, and by which a distinction is made between different odours, remain unknown. Several mutually exclusive theories have been put forward about the way odours are perceived, but none of them has provided a complete explanation or been experimentally proved, though each has some experimental evidence to support it.

If we bear in mind the acuteness of the sense of smell, and its high discriminatory power in most animals, it is no surprise to find that the number of olfactory receptors is immense, ranging from tens to hundreds of millions in different animals. Even in man there are far more nerve fibres running from the olfactory part of the nose to the brain than there are from the eye or the ear.[3]

When the stimulus to touch or pressure receptors in the skin is prolonged the impulses sent to the brain gradually reduce in frequency and finally stop – the receptors become fatigued. Similarly a continuous stimulation of the olfactory receptors results in declining sensation, either because of similar fatigue or because the stimulating molecules must be removed from the receptors before others can act. The result is that we quickly 'get used' to a particular smell and no longer notice it even if it is an unpleasant one; a newcomer to a stuffy room remarks upon the fug of which the occupants are unaware. This is also probably another reason for sniffing at an odour, as mentioned above; we present our olfactory receptors with small successive doses and give them the chance of recovering from their insensitivity of fatigue during the intervals. Other mammals, such as the carnivores, similarly sniff at odours that interest them, whereas lagomorphs and rodents open and shut their nostrils for the same purpose – the familiar 'winking the nose.'

This brief glance at the mechanisms of the receiving end of olfaction in the mammals must suffice here, but readers who are interested to explore them more deeply cannot do better than consult the Institute of Biology's booklet by D.M. Stoddart.[135] Turning now to what is received during olfaction, we may first note that the scent receptors must be bombarded with all kinds of molecules that convey information of no particular importance to the recipient. This background smell coming from all directions is ignored, probably partly by the fatigue of the receptors which no longer react to it, and partly by the suppression of any signals they may transmit in the brain itself. The brain receives a continual stream of signals from all the organs of special sense but is able to suppress and ignore those that are not relevant to the animal. The moment a signal that may be important arrives, however, the lower centres of the brain allow it to break through to consciousness and obtain the recipient's attention, just as we are unaware of the clock ticking on the mantle-piece unless it stops, whereupon we at once notice it.

Before considering the use of the olfactory sense in communication between animals it is appropriate to glance at its use in exploring the environment, particularly in seeking for food. Most of the carnivores are well known for locating and trailing their prey by scent, though the cats, as we shall see, rely more on their other senses. Most of the mustelids, with the exception of the otter when fishing, are trail followers, as the sight of a stoat hunting a trail of scent well illustrates. Insectivores such as shrews sniff out their food with the mobile snout that is lengthened almost to a miniature proboscis, and the hedgehog can sometimes be found rooting in the ground with its snout almost like a real hog, presumably searching for slugs. Some of the rodents, too, are adept at sniffing out their food; gardeners well know the way in which the wood mouse robs them of their newly sown broad beans and peas. The mouse does not dig at random but knows through its sense of smell exactly where each seed lies and digs directly down to it, leaving a row of holes along the row. Squirrels, which bury nuts in the autumn do not remember where they have put them, but later find them by the sense of smell, if indeed they find them at all.

All the mammals use the sense of smell to warn them of danger, and particularly the ungulates. Any mammal-watcher, whether he be a benign naturalist or a hunter approaching his quarry, knows that the first essential in stalking is to work up-wind, and that an unlucky change in the breeze carries his scent to the object of his interest and at once alarms it. A taint on the breeze ruins the sport of the deer stalker as much as that of the badger watcher, who may have to wait for hours to see the animal come out of its set, if it has been frightened by his scent when it first started to emerge.

Some of the scents received by one mammal from another give information about the sex, social status, age, individual identity and so on of the donor, and thus directly affect the behaviour of the recipient. Others act more subtly and produce physiological changes within the recipient that affect its behaviour not immediately but after a lapse of time. In the mammals these scents are nearly always complex mixtures of many substances, and most of them are thus not strictly 'pheromones', a term that is often loosely used for them. The word was introduced as a name for the chemical messengers used for communication by some insects, the well known example being the scent that certain female moths give out to attract the males from a great distance. They are generally single specific substances, not mixtures, and they are effective in extreme dilution. Their action appears to be specific on the males, which fly towards the source reflexly and without conscious volition – they are analogous with the hormones which, carried in the blood, evoke a particular response in the target organ. The scent of a bitch in heat might perhaps be regarded as a pheromone, for it appears to have a compelling effect on dogs, making them follow her to the disregard of other stimuli to which they usually react. But we do not know whether it causes an automatic and involuntary response, or whether it is consciously so seductively alluring that all else is forgotten. The phenomenon is practically universal among the mammals – George Borrow long ago[22] told how to make use of it for stealing a savage stallion out of a field by night, and alludes to the tale told in BC 445 by the Greek historian Herodotus, of its use by Oebares, the groom of Darius son of Hystapes, to secure the throne of Persia for his master.

Some of the scents produced by mammals are excretions, others secretions, the use of the former being the most primitive way of marking territory, for an animal cannot avoid leaving a record of its presence when it deposits urine or faeces. The development of special scent-producing glands was probably secondary to this, and added a specific or even personal flavour of identity. Yet even the special glands are themselves derived from structures already available, the sweat and sebaceous glands of the skin. The sweat glands produce a watery secretion that is mainly useful in regulating the temperature of the body by evaporation to prevent over-heating. Sweat glands are abundant in the skin of some mammals such as the horse, but scanty in others such as the dog which achieves the same end by evaporation from the lolled out tongue. Sebaceous glands produce an oily or greasy secretion that serves as a hair dressing to render the pelage supple and waterproof; there is one associated with every hair follicle.

Where these glands are modified into special scent producers the skin is thickened and generally folded to form a pocket in which the secretion accumulates. The secretion usually consists of an extremely complex mixture of esters, fatty acids, cholesterol, and their derivatives produced by the action of bacteria on the raw material secreted from the glands; some of them with a musky note are pleasing to our noses but others are repulsive stinks. An exception to the usual derivation of scent glands is shown by the chin scent gland of the rabbit, which is a modified part of the submaxillary salivary gland. Its secretion is entirely different in character and is inodorous to us; possibly it does not stimulate the olfactory receptors of the rabbit either, but acts upon the sensory pads of complex micro-structure that lie just inside the opening of the nostrils in the rabbit and other lagomorphs.

Skin scent glands can occur in almost any part of a mammal; among British mammals there are facial glands below the eyes, and interdigital glands between the toes in deer, lateral glands on the flanks of shrews and some voles, caudal glands above the tail in the fox and below it in the wood mouse, anal glands opening into the rectum or near the anus in many species, inguinal glands in the groin, preputial glands in the males of many species, and equivalent genital glands in some females, as well as the chin gland of the rabbit mentioned above. In addition many foreign mammals have scent glands in the skin of other parts of the body.

The secretions of these glands may be deposited incidentally in passing, as by the foot glands of ungulates or the flank glands of shrews squeezing through their burrows, or during defaecation as with the anal glands, or urination as with the genital glands of many mammals. On the other hand they may be deliberately deposited as markers of territory or signs of the presence – the scented faeces or urine are often used as deliberately deposited markers. The lamp-post habit of dogs is a good example, for dogs first examine the post to find out who has already been there and then give a squirt of urine to add their quota of information, not to empty the bladder. Similarly, fallow deer spread a spray of urine by means of the long tassel of hair through which the stream has to pass. The faeces too, are used for deliberately marking territory, as in the latrines of the badger. Neal[115] tells of the experiment of putting faeces from the latrine of one territory into that of another; when the rightful owner came upon the foreign matter it was 'very upset' and showed great emotion in superimposing its own markers and scratching vigorously with its hind feet.

The scent of other glands is deliberately set by rubbing the gland orifice against the object to be marked. Deer very carefully wipe the facial gland onto twigs, rabbits rub the opening of the chin gland onto herbage, and many carnivores, especially the mustelids, rub the openings of the anal glands on marking places. Most of the glands become highly active when the owner is sexually potent, and their secretions indicate this to others, either as an attracter of the opposite sex or as a warning to others of the same sex to keep away.

We have already suggested that it is interesting to reflect that these markings with the secretions of special glands are analogous to an early and primitive form of writing, without the necessity for having an articulate language. The marking leaves a message that can be understood by the recipient in the absence of the one that left it – and writing is no more than an elaboration of this basic principle.

In addition to the scents that are thus used in general communication there are those that play a prominent part in the sexual lives of the mammals. The secretions of the genitalia are altered when a female comes into oestrus – the pheromone-like effect of those of the bitch have already been mentioned, and similar scents are produced in all female mammals at and near oestrus. They inevitably become mixed with the urine which thereby attracts the males, and has led to a peculiar pattern of behaviour in the males of ungulates, carnivores and some others, even in the wombat, a marsupial mammal of Australia.[66] The male sniffs at the female's genitals, or at the urine she has passed, or even takes some urine into his mouth when she passes it; he thereupon makes a characteristic gesture that has no name in the English language but is known by the German term 'das Flehmen'. On sniffing or tasting he raises the head and parts the lips, without separating the jaws, and curves back the upper lip in a kind of sardonic grin while holding the breath.

The flehmen is believed to draw the odorous substances into contact with a special sensory structure, the organ of Jacobson or vomero-nasal organ. This lies in the fore part of the roof of the mouth and is connected by a duct with the nose cavity, or the mouth, or both, in different species, and is lined with a membrane containing sensory receptors. The organ is found in most mammals but some, including man, lack it, so that we can have no subjective knowledge of its use. It certainly indicates to those species that possess it the state of sexual receptivity of the female, and acts as a stimulus to the male.

Some scents produced by the male likewise serve as stimuli to the sexual processes of the female. These affect her physiology and act indirectly, and with a time lapse, on the reproductive organs. They are mediated by the brain and the anterior part of the pituitary body at the base of it which produces hormones that influence the secretion of the sex hormones in the ovary. These 'gonadotropic' hormones from the pituitary act upon the gonads of both sexes – the ovaries or testes and stimulate them to produce the sex hormones, the oestrogens and androgens. They not only stimulate the gonads but also the secondary sex characters, among them the scent glands which spring into increased activity. The scent glands contain a large proportion of modified sebaceous glands but they are not alone in responding to the action of the hormones, for the normal sebaceous glands of the skin also respond as 'target organs' – hence the adolescent acne commonly seen in boys when their blood carries unwonted quantities of sex hormone after they reach puberty. The excess sebaceous secretion often fails to be expelled and accumulates in the gland where it acts as a substrate for bacteria causing the characteristic pimply face.

The odour from the scent glands influences the behaviour of the opposite sex; the scent of a male mouse, for example, shortens the length of the oestrus cycle in females, and if a number of females are kept together the odour also tends to bring the cycle of the individuals into synchronism. On the other hand the odour of a strange male mouse has an inhibiting effect on a mated female, causing her to resorb her developing embryos if she is exposed to the scent within the first five days after she was impregnated. This peculiar reaction, which is known in some other rodents, is called the 'Bruce effect' after its discoverer.

Turning now to the sense of sight, which is so important to us, we find that it takes second place to olfaction or even third place in some species where hearing preceeds it. The eye is a camera whose lens throws an image on the back which is covered by the retina containing the light-receptors. We do not need to examine the structure of the eye in detail here, beyond noting that the light receptor cells are of two kinds, the rods and cones, so named from their shape. The rods are much more sensitive to light than are the cones, and consequently respond to lower intensities of illumination; they do not discriminate colour, whereas the less sensitive cones do. The rods and cones are scattered over the retina, and in some mammals there is a central area, the fovea, that contains cones only; this is the part we use when we concentrate on looking at anything. In general, however, there are few cones in the retinas of most mammals and consequently they have poor or no colour vision, but they are able to see in light so dim that we are baffled. The advantage of this arrangement to nocturnal mammals is obvious. On the other hand, small mammals that live most of their lives in underground burrows, such as the mole and some kinds of shrew, have little use for the sense of sight, as is shown by the small or even minute size of their eyes.

The sense of sight gives mammals general information about the topography of their surroundings but its most important use in most of them is the detection of movement. Both predator and prey species instantly react to slight movements seen by the eyes, though for opposite purposes. Hence comes the habit of both when alerted though not fully alarmed of remaining 'frozen' absolutely motionless. A cat stalking a bird freezes every time the prey shows signs of alarm, and a startled rabbit likewise freezes until reassured, or until approaching danger puts it to flight. Both 'hope' to avoid detection by refraining from the slightest movement that might attract attention.

This phenomenon leads to the question of what mammals see when they look at anything. If remaining frozen avoids detection we must conclude that although the image of the frozen rabbit falls onto the retina of the predator, the retina or the brain is unable to discriminate the rabbit from the background, and the picture is meaningless until movement attracts the attention and allows discrimination to occur. The lack of colour vision is thus a handicap to most mammals, for colour often picks out objects from the background, as can be seen by comparing a monochrome with a colour photograph or television picture. On the other hand mammals have the advantage of being able to detect movement at night when light intensity is low. Furthermore, the meaning of the picture thrown onto the retina has to be learned by experience. A new born mammal – including even the human baby – sees its surroundings, but until it has learnt about them by means of the other senses, particularly that of touch, the picture that it sees has no meaning. Even an adult seeing an unfamiliar object for the first time often has to touch it to learn what it is. Show a friend some new small gadget: he holds out his hand saying 'Let me see it', but he really means 'Let me touch it' so that he will know what it is when he sees it in the future. Seeing may be believing in popular opinion, but the sense of sight is the easiest to deceive and the most prone to jump to wrong conclusions – the art of conjuring and the tricks with optical illusions exploit its weaknesses.

With many mammals the sense of hearing is quite as important or even more important than that of sight, again for defence in prey species, and for offence in predators. The vibrations of the air that constitute sound are received by the complex structures of the middle and inner ear where they give rise to nerve impulses that are transmitted to the brain. But in considering the sense of hearing in the daily lives of the mammals it is the much simpler outer ear that mainly concerns us. The outer ear consists of the tube leading from the surface of the head inwards to the ear drum, together with the conch or ear flap, the 'ear' of common speech.

The conch is small in many species and so covered by the fur that it is almost invisible, but in others such as the wood mouse, the lagomorphs, the cat, the fox, and the deer it is a comparatively large moveable trumpet that directs the sound waves into the outer ear-passage. In these animals the large ear is an important aid to finding prey or detecting the presence of danger, that is, to gaining information about the environment. In particular the ears are direction finders, for by turning the head so that the sounds received in each ear are equally loud the direction from which they come is known. A subsidiary use of the ear conch is in regulating the temperature of the body, particularly in mammals that live in the tropics – the huge ears of the African elephant give a large surface area through which heat may be lost. On the other hand the ear conches of the mammals of cold climates are noticeably small and often hardly protrude beyond the surface of the fur; the field and bank voles which have small ears reach the arctic circle and beyond on continental Europe, whereas the wood mouse which has comparatively large ears is absent from northern Scandinavia, Finland and northern Russia.

The ear is also important in communication between animals of the same species – for receiving the sound of the voice of others. The voice is produced in the larynx, the upper part of the windpipe, by the rapid passage of air over the vocal cords, which are folds of the lining membrane that produce sound by their vibration in the stream of air. The voice is under voluntary control, and is modulated by the action of the muscles of the larynx, and by resonance in the air passages of the nose and mouth. Although the mammals apart from man have not articulate language, they do produce different sounds in different circumstances; thus different sounds may have more or less specific meanings to the recipients, though they may be obscure to us. Two kinds of call are almost universal; the alarm call made when an animal becomes aware of danger, such as the bark of deer or the squeak of a frightened mouse, and the scream given when in mortal danger. The function of the first in alerting other individuals is obvious, especially in gregarious species, but the meaning of the latter is obscure. It seems to be involuntary, even in man, and can bring no benefit to the screamer; with rare exceptions it cannot be a call for help – a rabbit for example when caught in a snare sits quietly after its first struggles to get free and screams only when man approaches to knock it on the head. Perhaps it is an extreme and involuntary form of the alarm call. The voice is not, however, always used in giving an alarm signal: the rabbit when alerted lets its neighbours know that danger may threaten by thumping the ground with the hind legs.

Between the alarm signal and the terror scream there is a great range of mammalian vocal sounds, most of which we understand but poorly or not at all. Some, such as the roaring of the red deer stag at the time of the rut, or the seasonal scream of the fox, may be territorial or sexual, or both, whereas others such as the growlings made by carnivores express aggression, and warn others to keep away, especially when the growler is feeding on captured prey. The sounds used in communication between a mother and her young are numerous, both those made by the young to attract the attention of the mother, and those made by her in reply, especially the greeting used when she returns to her young, which presumably reassures them that it is in fact their mother and not an aggressive stranger that approaches. The innumerable 'conversational' noises made by young animals and their dams before the family breaks up evidently serve to keep the group together, and to inform its members that each belongs to the group and is not a stranger to be attacked; they are thus important in maintaining the social bond.

The voices of many small mammals can produce sounds of so high a pitch that they are above the human range of hearing. Such ultrasonic noises are to be expected when we take into account the physical size of the larynx in small mammals – the smaller the whistle the higher the note – although such sounds were thought to be something unusual when they were first detected. Nevertheless, it has long been well known that the range of hearing in dogs goes far higher than that of people, so that one can train a dog to respond to a 'silent' Galton whistle; the dog can hear it but we cannot. Ultrasound is the normal medium of communication between mother and young among the small rodents, but sounds of lower frequency are used by the young of larger animals. Research workers in Australia[8] have found no evidence of the production of ultrasounds up to 40KHz by rabbits, but have recorded a variety of sounds in the 2 to 6 KHz range. They found that the young in the nest, where they are in complete darkness because the mother plugs the entrance after each of her visits, are particularly vocal. They produce a considerable variety of sounds including distress, attention-seeking, aggression, and satisfaction calls. The noisy young are, apparently, particularly vulnerable to being found and dug out of the nests by foxes. This is no doubt equally true of young rabbits and foxes in the British Isles, where there is a further danger to the young. Another predator not present in Australia, the badger, is well known for its skill in finding and digging out nests of suckling rabbits, and it is probable that the badger finds the nests by hearing the noisy young rabbits within.

One of the most interesting aspects of the use of sound by mammals is the phenomenon of echolocation or sonar. It is peculiar that the discovery of sonar among the bats had to wait until man had invented echolocation for himself before it was appreciated that bats were able to find their way about and catch their prey in darkness by similar means. Echo-sounding for finding the depth of water beneath a ship was developed during and after World War I, and although the principle was known, only one worker[79] suggested, on the strength of some preliminary experiments, that bats might be using something of the sort; unfortunately he did not pursue his investigation to the stage of proof. The development of radar shortly before and during World War II, using electromagnetic waves for echolocating aircraft, pointed to the probability that bats use a similar method employing ultrasonic sound waves. Two American zoologists, Galambos and Griffin, were the first to publish the results of experiments that proved the use of sonar by bats.[64] Their work has led to many investigations of the complexities of the sonar methods used by bats in those parts of the world where they are found.

The simplest kind of bat sonar consists of a stream of high frequency pulses emitted from the mouth and reflected from nearby objects. Each pulse is a burst of ultrasound, and the pulses are separated by short periods of silence lasting a fraction of a second. The time taken between the emission of a pulse and the receipt of its echo gives the distance of the object, and turning the head so that the loudness of the echo is equal in both ears gives the direction. A bat using its sonar is not consciously aware of these processes, but gains a mental picture of its surroundings through its ears just as we do by sight when we open our eyes. The ear flaps of bats are large when compared with the size of the body, and act as trumpets in concentrating received sounds into the ear passage; and the tragus, the equivalent of the small lobe in front of the entrance in our ears, is comparatively large, often being elongated or broadly rounded. This modification is concerned with focusing the received sounds, or perhaps rather with preventing ambiguities in the received echos hampering accurate direction finding.

In some bats the sonar system is more complicated. In the horseshoe bats, and others that possess nose-leaves, much longer trains of ultrasound are emitted so that range and direction are determined by use of the Doppler effect, the change in frequency in the received sound caused by the movement of the object or the receiver. The horseshoe bats take their name from the fancied resemblance to the shape of a horse-shoe of a flap of skin surrounding the nostrils; this flap is continued upwards into a pointed lancet and is further complicated by the presence of a small central blade pointing forwards in a fore-and-aft direction. This nasal complexity is concerned with directing the emitted ultrasound into a beam rather than a broadcast of sound, so that direction finding is made accurate. This kind of sonar differs from the first mentioned in that the sound is emitted through the nostrils and not through the open mouth, but its effect in giving a mental picture of the surroundings is similar. Bats possess eyes, and use them when there is light, but sonar allows them to 'see' in the dark as well as in the light. It may be that the eyes of the horseshoe bats, small compared with those of many other species, indicate a greater efficiency of, or reliance upon, their different system of echolocation.

The sense of touch may be regarded as the most primitive of the senses, for nerve endings responsive to touch or pressure occur all over the surface of the body – every hair of a mammal is connected with one. Touch thus gives the animal information about the surroundings with which it is in immediate contact and, as we have seen in connection with sight, it is necessary for learning the meaning of stimuli received by the other, more complex, senses. In most mammals the touch sense is more highly developed at certain points than it is over the general surface of the body. These points lie at the base of the long stiff hairs, the vibrissae, that form the 'whiskers' on the snout, and which are not the same thing as the whiskers of the male human face. Vibrissae are not confined to the snout but are commonly present also above the eyes or under the chin, and in some species on the elbow or forearm, the wrist, ankle, and elsewhere. The skin and underlying tissues are thickened at the roots of the vibrissae to form a sensory papilla in which the nerve endings surround the base of the hair.

The aggregation of the papillae on the upper lip produces a thickened pad that is prominent in the shrews and particularly large in aquatic mammals, such as the water shrew, the otter and the seals. It is probable that this unusually high development of the moustache, or mystacial, vibrissae is correlated with the denser medium in which the animals seek their food, and it is possible that they convey information about the surroundings by reacting to turbulences in the water, especially those produced by the prey. This suggestion is supported by the condition of blind grey seals that have been seen from time to time.[45] They have been found to be suffering from corneal opacity caused either by infection or accidental injury, and are certainly blind as judged by their reaction to the approach of people. Yet they are plump and well-fed, and not, as might be expected, dying of starvation; it is evident that they can find their prey without the use of sight. Furthermore a small population of common seals living in the upper waters of the Bristol Channel and Estuary of the Severn find their food in water so heavily laden with silt and mud that it is completely dark a couple of feet or so beneath the surface, as every swimmer in those waters well knows. These seals are not known to make use of sonar, and thus the probability that the vibrissae respond to small turbulences and in effect give 'touch at a distance' is strengthened.

The mole, too, may perhaps be able to locate objects at a distance by detecting changes in air pressure and minute air currents by means of special sense organs in its snout, as its minute eyes have little acuity and are useless underground.[105a] The snout is covered with tiny pimples known as Eimer's organs; they are richly supplied with nerve endings making the naked end of the snout a very sensitive organ of touch. Eimer's organs evidently collect information different from that supplied by the vibrissae which cover the rest of the snout.[126a]

The last in the popular classification of the 'five senses' is that of taste, which is produced by the impinging of molecules dissolved in the saliva on special receptors, the taste buds. The buds are of different kinds, each corresponding with a specific taste, of which there are only four – sweet, sour, bitter, and salt. The flavours of food are perceived by the smell receptors of the nose to which they are conveyed by gaseous diffusion in the pharynx; and qualities such as softness or crispness are perceived through the touch receptors. The sensation commonly called taste is thus a complex of taste, smell and touch. Taste tests the quality of food to a certain extent, but it does not discriminate between the poisonous and the wholesome, though it does help in the selection of food, as can be seen in a pasture where grazing animals have left tufts of the less palatable grasses standing alone. The sensation produced by taste varies between different mammals so that what is acceptable to one species may be rejected by another – goats for example seem to enjoy eating herbs so bitter that they are intolerable to us.

All herbivorous mammals, and some others, appear to enjoy sweet things, though sugar is not an essential ingredient of the diet; on the other hand they also have an avidity for salt, which with associated trace elements, is essential. The attraction of salt is particularly strong for the ungulates, which regularly visit 'salt-licks', places where the earth is alkaline and salty, which they greedily lick. Stock farmers ensure that their animals obtain the necessary salt and other minerals by throwing out salt blocks for them to lick. Rabbits too are attracted to gnaw wooden pegs impregnated with salt, and this propensity has been used in Australia[113] to kill rabbits by adding poison to the salt in attempts to control their numbers. There seems to be no information recorded about how mammals find natural or artificial salt licks; perhaps they can smell them, although salt is inodorous to the human nose. Nor is it known what stimulus starts them licking a substance so different from their usual diet, beyond the postulation of a 'physiological urge'. Whatever may be the way by which they receive the information, once they have found a salt-lick they regularly visit it. The proprietor of a deer forest in Scotland, who wished to sell his property, liberally supplied it with artificial salt-licks, thereby attracting an abnormally high population of red deer onto his hill, which in turn attracted a satisfactorily high price from the hoodwinked purchaser.

In addition to the generally recognised five senses, there are others that give an animal information about conditions within its own body. They are mostly connected with the autonomous nervous system, that part of the nerve network that responds to stimuli automatically without involving conscious perception. Thus the perception of the positions of the limbs and their joints and muscles does not enter consciousness in the act of walking or running, nor do the movements of the intestines during digestion. On the other hand some of the internal monitors do sometimes break into consciousness, for example those producing thirst or hunger. A deeper exploration of this interesting topic lies beyond the scope of the present work.

The conventional five senses are all concerned with the reception of external stimuli, a fact that gives meaning to the way the brain and nervous system are derived during the development of a mammalian or any other vertebrate embryo; this was emphasized by the late Professor Wood-Jones, the 'prince of anatomists'[31] and Conservator of the Hunterian Museum of the Royal College of Surgeons of England. In his fascinating work on the brain[92] he points out that in the simplest single-cell animals the whole surface responds to external stimuli, whereas in the 'higher' multi-cellular animals special nerve cells are set aside early in development. They are derived from the outer layer of cells, the ectoderm, that is formed in the early stages of development from the single cell of the egg. One of the earliest structures formed during the differentiation of tissues is a groove along the future back; its sides grow upwards and join to form a tube. Later the tube sinks inwards and becomes detached from the rest of the ectodermal layer, which grows together over it; the tube goes on to develop into the brain and spinal cord, so that the lining of the central canal of the spinal cord and of the ventricles of the brain represents the original outside of the animal. The nerves later grow outwards from the central nerve system to make contact with the peripheral sense organs, from which they convey messages to the centre. Other nerves grow out to the muscles, glands, and similar 'effector' structures to which they convey messages from the centre. The sense organs are themselves derived from the ectoderm, as are the outer layers of the skin, so that although the sense organs, brain, and nerves of adult mammals are embedded in, and appear to be inextricably mixed with, the tissues derived from other cell-layers of the embryo, they originate on the outside, the part in immediate contact with the environment on which all external stimuli must impinge.

CHAPTER 9

INTERNAL AND EXTERNAL RHYTHMS

THE daily lives of the mammals, like those of most animals, comprise many different activities, some of them occasional but others recurring at more or less regular intervals. The latter occur rhythmically and may be induced by external or internal stimuli, the most obvious external stimulus being the alternation of night and day, so that diurnal animals sleep at night but the nocturnal ones by day. The effect of external stimuli on the rhythm of activity is not, however, as simple as it appears at first sight, because animals forced to live in continuous light or darkness retain their rhythms for a while and sleep or become active at approximately the 'right' times.

On a larger scale the succession of the seasons through the year, with steady increase or decrease in day length and temperature, with the associated changes in weather, affect the daily lives of all animals from man to microbe – the seasonal variations being least at the equator and greatest at the poles. In temperate regions the seasonal growth of plants, on which all mammals are directly or indirectly dependent for food, can be said to govern the daily lives of all the mammals of the British Isles. The yearly alternating cycles of scarcity and plenty bring corresponding cycles in population size, the more regular fluctuations being modified by occasional natural disasters such as droughts or unusually severe winters.

The life spans of small mammals are short; the shrews provide a clear example of the correlation of a short-lived population structure with the cycle of the seasons. The young of the common and pygmy shrews are born during the summer, and live through the following winter as sexually immature subadults. In the next spring they become sexually mature, breed during the summer, and die in the autumn. Although a few early young may breed in the year of their birth, normally the winter population consists almost entirely of sexually immature animals – shrews are the equivalent of the gardener's hardy annuals. The death of the senile adults in the autumn is probably caused by their young, with which they cannot compete, excluding them from their territories so that they are literally 'left out in the cold' and die of starvation. The life cycle of the water shrew and of the white-toothed shrews is similar but perhaps not quite so sharply limited.

The cycle of daily activities in the great majority of human beings is closely correlated with the clock – or the sundial and its equivalents. Underlying our dependence on an external clock there is also a cycle or rhythm of bodily activities of which we are hardly aware, because we take them for granted unless they are upset by external causes. The long distance traveller by air suffers from 'jet lag' because his internal rhythms remain unaltered when he re-sets his watch to the local hour on entering a different time zone.

The activities of the other mammals, which have no external clock beyond the fluctuating lengths of day and night, are more obviously linked to their internal rhythms. Hence we have the expression 'internal clock' that is used as a convenient shorthand for recognising the existence of the rhythms and concealing our ignorance of their ultimate cause. No one has yet been able to identify or find the site of an internal or biological clock, though many ingenious theories have been postulated.

Although biological clocks go on running in the absence of external stimuli, as when an animal kept in constant light or darkness and at steady temperature continues its cyclic activities, after a while the internal clock does get out of phase with the time of day – the internal rhythm does not exactly fit the day-length. A new word has therefore been introduced to label the rhythms more exactly than by calling their results 'daily activities'; they are now called circadial, meaning 'about a day'.* As the circadial rhythms gradually get out of phase with the time of day in the absence of external stimuli, it is obvious that normally they are constantly being brought into phase by external stimuli, which re-set the biological clock, whatever it may be.

The activities of mammals are by no means constant throughout the day or night as the case may be, but differ in kind from time to time under the influence of the circadial rhythms, many of them linked with physiological processes. In particular mammals do not spend all their waking hours in feeding but divide their time between eating, resting, grooming themselves, marking and defending their territories, and so on. The deer, being ruminants, browse or graze mainly about dusk and dawn, and spend long periods of the day

* *circadial*, pronounced circadée-al, not circáy-dial.

resting and chewing the cud. Rabbits similarly are mainly crepuscular in feeding but when lying up in their burrows they re-cycle the
food they have gathered by eating the residue of the first process of
digestion. This is known as 'refection'; when the food on its first
passage through the gut reaches the large caecum it produces soft
moist pellets, which the rabbit takes from its anus and eats. They pass
through a second time and make the familiar hard and comparatively
dry 'rabbit pills'. Many of the small rodents similarly refect at least
part of their food, and shrews protrude the rectum through the anus
and lick it to obtain what appears to be not faecal pellets but creamy
partly digested food. The coypu, too, recycles nearly all its food by
refection during the day after the nocturnal active period of
swimming and feeding.[71]

The alternation of activity by night and rest by day in small rodents
such as the wood and house mice and the brown rat is correlated with
the alternation of light and darkness, but must also often be
correlated with internal rhythms, for how could a small mammal in
its nest deep in a tortuous burrow, where no light can penetrate, know
that it is light or dark outside? These animals, moreover, are not
continuously active during their periods of activity, but alternate
activity with periods of rest, so that there is a lesser rhythm of activity
within the greater circadial one.

Unlike many other mammals the shrews are active both by day
and night, though they do show an overall circadial rhythm. 'A
common shrew alternately wakes and sleeps at regular and quite
short intervals throughout both day and night'.[43] Nevertheless some
common shrews will be awake and active at any hour while others are
asleep because their short-term rhythms are not in step. The short-
term rhythm consists of active periods lasting about two hours
alternating with approximately two-hour periods of rest. There is,
however, a circadial rhythm of two periods of greater activity, the first
and longer one in the evening and early part of the night, with a
second period of lesser intensity in the early morning and forenoon;
they are probably correlated with the times of sunset and sunrise.

The field vole shows a similar alternation of short periods of activity
and rest each lasting about two and a half hours throughout the
twenty four hours[47] so it is neither diurnal nor nocturnal. On the
other hand the mainly nocturnal house mouse and wood mouse are
not continuously active during the night, but also show periods of
activity lasting about two and a half hours alternating with rest

periods of similar length. The much larger brown rat also is nocturnal but has longer periods of activity lasting about four hours. It thus appears that in general the smaller mammals have shorter periods of activity and rest than the larger ones. This is confirmed by the rhythms of the water shrew, the mole, and others. The mole has three periods of activity and three of sleep every twenty-four hours, so that in effect it has three 'mole days' in every 'man day'.[66a, 105a]

It was formerly supposed that hunger is the stimulus controlling the short-term rhythm of activity; it may well be, but not in the simple manner first proposed, for the rhythm is not due to the periodic emptying of the stomach. The ultimate control of the circadial and shorter rhythms is much more deep-seated, and lies in the activity of the brain, particularly in the action of the hypothalamus, in relation to the physiological states of the various organs of the body.

The circadial rhythms of the bats are particularly well marked; in the British Isles they were first studied in some detail by several naturalists in the closing years of the last century and the opening ones of the twentieth.[4, 41, 117] They established that in most species there is an evening period of activity lasting up to about two hours followed by another before dawn, thus correcting the previous mistaken assumption that bats continue flying all night once they have left their roosts. Recent studies on the pipistrelle[138] have shown that bats leave their roosts when the light intensity reaches a critical level after sunset, and that weather vagaries do not affect the emergence time. In early and late summer most of the bats leave the roost only once each night soon after dusk, but in the middle of the summer, when the females are suckling their young and thus have greater energy requirements, they make two flights each night, one after dusk and a second before dawn. These two flights correspond with the flight times of the insect prey, which is most abundant in those periods as shown by insect traps set in the feeding area of the bats.

The early naturalists had to make their observations with unaided eyes and ears, and consequently could achieve little more – most of the information they recorded was about bats in their roosts when they are simply hanging up doing nothing in particular apart from sleeping. The important aspect of bat behaviour – what they are really doing when they are active, has until recently been quite unknown. Now the invention of instruments based on modern technology has given a new generation of naturalists the chance to find out; the use of ultrasonic detectors, miniature radios, radar, and night vision apparatus for seeing in the dark, will doubtless produce a large amount of new natural history information that within a decade will tell us more about the lives of bats than has been discovered during the last century.

One interesting point that the earlier naturalists did know throws some light on the control of the circadial rhythms of bats, and indicates that it is the internal physiology of the animals, and not merely the succession of light and darkness, that produces the rhythm. In the first place bats are often in total darkness during the day when asleep in their roosts, where day and night cannot be distinguished. Furthermore, when asleep in their roosts they are not just sleeping but are torpid; their temperature falls, the rate of the heartbeat and breathing is slowed, and all their physiological processes are reduced, yet at the appropriate hour activity returns. It was well known that for about half an hour before a roost of bats started the evening flight there was scuffling and squeaking as they warmed up and returned to life from the regions of 'suspended animation'.

The circadial rhythms of many species are greatly modified during the breeding season, when reproduction takes precedence over the more general activity of feeding. Territorial behaviour is then intensified even in small mammals. Among the larger species the red deer exemplifies the complete change from the usual behaviour during the rest of the year. As the rut approaches the herds of stags break up and the stronger animals take up territories which they defend from rivals, and on which they maintain a harem of hinds. Their attention is so completely engaged that they feed little, and use so much energy that in three to six weeks they are exhausted or 'run out', and retire from the turmoil of the rut. Similarly bull grey seals drive rivals from the breeding grounds, though the cows with which they associate do not form private harems. Nevertheless the bulls are so preoccupied with holding their positions that they do not feed for six weeks or more, and use their reserves of blubber to provide the energy they need during their fast.

The breeding season likewise imposes a different pattern of behaviour on female mammals; their heat periods are brief compared with the rut of the males, but their occupation in preparing a nest as a cradle for the young, in suckling, and in some species in feeding or guarding the young after weaning, is added to their usual behaviour.

In many species a heat period, the post-partum oestrus, occurs shortly after the birth of the young so that among small rodents and insectivores a second or third litter can be produced in a single season. Most of the British carnivores produce only one litter a year, for birth of the young is followed by a post-partum anoestrus in which the female is not receptive to the male until she has finished lactation and raising her family. In some of the mustelids fertilisation of the eggs and the formation of the blastocyst, the earliest stage of the embryo, is followed by a period of suspended development or 'delayed implantation' during which the blastocyst lies unattached in the uterus for weeks or even months, so that the apparent length of gestation is much prolonged. When development is resumed with the attachment of the blastocyst to the lining of the uterus gestation goes on comparatively fast. In the stoat implantation is delayed from the summer, when fertilisation occurs, until the following spring, so that a single litter is born each season. In the weasel, a smaller animal, there is no delayed implantation, but the female is in anoestrus from autumn until early spring. She then comes into heat and is inseminated, giving birth to a litter after a gestation of about five weeks. Those females that have young early in the season are thus able to bear a second litter later in the summer.

In the seals, and especially the grey seal, the occurrence of delayed implantation effects an economy in the yearly life cycle, for the female is impregnated at the post-partum oestrus a fortnight to three weeks after the birth of her pup. The annual assembly or 'haul out' for the birth of the pups is thus also used for the conception of the pup to be born the following year, gestation being resumed after a delay of about a hundred days. This arrangement is an obvious advantage to a marine mammal that is compelled to spend a few weeks ashore, to give birth and suckle its young, where it is 'out of its element' and specially vulnerable to disturbance and destruction by man, its chief enemy. The breeding cows are necessarily concentrated into comparatively small areas of suitable territory, and so the bulls which can serve up to twenty cows, though their average is much less, do not have to search far and wide for cows a hundred days after they have dispersed and returned to the sea. On the other hand, the advantage of delayed implantation to the common seal is less obvious, for the cows give birth on tidal banks or rocks and the pups can swim from the first, and indeed are sometimes actually born in the water. There is thus no need for a breeding haul-out, nor do the seals disperse widely afterwards, but remain loosely gregarious thoughout the year. Furthermore common seals, like grey seals, are promiscuous in pairing, and often copulate in the water.

Delayed implantation also occurs in the roe deer, the only ruminant in which it is known, but its correlation with the breeding cycle is obscure. The does are impregnated during the summer but the blastocyst remains unimplanted until the end of the year when gestation is resumed, and the young are born in late spring or early summer. Lactation is prolonged so that the does may suckle the young throughout the winter. There seems to be no correlation between the lengths of the delayed implantation and of suckling in the roe, for in the red deer, which has no delayed implantation, the calves are suckled for eight or ten months after their birth in the summer, and the hinds can come into oestrus and be impregnated during the autumn while they are still lactating.

All these sexual activities are controlled by the action of various hormones circulating in the blood, the amounts and kinds of hormones being ultimately determined by stimuli from the brain, particularly the hypothalamus. The pituitary body or gland is closely connected with the hypothalamus, and its front part, the anterior pituitary, secretes certain hormones that mediate the activity of many other organs. Two of the anterior pituitary hormones, the gonadotropic hormones, act upon the gonads, or sex glands, the ovary in the female and the testes in the male. The first, the follicle stimulating hormone (FHS) in addition to stimulating the growth of the follicles containing the egg cells in the ovary of the female, acts upon certain cells in the testis of the male, so that in both sexes the gonad produces the appropriate sex hormone, androgen in the male and oestrogen in the female.

The sex hormones have a profound effect on reaching the 'target' organs that are able to respond to them; they cause proliferation in the genital tract of both sexes, and in the accessory glands such as the prostate of the male. They also bring about the enhancement of the secondary sexual characters such as the mane of the rutting stag, the descent of the testes into the scrotum of some male mammals; and equally they are responsible for the development of sexual behaviour. Thus in the female the sex hormone brings her into oestrus and makes her receptive to the male, and in the male it enhances the aggressive and territorial behaviour that is so well-marked in the deer and the seals, and has become proverbial in the 'mad March hare'.

The second gonadotropic hormone secreted by the anterior pituitary, the luteinising hormone (LH), causes the cells of an ovarian follicle from which an egg cell has been discharged to enlarge and secrete another sex hormone, progesterone. This stimulates changes in the uterus in preparation for the reception of the embryo and for its gestation, and also influences the maternal behaviour, as for example in preparing a nest to cradle the as yet unborn young. Another hormone secreted by the anterior pituitary, prolactin, acts on the mammary glands, stimulating them to proliferation and the secretion of milk.

Discussion of the many other hormones lies outside the scope of this book, but before passing to other matters we should note that their actions are not as simple and straightforward as the preceeding paragraphs might imply, for they constitute a most complex web of feed-back mechanisms and chain-reactions. Furthermore, as most of them are brought into action by the hormones secreted in the pituitary, which is closely linked to the hypothalamus and thence to other parts of the brain, their production can be affected by stimuli received through the sense organs. Thus in some mammals such as the polecat and many others, the length of daylight controls the onset of oestrus in the female; in addition the whole of the sexual behaviour of mammals called 'courtship behaviour' results in stimulating the pituitary, and hence indirectly the production of sex hormones in both sexes.

The stimuli are received through any or all of the special sense organs, and may be produced by sight, sound, scent, taste or contact. Stimuli are not solely derived from the presence of the opposite sex, but from the environment in general; keepers of wild animals in captivity well know the importance of the right 'psychological atmosphere', and that animals that will not breed in close confinement often breed successfully when put into surroundings more nearly resembling their natural environment. There is, too, a further psychological effect in that some animals show individual preferences or dislikes for others of the opposite sex, probably mediated by individual variations in the stimuli received by the special sense organs. We have already noted that the scent of a strange male can prevent or stop gestation in the house mouse; similarly reaction to an unfavourable environment, such as may be caused by an over-crowded population, can result in the death of the foetuses of the rabbit. The dead foetuses are not aborted but are resorbed by the

uterus through the action of certain of the white blood cells, so that
the material that went into their making is recycled by the mother's
metabolism.

Moulting of the coat is a seasonal rhythm of metabolism that is very
conspicuous in a few mammals, less obvious but universal in the rest.
The conspicuous examples among the mammals of the British Isles
are the changes to a winter white coat in the mountain hare, and in
the stoats of the northern parts of the islands. Among our other
mammals there is at least one annual change of coat; in all it consists
of the shedding of the existing coat and its complete replacement by a
new one. Thus moulting brings changes adapted to the environment
in the colour and in the heat insulating property of the coat. The
growth and replacement of hair is 'regulated by the endocrine system
in such a way that it is geared to seasonal changes in the
environment'.[91]

The first coat or pelage grown by a young animal differs from that
of the adult, being usually finer, different in colour, and having
relatively longer hairs. This juvenile coat is always present at birth,
although the hairs may be so short that the new born animal, as in the
young of the rabbit, the mole, most small rodents and many others,
appear at first to be naked. The juvenile coat grows quickly and is
generally retained by small mammals until the autumn after their
birth, when the moult into winter coat brings the first adult pelage.

In the seals the first moult occurs at a much earlier age; the young
of the grey seal are born with a white, silky and fluffy juvenile coat
under which the hairs of the replacing pelage are already sprouting.
The white fluff is retained for no more than three weeks and is actively
shed from about twelve days of age onwards. The subadult coat
revealed when the white coat comes off lasts until the autumn of the
following year. The white coat of the young common seal is lost at an
even earlier age, most of it before birth. The shed hairs float in the
amniotic fluid which bathes the foetus, and many of them find their
way into its stomach, for the foetal seal, like all foetal mammals and
the human baby, drinks its bath-water.

The coat of the new-born calf of the red deer also differs greatly in
colour from that of the adult, being reddish-brown covered with white
spots on the upper side. This coat, which is softer and fluffier than that
of the adult, is replaced with a second coat by the age of about two
months, and the spots are lost with it. The young of the roe, too, are
spotted in their first coats, but resemble the adults after the first coat is

lost in the autumn. The first coats of both species thus resemble the adult summer coats of the fallow deer and several foreign species. It has been suggested that the coats of all ancestral species of deer were spotted, but that in the course of evolution the self-coloured coats of the adult of many species have been developed. This may be so, but the spotted coat of the young of those species may equally have been selected as a disruptive pattern that camouflages the young in its first week or ten days when it is hidden by the mother in dense herbage, and visited for suckling only at comparatively long intervals.

The summer and winter coats of the self-coloured deer do not differ greatly, though the winter coat is darker. In the fallow deer the light-coloured spotted summer coat contrasts markedly with the dark practically unspotted winter coat, though some herds contain animals that do retain spots in the winter. Few of our smaller mammals, apart from those that turn white in winter, differ conspicuously in their summer and winter garbs. The squirrels, however, are an exception, both the native red squirrel and the introduced grey. In the red squirrel the autumn moult produces a greyish brown winter coat with long dark tufts on the ears and nearly black bushy tail, the underparts being white. The colour of the coat fades or bleaches during the winter; at the spring moult the body coat is replaced by the red summer coat, but the hairs of the ear tufts and the tail are retained. The bleaching of the tufts and tail continues so that by mid-summer they are white in many individuals, and by loss of hairs much sparser. The grey squirrel is not uniformly grey in the summer but has a chestnut streak along the sides, and similar colour on the feet and edges of the legs; in winter it is also brownish on the head and along the back, though the feet are grey. The yellow-brown colouration sometimes misleads people into mistaking well-tinted individuals for red squirrels.

The moult of the pelage in the mammals of the British Isles, usually twice a year to produce a thick winter coat and a thinner summer one, generally takes several weeks; the old hairs are not shed all at once but are gradually replaced from one end of the body to the other, the moult thus appearing to creep over the surface. In the small rodents, and in the larger mammals that have coats with a direction of lay with the hairs in front overlapping those behind, the progress of the moult is generally not conspicuous. It can, however, be easily traced by examining the flesh side of the skin when removed, for the areas where new hairs are growing or about to grow are darkly pigmented; thus a succession of skins taken throughout the year shows the average progression of the moult. In some species it may start on the head, in others near the tail, or it may spread outwards from patches in other parts. In the squirrels the moult starts at the head for the spring moult, but at the tail for the autumn one. In mammals with velvety pelage having no direction of lay, such as the mole and the shrews, the progress of the moult is sometimes highly conspicuous because the longer hairs of the winter coat do not overlap the shorter ones of the summer coat. In these animals it is thus often possible to see a distinct line across the body where the new coat abuts against the remains of the old one.

Among the winter-white mammals the stoat has the usual two moults annually, in spring and autumn. The spring moult starts on the head and back, and spreads slowly over the rest of the body, producing the summer coat of brown above and white below with black tail tip. The autumn moult is much quicker, almost sudden; starting at the hind end of the body and sweeping forward it produces the thicker winter pelage. In England, Wales, and Ireland the winter coat is usually brown, rather paler than that of the summer, but in the north of Scotland it is often white, excepting the black tail tip. In southern Scotland and northern England some stoats are white in winter, some are not, and others are partly white and partly brown. Elsewhere in England, Wales, and Ireland the occurrence of white or partly-coloured stoats is less common, irregular and sporadic. The change to winter whiteness is roughly correlated with the general climate of the different regions, but it is not directly controlled by temperature – keeping southern stoats in low temperatures does not necessarily make them turn white in winter. Furthermore the weasel does not turn white in winter in the British Isles, but in the northern part of continental Europe it does.

The mountain hare, our only other mammal that bears a white winter coat, moults in a different way. The winter white coat is shed in spring, starting on the head and back and spreading downwards, and is completed fairly quickly. The greyish-brown coat that replaces it is not retained for long; it is shed in another moult from midsummer to autumn, and replaced by another brown coat. This moult is thought to be the equivalent of the autumn moult in which the brown hare obtains its winter pelage. The white winter coat with longer and denser hair is produced by yet another moult in the late autumn and early winter. There are thus three moults a year, in contrast with the two that are normal in most mammals, the third producing the white winter coat. Very few Scotch mountain hares turn completely white in winter, and even in them the ears remain dark. The majority always have some brownish grey colour on the face and back, and have dark ears; some do not complete the moult and remain partly coloured, as do those of the Irish subspecies, not all of which show any white in winter. The moult to the white coat is stimulated through the endocrine system of hormones by decreasing day length, and the moult from white to brown by the increasing length of day in spring, but in addition to the stimulus of light the rate of moulting to white is hastened by low temperatures.

The growth of a dense white pelage protects the animals from cold by thermal insulation of the body, and from predators by camouflage in regions where snow cover is wide and long lasting. There are, however, other ways of getting through the difficult cold season than by brazening it out. Some mammals give up the attempt and opt out of active life by hibernating; they enter into a winter 'sleep' in which all the physiological processes are reduced to the minimum necessary to preserve life. The only mammals in the British Isles that hibernate are the bats, the dormice, and the hedgehog – some others that are popularly supposed to hibernate, such as the red squirrel or the badger, do not, as any naturalist with his eyes open can see.

In hibernation the body is subjected to a controlled or voluntary hypothermia in which the normal temperature of about 37°C drops to only five or six degrees. At the same time the rates of breathing and of the heart beat are drastically reduced, and all the metabolic processes are accordingly slowed down so that the popular conception of 'suspended animation' is approximately but not entirely true.

The dormouse and the hedgehog hibernate in sheltered winter nests that they have prepared, usually underground because hibernating mammals cannot withstand being frozen; if the ambient temperature drops so low as to threaten freezing they are aroused, and then at least have the chance of seeking better accommodation. A hibernating hedgehog adopts the well-known defence attitude, rolled into a ball with snout and limbs tucked inside and secured by the action of the highly developed skin muscle or *panniculus carnosus* which functions almost as might an elastic band in keeping the opening into the ball shut. A hibernating dormouse similarly rolls up into a ball; the head is bent down onto the abdomen, the hind feet brought forward, the fore feet are clenched into fists and held under the chin or alongside the cheeks, and the tail is wrapped forward covering the head and back. The body temperature is so low that the dormouse feels cold to the touch, and the pose is so rigid that the animal can be rolled along a flat surface without arousing it.

The bats hibernate without preparing any winter nests; most of them creep into crevices in hollow trees, in caves, or roofs and other parts of buildings where there is some protection from extremes of low temperature. The horseshoe bats, however, hibernate hanging free from the roof in caves by the hind feet, and wrap their wings around them to make a neat bundle. They then look much like the fruit-pods of some exotic plant, or loosely rolled umbrellas. The other species of bat hiding in some crevice, cling to the surface, usually head downwards, with the wings closed at the sides and the ears folded back.

The torpidity of hibernation does not necessarily, or even generally, last continuously throughout the winter. The hedgehog is often late in hibernating, not lying up until the end of the year, and waking at intervals to forage around during mild spells of weather. The bats, too, wake at irregular intervals and move from one position to another within the hibernating cave, or sometimes move from one cave to another. Their arousal cannot be in order to feed, for there are few insects about at that time of year, but it may be that they drink. During the summer and autumn when food is abundant the hibernating mammals accumulate large amounts of fat, laid down under the skin and in the abdomen; this is gradually drawn upon as fuel to produce the energy needed to keep the metabolism going at the reduced rate of hibernation.

A second kind of fat, the 'brown fat', is prominent in mammals that hibernate, and is present to a lesser extent particularly in the young, of other mammals. It consists of masses of adipose and lymphatic tissue around the blood vessels in the neck and chest and especially on the back between the shoulders. The brown fat is not used for general metabolism but for producing heat on arousal, the rate of its oxidation being then greatly raised; it is similarly used by the young of non-hibernators to produce heat as their temperature-regulating mechanisms become established. In addition, the increased rate of the heart beat, and shivering of the muscles, help to produce heat and bring the body temperature up to normal.

The stimuli that start hibernation are both external and internal. The accumulation of body fat in the autumn is brought on by the seasonal availability of abundant food, but the later scarcity of food and lowered temperature are not the immediate causes of hibernation. The presence of fat stores, together with the reaction of the feeding physiology to them, appear to be part of the stimulus, but the final word lies in the central nervous system, because the temperature regulating centre in the hypothalamus is the basic control. In some hibernators, and possibly in all, there is an innate hibernating rhythm, for experiments on certain American ground squirrels[123] have shown that hibernation occurs at the right time of year even if the animals are kept in a constant warm temperature with artificial day and night lengths of twelve hours each.

Although bats arouse from hibernation for short periods from time to time they can continue torpid for a long while; in the laboratory bats have been kept in continuous torpidity at low temperature for six months without ill effects on arousal. The dormouse, too, has been kept in a torpid state for even longer, though in the wild it probably arouses now and then, because it lays up stores of food in the autumn, though they could be used as a first resource on spring arousal. Some of the non-hibernating mammals also lay up stores of food for winter use.

In general the carnivores do not lay up winter stores, though some do cache excess food but not particularly for winter use, as they may do so at any time of year when food is abundant. Tinbergen's and Kruuk's researches have shown how foxes exploiting a gullery of black-headed gulls cache some of the food they cannot immediately consume.[96, 145] Similarly the mole accumulates stores of worms, immobilised by being bitten through the nerve ganglia in the front end, at any time of year and not necessarily as winter stores.

The mole probably does use its stored worms for food, but the carnivores often do not retrieve even the food they have cached, and abandon most of the kill excessive to their immediate need. Some students of behaviour have embarked on lengthy discussions about the biological 'meaning' of excess killing, and how the phenomenon has evolved. To an unprejudiced observer, on the other hand, excess killing appears to be no more than the normal instinct to kill taking advantage of an unusual opportunity. The presence of large numbers of the prey in conditions where they cannot escape releases the carnivore's instinct onto a wild orgy of killing; is it necessary to look for more complicated reasons?

Excess killing occurs only when an abundant prey cannot escape;

it does not occur when the carnivore has to use all its skill to stalk or run down a single victim, but everyone knows what happens if a fox, stoat, or badger breaks into a hen house. Similarly well fed dogs whose owners do not trouble to control them do enormous damage every year by sheep-worrying. Even human picnickers coming upon a wood full of bluebells or a field of mushrooms often gather far more than they can use, simply because the excess is there. As for the release of aggressive behaviour by the opportunity for its expression, what of the hooligans and vandals who break all the windows of an unoccupied house or smash up public telephones? Excess killing by wild carnivores seems to be much the same. We may remember, too, that respectable millionaire business men call a successful deal, especially if it over-reaches a rival, 'making a killing', and pile up so much money that they cannot spend it but have to give it away to charities and political parties thereby obtaining peerages and other honours that promote them in the peck-order.

The squirrels are well known for laying up provisions for the winter, but they are less methodical than popularly supposed. They are 'scatter-hoarders' and thus do not accumulate stock-piles, but bury items of food apparently scattered at random over a wide area. The scattering, however, may not be so haphazard as it appears. I have watched grey squirrels busily collecting hazelnuts and walnuts from the trees and carrying them to a small area of clear grass plot some hundred yards away, where they buried them separately an inch or two deep. Squirrels are said to find such buried food by scent and searching at random when other food is scarce. But in this particular area of Suffolk grey squirrels are present only during an autumn invasion from the west and thereafter disappear, so that the nuts buried with such apparent compulsiveness are never retrieved – at least by squirrels.

Several others of our rodents hoard food in a more definite way, and the behaviour of the brown rat shows how the habit may have been evolved. The brown rat on finding something edible picks it up and carries it to a safe spot to eat it; if the food is a comparatively large object the rat drags it to the safety of cover before starting its meal. Sometimes such objects – for example a bone, a corn cob, or a fish, are carried into the safety of the nest, and after the edible parts are eaten the remains are not thrown out. Similarly there is some tendency to food hoarding in the bank vole and the water vole, but it appears that large stores are not built up.

The wood mouse and yellow-necked mouse are the great hoarders of winter food among the small mammals of the British Isles. Both species make extensive burrow systems; in one instance the burrows of wood mice were found to be centred round the stools of coppiced hazel trees,[88] with the nest chambers lined with dead leaves, grass, and moss, built under it. A store chamber nearby was stocked with hazelnuts and acorns together with the shells of snails and the wing-cases of beetles that had been eaten. There were up to eight entrances to the burrow system but some of the entrances were generally blocked up with leaves, twigs, lumps of soil and small stones, though at least two were always open. The hoarding habit seems to be innate; I have several times found hoards containing up to a quart (about a litre) of hazelnuts, all accumulated by the mice bringing in one nut at a time.

The wood mouse, and particularly the yellow-necked mouse which regularly comes into houses in the autumn, show a peculiar abberation of the hoarding habit when they come across food that cannot be taken away, such as barley meal – or a pan of warfarin bait – or things too large or awkwardly placed for removal. The mice then hide the food where it lies by covering it with dead leaves, twigs, shreds of torn-up paper, small stones, bits of plaster removed from walls, and other small objects that may be available, as though to make a cache. Such accumulations of miscellaneous rubbish often puzzle people when they come across them in their outhouses and garden sheds, but they may be sure that they are the work of yellow-necked or wood mice.

The evolution of hoarding behaviour has been considered theoretically by Andersson and Krebs[7] who have made mathematical models which tell us that 'the energy cost-benefit ratio per food item could be estimated via its metabolisable energy content and the energy required to hoard and recover it. However, it is difficult to specify how these measures relate to fitness. In many cases energetic considerations might be inadequate, because a fixed amount of energy represents a lower fitness cost (or gain) when food is common than when rare.' Further clarification is unnecessary.

We have noted that hibernation is not usually uninterrupted, and that hibernating mammals arouse at intervals, move about and may feed before returning to torpidity. The converse also is true; the temperature of mammals is not constant but varies slightly throughout the twenty-four hours, and in the small mammals particularly the temperature falls during periods of inactivity. This tendency to temporary torpidity is highly developed in the bats which, during normal day-time sleep, generally become semi-torpid with reduced respiration and heart rates and reduction in overall metabolism. Thus bats, which may spend as much as nine-tenths of the summer in torpid sleep and all of the winter in hibernation, are able to reach ages of up to twenty years and more in the wild, whereas a shrew of similar weight, which is on the go in spells of about two hours of alternating rest and activity through the twenty-four hours all the year round, is lucky to exceed eighteen months. It may be questioned whether a long life spent mainly in unconscious torpidity is more satisfactory than a short one spent in frequent short bursts of great activity. Natural selection, or rather natural elimination, has presumably been the cause of the evolution of the different ways of life, both of which, however, 'await alike the inevitable hour.'

The process of ageing appears to be more than a mere mechanical wearing out of the body; some of the simpler invertebrates can divide, regenerate, and renew tissues so that they avoid senescence, but in mammals, as in all vertebrates, only the genes in the reproductive cells avoid ageing and are thus potentially immortal. The genes are replicated in all the cells of the body, not always with precise accuracy so that the suggestion has been made[95] that increasing inaccuracy of transcription with advancing age may determine longevity. It may be an advantage for the higher mammals to save energy by tolerating reduced accuracy in the somatic, or body cells, and speeding up reproduction and development, although the result for the individual is degeneration with advancing age followed by death. 'This "disposable soma" theory of the evolution of ageing also proposes that a high level of accuracy is maintained in immortal germ line cells, or alternatively, that any defective germ cells are eliminated.'

The genes in the germ cells are thus not minor parts of the mortal body – the 'disposable soma' – which is merely a nest for sheltering, and a vehicle for transmitting what really matters, the double helix of DNA forming the genes. The body is only its temporary habitation, and it seems strange that DNA has found it necessary to build such an infinite variety of houses to be abandoned as they become dilapidated. Although the DNA of the germ cells is potentially immortal, can we really regard the enormous coiled molecule as living in the sense that we say animals are living – until they die?

CHAPTER 10

MAN AND THE OTHER MAMMALS

WE saw in chapter 2 that in the course of the last 5,000 years man has modified the environment in the British Isles at an increasing rate so that today it is in effect not natural but wholly artificial or man-made; the government nevertheless maintains a Natural Environment Research Council although there is no natural environment in the British Isles on which to conduct research. Yet the effects of man's activities, though they had a profound influence in determining the character of the environment, inflicted little deleterious or degrading results on it before the growth of the large towns and of industry began some two hundred years ago. Until then, apart from general deforestation, the felling of trees for use in smelting iron, lead, and other metals, and for ship-building, destroyed a capital asset that might have been preserved by replanting. The growth of the human population from about ten million in 1780 to the fifty five million of 1980 and its concentration in industrial areas, produced an ever growing degradation and pollution of the environment, the effects of which on our mammalian fauna we shall now consider.

During the eighteenth century industry and domestic chimneys fouled the air with soot and harmful gases such as sulphur dioxide, and the growing population fouled the rivers with sewage and industrial wastes. At the same time the enclosures of the countryside brought an enormous improvement in agricultural production although, as Malthus[105] had predicted, its growth could not keep up with that of the human population and produce all its food. The fouling of the waters got so bad in the nineteenth century that epidemic diseases, especially cholera, became widespread, forcing the towns to build sewers and to improve the water supply, though they still used rivers and inshore sea waters for the discharge of untreated sewage.

In the first half of the twentieth century there was little change beyond some improvements in the treatment of sewage to make the effluent less foul. During the last forty years, however, a revolution in land use has brought great changes. Clear air legislation has greatly reduced the fouling of the atmosphere, and improved sewage treatments are gradually reducing the fouling of most rivers; many species of fish now live in the lower Thames that was formerly lifeless, and even a few salmon have blundered into the estuary.

The agricultural revolution is even more spectacular; the destruction of many hedges planted at the time of the enclosures has given bigger fields so that the larger machines of mechanised agriculture can work. This, together with the use of fertilisers, herbicides and insecticides, and the introduction of improved strains of cereals, has produced those beautiful broad acres of crops free from the contamination of countless weeds that made the corn fields of the past so colourful, and so unthrifty. If making two blades grow where only one grew before is laudable, the triumph of the agricultural scientists is beyond praise. Likewise the improvements in raising livestock, denigrated by the ignorant as 'factory farming', have enormously increased the production of poultry and eggs, pork, bacon and beef. Some agricultural productivity has been lost to the towns, around which much good agricultural land is yearly permanently sterilised by building to house the still growing population – there are now nearly 600 people to every square mile in the British Isles whereas in the United States of America there are only twenty-six.

We should not forget that since neolithic times man has been struggling to improve and adapt his environment to suit his needs, and has succeeded in turning the howling wilderness into a land flowing with milk and honey over much of the earth's surface, bringing civilization in place of savagery. The romantic delusions of people cradled in all modern amenities that the wilderness is a place where everything is beautiful and unspoiled would soon be dispelled if they had to fend for themselves in the majestic cathedral of a tropical forest, or among the glittering ice pinnacles of the polar regions. All wild environments are hostile to man, and his success in taming and modifying them distinguishes his humanity from the ways of the brutes.

One might expect such great changes to have had a deleterious effect on the mammalian fauna of the British Isles, but with few exceptions they have not, and most species are able to co-exist with man and his works, or even take advantage of changed conditions. Only four species, all large and incompatible with human occupation of the land, the brown bear, wolf, wild boar, and beaver, have been exterminated in historic times – all the rest of our indigenous mammals are still with us. The resilience of the mammals to environmental change contrasts with what has happened to some of the birds, insects, and plants, which have undoubtedly been locally exterminated or driven away from former habits by human interference with the environment, though some may be merely showing the often cyclic alterations in numbers due to natural causes, for nothing in nature is static.

Most of the changes in the size of the populations of our mammals have been caused by the deliberate action of man against them, rather than by unintended side effects of his industrial or agricultural activities. The carnivores have been the chief victims of deliberate persecution, either for their destructiveness to domestic livestock and game, or for the value of their fur. The polecat, once widely distributed, has been exterminated over much of its former range for the first reason, and the marten for the second; both species, however, are increasing in numbers now that the pressure against them has been reduced. On the other hand the stoat and the weasel, vermin which have both been subjected to intense and prolonged persecution – and still are – have been able to maintain their positions, and are widely distributed and common throughout most of the land. Perhaps their smaller size has helped to preserve them.

The fox and the badger both stand in a peculiar relationship to man. The fox, universally hated by poultry- and game-keepers for its often devastating destructiveness, is nevertheless tolerated in many parts of the country for the sport its pursuit affords to those who ride to hounds or enjoy the spectacle of others doing so. In the highlands of Scotland, however, it is treated as vermin by gamekeepers and shepherds so that shooting foxes is not there a 'crime' against civilised behaviour. In the last thirty years, perhaps partly because of the scarcity of rabbits caused by myxomatosis after it arrived in the early 1950s, foxes have taken up a new habitat in the suburbs of large towns, and even in derelict areas within them – derelict through the destruction of war, of slum-clearances, or of industrial disputes such as those in the once thriving Port of London. Here foxes have insinuated themselves into the human environment, their wariness enabling them to remain largely unnoticed by most people; though they cannot be said to have become commensals, they are certainly scavengers, as they find their food largely in the garbage discarded by their unwitting human hosts. It is said that there are more foxes to the acre in the east end of London than in the Shires; whether or not this is correct the statement indicates that a large population now lives in urban surroundings.

The suburban population of foxes might be even larger were there not an unexpected curb on their reproductive rate. More than 34 per cent of the yearling vixens in suburban London are barren because, it is believed, in some areas foxes live in social groups of one dog fox with several vixens, only one of which breeds a litter.[76] The adoption of the new habit of urban life, though as far as we know it is not genetically determined, is an example of evolution going on before our eyes, and is perhaps similar to the fairly recently learned habit of opening milk bottles, most appropriately, by tits.

Foxes, and particularly urban foxes, would become a serious threat to human welfare if the epidemic, or more correctly epizootic, of rabies is introduced from the continent. Most mammals are susceptible to rabies, but the present epizootic is carried by foxes; it started in Poland nearly forty years ago and is advancing westwards at the rate of about 30 kilometres a year. The virus of rabies in the saliva passes into a new victim if it is bitten by an infected animal; it multiplies in the nervous system producing paralysis or 'dumb' rabies, often passing into restless activity and aggression in 'furious' rabies. In man it produces hydrophobia which, once the symptoms had developed, was invariably fatal until the recent production of effective vaccines. The dreadful course of the disease is well described by the nineteenth century naturalist W.J. Broderip in his fascinating but long forgotten 'Zoological Recreations';[24] he adds that Bewick's vignette of a rabid dog[20] is a vivid representation of a mad dog's typical gait.

The epizootic has now reached western France, and the British authorities hope to keep it out of the British Isles by strict customs and quarantine control backed by heavy penalties. If some irresponsible fool smuggling a pet dog, cat, or other animal, brings in the disease plans are ready to contain and stamp it out by the extermination of foxes and other wildlife in the affected area. Yet rabies was endemic in the British Isles for hundreds of years and was eradicated only at the beginning of this century. During the 1890s about thirty people died from hydrophobia every year; in 1897 a muzzling order required all dogs to be muzzled, and the police to seize and destroy all dogs found without muzzles. In two years the disease had disappeared. Before the disease was stamped out dogs transmitted it not only to people but also to sheep, cattle, horses, and cats, and must have given it to foxes and other wild mammals from time to time. It is therefore surprising that no reservoir of infection was left in other species from which the disease could spread again after the dogs were relieved of their muzzles in 1899. It has been suggested that the success of the order was due not so much to preventing dogs from biting by muzzling them, as to the destruction of all those found without muzzles. A new method for the control of rabies has now been devised: to vaccinate wild foxes by putting out baits containing an oral vaccine so that animals eating them would immunise themselves.[10] Unfortunately the live vaccine that immunises foxes can actually give rabies to other animals, even to rodents, that may eat it. This method has, nevertheless, been successfully used to keep rabies from infecting foxes in certain narrow Swiss valleys, but it is far too dangerous for general use.

The population of the badger may have increased since the beginning of the century, but there are no figures to support the suggestion; it is equally probable that the more recent growth in the numbers of people interested in them has revealed its size, for the badger is an expert at keeping out of the sight of casual observation. The badger, almost harmless to human interests, has for long been regarded as vermin, partly to justify the hard labour of 'badger digging', with its corollary of badger baiting, formerly considered a rural sport but now illegal. A badger once captured is practically useless to man except for its hair, which is used in the manufacture of artist's and the best shaving brushes – indeed 'blaireau' in the French language means both a badger and a (shaving) brush. In the last few years, however, the badger has become of serious importance to the dairy industry in parts of south-west England because it is a carrier of bovine tuberculosis.

After more than twenty-five years of intense official effort had eradicated the disease from Great Britain's cattle, over ninety per cent of which were suffering from it in 1945, it was disconcerting to know that serious outbreaks of bovine tuberculosis were being spread by infected badgers. The only possible remedy appeared to be the local extermination of badgers in the infected areas, and this was officially adopted. Opposition by certain 'animal lovers' who, apparently, love tuberculous badgers as much as they love clean ones, and are indifferent to the anguish of the farmer who sees his reactor cows sent away for slaughter, led to an official re-examination of the problem in 1980. Lord Zuckerman's report confirmed that destroy-

ing badgers by gassing them in their sets is the appropriate policy, so
we may hope in due course to have a population of badgers in the
areas concerned as free from infection as the cattle. The protesters
might remember that the Jews in the wilderness of Sinai on their way
to the promised land did not protest against the word of their Lord
that he would 'rid evil beasts out of the land'.[99]

The only British mammal that seems to have been seriously
affected by man's development of the countryside in recent times is
the otter. During the last thirty years there has been a marked decline
in the number of otters in much of lowland England, from parts of
which they have completely disappeared. The otter is a naturally shy
animal that needs plenty of cover around its aquatic habitat in order
to survive. The enormously increased use of the country for recreation
by the town-dwellers, brought about by the mobility conferred by the
motor car, is one of the main causes of the disturbance of the habitat
that has driven the otters away. Apart from the trampling of noisy
picnickers, even the quiet and contemplative anglers have so grown in
numbers that the otter habitat is unwittingly disturbed – and motor
boats, speedboats, and water-skiing make conditions impossible for
otters.

The greatest disturbers of the otter habitat, however, are the
Regional Water Authorities, which are responsible for the water
supply, the disposal of sewage, land drainage, and the reduction of
pollution. In carrying out their duties the Water Boards clear the
channels of rivers and streams by dredging the silt and depositing it
on the banks from which they clear overhanging trees and bushes, so
that the water has a clear run through unobstructed channels with
neat bare banks. The Water Authorities do no more than carry out
their statutory duties; if every human habitation, rural as well as
urban, is to have piped water and main drainage we must be
reconciled to doing without otters. The operations completely destroy
the habitat of the otter, which though shy in the sense that it is an
expert at keeping out of sight, is not incompatible with the human
presence. Before the general tidying-up otters commonly lived in
streams with banks overgrown with scrub close to houses, and even
made their holts in drains and under farm buildings – one holt was
found under the seat of an earth-closet at the end of a Welsh cottage
garden path.[134] Most people were completely unaware of the
presence of their otter neighbours.

The decrease of otters is so great that most masters of otter hounds have called off hunting, and many have turned to the introduced wild mink as an alternative quarry. At the same time conservationists have constructed artificial holts and refuges to which they hope otters may be attracted and so recover their numbers. Otters adapt fairly easily to captivity and it may be possible for them to take to such artificial homes; but the general habit is not what it was – people might formerly have been nearby but they did not trample over it in such numbers, nor neaten up the streams by canalising and clearing channels and removing all the cover from the banks. In places untouched by such modern improvements, as in much of the west coast of Scotland, otters are still common.

In contrast with the decline of the otter both our species of seal have shown a remarkable increase in numbers during the last sixty years. This is not due to legislative protection, although there has been a legal close season for the grey seal since 1914. The later protection acts were not passed until after the numbers of seals had so increased that they were seriously damaging some fisheries, particularly the salmon netting on the east coast of Scotland. During the nineteenth century the inhabitants of remote islands off the west coasts of Scotland and Ireland, who made a primitive and precarious living from fishing and small-scale farming, used to hunt grey seals to extract oil from the blubber and use the skins for various purposes. With the improvement in living standards on the mainland and the benefits of the welfare state, the hard life of the subsistence farmer and fisherman became more unattractive than ever; the people left many of the smaller islands which were left uninhabited, abandoned to the wild birds and the seals.

On the other hand, the grey seals of the Farne Islands off the coast of Northumberland equally increased in numbers although human disturbance of the habitat seems to have changed little; and the common seal herd of the Wash has likewise multiplied although until recently it has been cropped every year for the commercial value of the skins of the young.[137] It is possible that these changes in size of seal populations may be caused by some natural cyclic changes of which we are ignorant. It is peculiar that the seals were given full legal protection at the one time in their history over the last few centuries when they least needed it. Indeed, in the 1920s the government actually paid a bounty for killing common seals in the Wash, and in Ireland, where seals are not protected, a bounty was likewise paid for grey seals.

The seals are among the few species of native mammals other than the fur-bearers that have been commercially exploited by man. The hare, deer and fox have been valued more for the pleasures of the chase, though the inflation of the last decade or so has seen the rise of a well organised black market in poached venison and other game. Some of the indigenous mammals are vermin or pests to agriculture. The carnivores either from prejudice or ignorance have long been regarded as the enemies of man to be killed on sight as vermin; the poultry-keeper in the country sees them in a different light from that of the holiday intruder from the town.

The field vole, when its numbers occasionally build up to 'plague' proportions, damages turf and rough grazing, but such outbreaks of population explosion are always local and of short duration. The bank vole is sometimes a pest to the gardener, eating seeds and seedlings, ripening fruit, and barking small trees and branches in the winter. The water vole damages river banks by its burrowing, but the trouble is seldom extensive or serious. The wood mouse is by far the most troublesome pest among our small animals, for it not only frustrates the gardener as noted in chapter 8, but inflicts serious damage on agriculture, digging up the seeds of sugar beet and other crops, and sometimes grazing young cereals to the ground.

The native red squirrel is a pest to the forester, particularly through the damage that it does to plantations of conifers. The destruction of pine cones to obtain the seeds may be of little importance, but the squirrel also feeds on the buds of trees and is partial to the succulent leading shoot of conifers in the spring. This destruction of the leader mutilates the tree so that it becomes 'stag-headed' and valueless as timber; similar damage is inflicted by stripping the bark of young shoots in springtime to obtain the juicy cambium layer beneath.

Of the insectivores the mole is more of a nuisance than a pest, both to the gardener and the farmer. In the days before the combine harvester mole heaps among cereal crops were a hindrance to the mower, or self binder, still more to the scythe, but the old country trade of the mole-catcher is now practically extinct; only a few people trap moles for the small commercial value of the skins. The shrews, apart from the water shrew whose presence in trout hatcheries is unwelcome, have never been pests. The common shrew, however, was formerly thought to be venomous and was used in certain superstitious rituals. A living shrew was plugged into a hole bored in an ash tree which thereupon became a 'shrew ash', the twigs of which when stroked on the limbs of domestic animals were believed to cure the pains resulting from a shrew happening to run over them. Gilbert White[52] saw such a shrew ash felled by order of the local parson in about 1755. Superstition also persecuted the harmless hedgehog until the nineteenth century, as is shown by numerous entries in the books of country churchwardens recording the payment of small rewards for killing hedgehogs.

The bats are all completely harmless to man, at least in the British Isles, though some tropical species carry rabies. At worst they may be a nuisance, as when the droppings from a bat roost offend those who worship in church; and at best they may be regarded as the beneficient destroyers of large quantities of noxious insects. But man has not been kind to bats; he has looked upon them with superstitious horror – many people still do – and wantonly driven them from their roosts. The decline in the numbers of greater horseshoe bats is attributed at least in part to the unintentional disturbance of their habitats by pot-holers and other cave enthusiasts, and to excessive handling by bat-ringers and other chiropterists who intend them no harm. The use of agricultural insecticides also takes its toll, for several species of bat have been found to be carrying a third of the lethal level of DDT residues in their tissues during the summer and a higher amount, just under the lethal level, after hibernation.[89]

Although man has looked upon most of our native mammals with unfriendly eyes he had, on the whole, little serious cause for doing so. On the other hand, most of the species introduced accidentally or on purpose during the last thousand years have turned out to be destructive pests with a resilience and toughness against which all human efforts to get rid of them have been powerless.

The original home of the house mouse was probably somewhere in central Asia, where it inhabited open country. Several thousand years ago races of house mice evolved that became commensal with man, living in his habitations and feeding on his stored food. Commensal house mice presumably did not evolve until after man had invented agriculture and the need for storing the harvest and, particularly the seed corn for the next season. Once it became commensal the mouse accompanied man wherever he travelled, and was in the British Isles by the beginning of the iron age and probably long before that; it has thus been with us for at least more than two thousand years. It has accompanied man to all parts of the world and differentiated into many subspecific races, some of which have deserted man and returned to the wild. The house mouse is not only destructive to stores but carries the germs causing food-poisoning and spreads them to man by fouling his stored food products. In spite of millenia of persecution, including all the control methods of modern science, the house mouse is still with us and as flourishing as ever.

The black and brown rats are similarly commensals but are relative late-comers compared with the house mouse. The black, or ship, rat came to Europe from south-east Asia, arriving in the British Isles soon after the norman conquest, and became widely distributed in human dwellings. In addition to the damage and fouling it caused to food stuffs it carried the germs of bubonic plague, which were transmitted to man by its fleas and brought the pandemic 'black death' of the middle ages and the 'plague year' of 1665–66.

The brown rat probably originated in central Asia and spread across Europe, arriving in the British Isles around the end of the first quarter of the eighteenth century. In about a hundred years it had displaced the black rat, and was common nearly everywhere, probably because it is more adaptable to varying conditions and is able to live out of doors as well as within houses and other buildings. The damage that brown rats cause is enormous, and although anti-rat campaigns have destroyed vast numbers the best way of defeating them is to house stores in rat-proof buildings. The poison 'warfarin' which contains dicoumarin, cumulative doses of which cause death from internal haemorrhage, has for years proved an excellent medium of control though not of extermination. Now strains of brown rat genetically immune to the action of warfarin have appeared, and it is said, perhaps facetiously, that some cannot live without eating the 'poison' so that they die if they cannot obtain it. It was only to be expected that killing off the susceptible part of the population would make room for the spread of the immune minority. On a Welsh farm rats living in hedgerows were found to have home ranges less than 100 m. in length, though most of them perished without establishing permanent home sites. The few that survived must have been responsible for spreading the gene giving resistance to warfarin poisoning at a rate of 4 to 5 kilometres a year.[78]

Although the brown rat replaced the black rat throughout most of the country, small colonies of the latter persist, or persisted until recently, in various seaports. This limited distribution strongly suggests that the isolated colonies are frequently replenished by new arrivals brought by shipping, in spite of all the precautions taken to prevent them getting ashore.

The rabbit was introduced from its native Iberian peninsula about A.D. 1300, and for several centuries was kept in enclosed warrens for the sake of the meat and fur. It seems to have become feral in the eighteenth and early nineteenth centuries when this system of husbandry gradually fell into disuse. It is noteworthy that Parson Woodforde's diary, written from 1758 to 1803, although it records coursing many a hare in Norfolk and notes presents of game between neighbours, mentions rabbits only when they appear on the table, usually served 'smothered with onions', except once when his greyhound Hector out coursing hares 'also killed one rabbit'.[152] The huge increase in the rabbit population appears to have coincided with the agricultural slump soon after the middle of the nineteenth century, when formerly prosperous farms were neglected, and much land reverted to rough grazings and scrub. The gross infestation of the countryside by rabbits spread slowly northwards so that by the end of the century the most northerly parts of Scotland were occupied. The rabbit thus became an agricultural pest inflicting such damage that the Ground Game Act of 1880 was passed to give the farmer the right of destroying rabbits on the land he occupied, a right that in the depression of the 1930s helped many a farmer to pay his rent, avoid bankruptcy, and scrape a bare living from his holding.

The rabbit remained a major agricultural pest in spite of the efforts made to reduce its numbers during World War II and after 1945. Myxomatosis, a pox caused by the myxoma virus, is endemic in, and not fatal to, South American rabbits of the genus *Sylvilagus*, but extremely virulent and fatal if transmitted to the European rabbit *Oryctolagus*. It was brought to Australia in the hope of destroying the millions of rabbits descended from early introductions; it succeeded well and caused a pandemic that cleared large areas of the pest. In the early 1950s it was introduced into an estate over-run by rabbits in northern France, and in 1953 it appeared in England – who brought it and released it has never been disclosed.

The Ministry of Agriculture, Fisheries and Food, which had spent hundreds of thousands of pounds in unsuccessful efforts at clearing land of rabbits, for clearances merely left a vacant habitat quickly occupied by newcomers, at once illogically started frantic attempts to contain the outbreak and stamp out the disease. It would not do: the disease escaped and spread like wildfire, soon wiping out over 90 per cent of the rabbits at no cost at all. A determined effort to destroy the few survivors was not pressed home, so a residue was left from which a new population built up. In the course of time strains of rabbits resistant to the disease appeared so that they recovered from infection instead of being rapidly killed, and at the same time strains of the virus of reduced virulence spread through the population. The rabbit is now again widespread and abundant in many places, but when local populations reach a peak they are generally cut down by a fresh outbreak of the disease which leaves a few survivors to start the cycle again.

Myxomatosis virus is transmitted from one animal to another by blood-sucking insects. In Australia it was carried by mosquitoes, but in the British Isles the transmitter is the rabbit flea. An early attempt to introduce myxomatosis for exterminating rabbits on the Welsh island of Skokholm in 1938 was not successful because, it has subsequently been said and improbable as it may seem, there were not any fleas on the rabbits there. The symptoms produced by myxomatosis in a pox-stricken rabbit are highly repulsive to human eyes, and there was much ill-informed public concern among those who regarded rabbits not as destructive pests but as endearing furry bunnies, as well as protests from those who enjoyed shooting them. A similar pandemic among brown rats would have been welcomed, for rats are 'not nice'. Myxomatosis is an ideal means of controlling the population of rabbits, because the rabbit is the only species susceptible to it – even the hare, with the exception of one or two isolated records, is immune.

The effects on the flora and fauna of the dearth of rabbits at the height of the epidemic showed dramatically how the hordes of the pest had influenced the ecology of the countryside. 'Bare ground was covered [with grasses]; better grasses and clovers, even uncommon species, appeared; there were sheets of orchids at Old Winchester Hill and a great reduction of pernicious weeds like ragwort . . . The turf increased in height and changed to a much greater proportion of palatable grasses and clovers. There was much spread of tree and shrub seedlings'.[142] The indirect effect on other animals was equally great: foxes ate larger numbers of small rodents and more vegetable matter – it seems possible that the adoption of the urban habitat by foxes may have been connected with the enforced change of diet. More indirectly the tawny owls in an Oxfordshire wood suffered in 1955 a reduction in reproductive success attributed to a shortage of their normal food of small mammals caused by the increased predation upon them by foxes.[9] Buzzards too, which apparently depended largely upon rabbits for food declined in numbers, but badgers, which commonly dig out nests of young rabbits, are so omnivorous that they seem to have been unaffected by the lack of a favourite delicacy.

The grey squirrel, introduced by irresponsible people who should have known better, was released at some thirty different places during the period between 1876 and 1929. Many of the introductions gave rise to flourishing populations which increased and finally merged with each other, especially after about 1930, so that the grey squirrel is now widespread over much of England and Wales and parts of Scotland and Ireland. Although the population was reduced by an epidemic of disease in 1931 the area of distribution increased from about 10,000 square miles in 1930 to over 21,000 in 1937,[121] and since then has greatly extended. All attempts at extermination or even control of numbers of the grey squirrel have failed; the official supply of free cartridges to 'squirrel clubs' and a bounty of a shilling a tail were abandoned when their ineffectiveness became obvious. It is now illegal to keep grey squirrels in captivity – but it is the huge non-captive population that does the damage.

Coypu escaped from fur farms in the late 1920s and established small populations in several places; they were at first regarded as harmless curiosities but when they over-ran East Anglia they became a serious pest. They have done immense damage to cereals, sugar beet, and other crops, and have undermined roads and damaged drainage channels with their large burrows. In a single year the cost of repairing the damage in Norfolk and Suffolk has amounted to half a million pounds. In addition they have altered the character of aquatic plant communities by their selective feeding on certain species, thereby affecting the general ecology of the regions inhabited.

The existing coypu pest-control area was to be extended in 1980 westwards from eastern Norfolk and Suffolk in a new government campaign intended to exterminate the animals; the work will cost nearly a quarter of a million pounds but will be money well spent if it succeeds. Coypu are controlled by trapping; occasional shooting by farmers and landowners has little effect on the population so that systematic trapping by professional trappers is the only practicable method. The animals have no natural enemies in the British Isles;

their large size and weight and huge incisor teeth enable them to defeat attack by most dogs or foxes. They are, however, sensitive to cold weather and often suffer damage from frost bite in winter – in exceptionally severe winters their numbers have been drastically reduced, but unfortunately not to the level of extermination.

The porcupine is an accidentally introduced animal that might become a pest but is at present little more than an unexpected curiosity. Porcupines are breeding at large in parts of the Devonshire countryside; they are descended from a pair of Hodgson's porcupines, natives of China and Mongolia, that escaped from a zoo near Okehampton in the early 1970s. At first they were almost unnoticed, but they have now increased in numbers and damage forestry plantations by stripping the bark from young conifer trees, and attack field and garden crops of potatoes, sugar beet and other root vegetables.

The edible dormouse has not spread far from its centre of introduction in Bedfordshire and, although a nuisance to fruit growers, has not assumed the proportions of a pest. Similarly the few capybara, chinese water deer, and wallabies that are at large in various parts of the country have not yet reached numbers large enough to cause any serious damage to man's interests.

On the other hand the muntjac, or barking deer, which has been regarded as a 'harmless introduction', is fast increasing, and threatens to become a forestry pest if it is not controlled. It is supposed to have escaped from Woburn park and occupies East Anglia, the home counties, and most of the east and central midlands.[23] Muntjac live in groups, each comprising an adult pair with a fawn and a yearling which is driven away when the fawn grows up. The gestation period is seven months, and breeding is continuous so a doe can produce three fawns in little more than twenty-one months – say three in two years. When the yearling leaves its group it finds another muntjac of opposite sex, thus starting a new group; the species is consequently rapidly increasing its range of distribution. These small deer establish their territories in dense thickets of bramble or gorse and similar places, where they feed on bramble, grass, ivy, acorns and beechmast. In severe winters, particularly when snow blankets their usual foods, they take to browsing on seedling and sapling timber, causing serious damage and loss if they are present in anything but sparse numbers. The rapid increase in size and distribution of the population is likely to make them a pest needing strict control.

If a serious attempt to exterminate the introduced North American mink had been made when the animals first established a foothold among our fauna, having escaped from fur-farms in southern England during the late 1950s, we should have been spared much controversy. The opportunity was however missed, and the feral population rapidly increased so that there is now a wild population throughout most of the British Isles, in which the parts still free will soon be occupied. The American mink is thus as much an established part of our mammalian fauna as the rabbit or grey squirrel, and there is no prospect of eliminating it.

Mink prey upon any animals that are not too large or powerful to resist them. The diet ranges from crayfish to fishes, birds and small mammals up to the size of young rabbits. In England and Wales moorhens and coots together with small mammals and, to a lesser extent, fish make up the bulk of its food,[32, 49] whereas in Scotland fish, especially trout and small salmon, are more important.[5] Ornamental waterfowl have sometimes been attacked, as have domestic poultry and young game birds; such predation has led some people to exaggerate the potential destructiveness of the mink, calling it[98] a 'voracious alien carnivore' which has 'caused immense harm to wild and domesticated land birds, to resident and migratory wildfowl, to game and coarse fish, and to small mammals.' Such general statements, apparently based more on emotion than on fact, are not supported by objective scientific enquiry.

Although the mink can make full use of its habitat because it is semi-aquatic, it is equally active on land, is a nimble climber, and is an opportunist predator taking whatever is available, it cannot be regarded generally as a pest in the British Isles.[101] Nevertheless at certain places and at certain times it can cause serious destruction, as in colonies of ground nesting sea birds, many of which, however, are on small off-lying islands and thus safe from such predation. Economic loss to human interests occurs when mink break into fish farms and hatcheries, and into poultry farms and game-bird rearing pens, but they are no more destructive than our indigenous carnivores such as otters, foxes, stoats, and weasels. While mink have been spreading otters have declined in numbers, but the allegation that mink have driven out otters is unproved and improbable, for there is strong evidence that there is no connection between the two events.[101] One result of the change in relative numbers of the two species has been that some Masters of Otter Hounds have taken to hunting mink in order to preserve their sport without further harassing the declining population of otters. Whether or not people like mink, the species is now so firmly established that it must be accepted as a new addition to our mammalian fauna in which, although it is not the grave menace that some believe, is on the whole an undesirable alien that we could well do without.

A similar view applies to all our immigrants, whether introduced deliberately or unintentionally, for nearly all our serious mammalian pests are foreigners. Some of our indigenous species present fully enough problems of control to the farming industry, the basic activity on which everyone's life depends, without having immigrants and undesirable aliens making its work more difficult.

Much of our mammalian fauna is thus as artificial and man-made as the rest of the environment of which it makes a part. There is no need, and indeed it is futile, to try to make time stand still by enacting laws for 'conservation'; although nothing should be wantonly destroyed everything flows inexorably on, and if instead of looking back in sorrow we turn our gaze upon the present we have the absorbing spectacle of evolution in progress – not, perhaps the evolution of new species among our mammals, but the evolution of new habits and habitats and ways of co-existence between the wild mammals and man. Nothing is static, for new and unexpected things are constantly turning up; in the last quarter century we have seen the near-extermination of the rabbit and its remarkable recovery, the unexpected population explosion of the grey seal, the establishment of mink as a British mammal, and the decline of the otter. Finality can never be reached, there is always something new to engage the attention of the naturalist; it is this that makes the study of the biology of our mammals, as indeed of the rest of our flora and fauna, an ever absorbing and fascinating pursuit.

APPENDIX

A list of the named subspecies of British wood mice and voles. Although a few of these names are retained by some writers, with one or two exceptions they are valueless and give a false appearance of scientific exactitude.

Wood mice

Apodemus sylvaticus sylvaticus. Mainland.
A.s. butei. Bute.
Apodemus hebridensis hebridensis. Lewis.
A.h. hamiltoni. Rum.
A.h. cumbrae. Great Cumbrae.
A.h. maclean. Mull.
A.h. fiolagan. Arran.
A.h. tirae. Tiree.
A.h. ghia. Gigha.
A.h. tural. Islay.
A.h. larus. Jura.
A.h. nesiticus. Mingulay.
Apodemus hirtensis. St. Kilda.
Apodemus fridariensis fridariensis. Fair Isle.
A.f. grantii. Yell, Shetland.
A.f. thuleo. Foula, Shetland.

Bank voles

Clethrionomys glareolus glareolus. Mainland.
C.g. skomerensis. Skomer.
C.g. alstoni. Mull.
C.g. erica. Raasay.
C.g. caesarius. Jersey.

Field voles

Microtus agrestis agrestis. Mainland: England and Wales.
M.a. macgillivraii. Islay.
M.a. exsul. North Uist.
M.a. mial. Eigg.
M.a. neglectus. Scotland.
M.a. luch. Muck.
M.a. fiona. Gigha.

Orkney voles

Microtus orcadensis orcadensis. Pomona, Orkney.
M.o. ronaldshaiensis. South Ronaldshay.
M.o. rousaiensis. Rousay.
M.o. westrae. Westray.
M.o. sandayensis. Sanday.
Microtus sarnius. Guernsey.

REFERENCES

1. ADAMS, M.G. & JOHNSON, E. (1980). Seasonal changes in the skin glands of the roe deer (*Capreolus capreolus*) *J. Zool., Lond.* **191**, 509.
2. ADRIAN, E.D. (1947). *The Physical Background of Perception*. Oxford.
3. — (1948). The sense of smell. *Advanc. Sci., Rep. Brit. Ass.* **4**, 287.
4. AGASSIZ, L. (1837). Discours prononceé à l'ouverture des séances de la Société Helvétique des Sciences Naturelles. *Act. Soc. Helvétique Sci. Nat.* **2**, V.
5. AKANDE, M. (1972). The food of feral mink (*Mustela vison*) in Scotland. *J. Zool., Lond.* **167**, 475
6. ALCOCK, N.H. (1899). The natural history of Irish bats. *Irish Nat.* **8**, 29, 53, 169.
7. ANDERSSON, M. & KREBS, J. (1978). On the evolution of hoarding behaviour. *Anim. Behav.* **26**, 707.
8. ANON. (1979). *Rabbit*. CSIRO Div. Wildlife Res. Rep. **1976-78** Canberra.
9. BACKHOUSE, K.M. & THOMPSON, H.V. (1955). Myxomatosis. *Nature, Lond.* **176**, 1155.
10. BACON, P.J. & MACDONALD, D.W. (1980). To control rabies: vaccinate foxes. *New Scient., Lond.* **87**, 640.
11. BARCLAY, R.M.R. & THOMAS, D.W. (1979). Copulation call of *Myotis lucifugus*: a discreet situation-specific communication signal. *J. Mammal.* **60**, 632.
12. BARRET-HAMILTON, G.E.H. (1899). On the species of the genus *Mus* inhabiting St Kilda. *Proc. zool. Soc. Lond.* **1899**, 77.
13. — (1900). On geographical and individual variation in *Mus sylvaticus* and its allies. *Proc. zool. Soc. Lond.* **1900**, 387
14. — (1903). Additions to the list of British boreal mammals. *Proc. roy. Irish Acad.* **24**, 315.
15. — & HINTON, M.A.C. (1910–1921). *A History of British Mammals*, London.
16. — (1913). Three new voles from the Inner Hebrides, Scotland. *Ann. Mag. Nat. Hist. Lond.* (*8*), **12**, 361.
17. — (1913). On a collection of mammals from the Inner Hebrides. *Proc. zool. Soc. Lond.* **1913**, 821.
18. BATES, H.W. (1878). Presidential Address. *Trans. ent. Soc. Lond.* **1878**, lxiii.
19. BEATY, C. (1978). Ice ages and continental drift. *New Scient. Lond.* **80**, 776.
20. BEWICK, T. (1790). *A general History of Quadrupeds*. Newcastle upon Tyne. (vignette p. 324).
21. BONESS, D.J. & JAMES, H. (1979). Reproductive behaviour of the grey seal (*Halychoerus grypus*) on Sable Island, Nova Scotia. *J. Zool., Lond.* **188**, 477.
22. BORROW, G. (1857). *The Romany Rye*. 2 Vols. London.
23. BRAY, D. (1980). Lest the muntjac run amok. *Field Lond.* **256**, 742.
24. BRODERIP, W.J. (1847). *Zoological Recreations*. London.
25. BUCHLER, E.R. (1980). Evidence for the use of a scent post by *Myotis lucifugus. J. Mammal.* **61**, 525.
26. BUCKLAND, F.T. (1882). *Curiosities of Natural History*. Fourth series. London.
27. BUCKLAND, W. (1823). *Reliquae Diluvianae*. London.
28. — (1841). The former existence of glaciers in Scotland and in the north of England. *Edinb. new phil. J.* **30**.
29. BURT, W.H. (1943). Territoriality and home range concepts as applied to mammals. *J. Mammal.* **24**, 346.

30. CAMPBELL, J.B. (1978). *The Upper Palaeolithic of Britain*. 2 vols. Oxford.
31. CAVE, A.J.E. (1980). A constellation of conservators. *Ann. r. Coll. Surgeons Eng.* **62**, 66.
32. CHANIN, P.R.F. & LINN, I. (1980). The diet of the feral mink (*Mustela vison*) in southwest Britain. *J. Zool. Lond.* **192**, 205.
33. CHARLESWORTH, J.K. (1957). *The Quaternary Era with special reference to its Glaciations*. 2 vols. London.
34. CLARK, J.G.D. (1936). *The Mesolithic Settlement of Northern Europe*. Cambridge.
35. — (1954). *Excavations at Star Carr*. Cambridge.
36. CLUTTON BROCK, T.H., ALBON, S.D., GIBSON, R.M. & GUINNESS, F.E. (1979). The logical stag: adaptive aspects of fighting in red deer (*Cervus elaphus L.*) *Anim. Behav.* **27**, 211.
37. CORBET, G.B. (1961). Origin of the British insular races of small mammals and of the 'Lusitanian' fauna. *Nature, Lond.* **191**, 1037.
38. — (1964). Regional variation in the bank vole *Clethrionomys glareolus* in the British Isles. *Proc. zool. Soc. Lond.* **143**, 191.
39. — & SOUTHERN, H.N. (1977). *The Handbook of British Mammals*. Oxford.
40. CORKE, D. (1977). The distribution of *Apodemus flavicollis* in Britain. *Mammal Rev.* **7**, 123.
41. COWARD, T.A. (1907). On some habits of the lesser horseshoe bat (*Rhinolophus hipposideros*). *Proc. zool. Soc. Lond.* **1906**, 849.
42. COWPER, W. (1817). *The Task*. Book III. London.
43. CROWCROFT, P. (1957). *The Life of the Shrew*. London.
44. DARLING, F.F. (1937). *A Herd of Red Deer*. Oxford & London.
45. — (1938). Atlantic seals. *Ctry Life, Lond.* **42**, 502.
46. DARWIN, C. (1859). *The Origin of Species*. London.
47. DAVIS, D.H.S. (1933). Rhythmic activity in the short-tailed vole, *Microtus*. *J. Anim. Ecol.* **2**, 232.
48. DAWKINS, R. & KREBS, J.R. (1979). Arms races between and within species. *Proc. roy. Soc. B.* **205**, 489.
49. DAY, M.G. & LINN, I. (1972). Notes on the food of feral mink *Mustela vison* in England and Wales. *J. Zool., Lond.* **167**, 463.
50. DELANY, M.J. (1964). Variation in the long-tailed field-mouse (*Apodemus sylvaticus* (L) in north west Scotland. 1. Comparison of individual characters. *Proc. roy. Soc. B.* **161**, 191.
51. — (1965). The application of factor analysis to the study of variation in the long-tailed field-mouse (*Apodemus sylvestris* (L.)) in northwest Scotland. *Proc. Linn. Soc. Lond.* **176**, 103.
52. — & HEALY, M.J.R. (1964). Variation in the long-tailed field-mouse (*Apodemus sylvaticus* (L.)) in north-west Scotland. II. Simultaneous examination of all characters. *Proc. roy. Soc. B.* **161**, 200.
53. DE WINTON, W.E. (1895). The long-tailed field-mouse of the Outer Hebrides: a proposed new species. *Zoologist.* (*3*), **19**, 369.
54. EAST, K. & LOCKIE, J.D. (1964). Observations on a family of weasels (*Mustela nivalis*) bred in captivity. *Proc. zool. Soc. Lond.* **143**, 359.
55. — — (1965). Further observations on weasels (*Mustela nivalis*) and stoats (*Mustela erminea*) born in captivity. *J. Zool., Lond.* **147**, 234.
56. EINON, D. (1980). Rats at play. *New Scient. Lond.* **85**, 934.
57. ELLENBROCK, F.J.M. (1980). Interspecific competition in the shrews *Sorex araneus* and *Sorex minutus* (Soricidae, Insectivora): a population study of the Irish pygmy shrew. *J. Zool. Lond.* **192**, 119.
58. ELTON, C.S. (1966). *The Pattern of Animal Communities*. London.
59. FAIRLEY, J.S. (1971). The present distribution of the bank vole *Clethrionomys glareolus* Schreiber in Ireland. *Proc. R. Irish Acad.* **71** B, 183.
60. FERNS, P.N. (1967). The classification of animal habitats. *Bull. Mammal Soc.* No. 28.
61. FLINT, R.F. (1957). *Glacial and Pleistocene Geology*. New York.

62. FORD, C.E., HAMERTON, J.L. & SHARMAN, G.B. (1957). Chromosome polymorphism in the common shrew. *Nature, Lond.* **180**, 392.

63. FROHAWK, F.W. (1914). *The Natural History of British Butterflies.* 2 vols. London.

64. GALAMBOS, R. & GRIFFIN, D.R. (1942). Obstacle avoidance by flying bats: the cries of bats. *J. Exp. Zool.* **89**, 475.

65. GARSON, P.J. (1975). Social interactions of woodmice (*Apodemus sylvaticus*) studied by direct observation in the wild. *J. Zool., Lond.* **177**, 496.

66. GAUGHIN, M.D. (1979). The occurrence of flehmen in a marsupial – the hairy-nosed wombat (*Lasiorhinus latifrons*). *Anim. Behav.* **27**, 1063.

66a. GODFREY, G. & CROWCROFT, P. (1960). *The Life of the Mole (Talpa europea* Linnaeus). London.

67. GODWIN, H. (1956). *The History of the British Flora.* Cambridge.

68. GOSLING, L.M. (1974). The coypu in East Anglia. *Trans. Norfolk Norw. Nat. Soc.* **23**, 49.

69. — (1977). Coypu. See 39.

70. — (1979). The twenty-four hour activity cycle of captive coypus (*Myocastor coypus*). *J. Zool., Lond.* **187**, 341.

71. GREEN, R. (1979). The ecology of woodmice (*Apodemus sylvaticus*) on arable farmland. *J. Zool., London.* **188**, 357.

72. GUNERNICK, D.J. (1980). Maternal 'imprinting' or maternal 'labelling' in goats. *Anim. Behav.* **28**, 124.

73. GUINNESS, F.E., HALL, M.J. & COCKERILL, R.A. (1979). Mother–offspring assoociation in red deer (*Cervus elaphus* L.) on Rhum. *Anim. Behav.* **27**, 536.

74. HALTENORTH, T. (1953). *Die Wildkatzen der Alten Welt.* Leipzig.

75. HARPER, R.J. (1977). 'Caravanning' in Sorex species. *J. Zool., Lond.* **183**, 541.

76. HARRIS, S. (1979). Age-related fertility and productivity in red foxes *Vulpes vulpes* in suburban London. *J. Zool., Lond.* **187**, 195.

77. — (1979). History, distribution, status and habitat requirements of the harvest mouse (*Micromys minutus*) in Britain. *Mammal Rev. Lond.* **9**, 159.

78. HARTLEY, D.J. & BISHOP, J.A. (1979). Home range and movement in populations of *Rattus norvegicus* polymorphic for warfarin resistance. *Biol. J. Linn. Soc. Lond.* **12**, 19.

79. HARTRIDGE, H. (1920). The avoidance of obstacles by bats in their flight. *J. Physiol.* **54**, 54.

80. HEDIGER, H. (1950). *Wild Animals in Captivity.* London.

81. HEWER, H.R. (1974). *British Seals.* London.

82. HICKLING, G. (1962). *Grey Seals and the Farne Islands.* London.

83. HINTON, M.A.C. (1924). On a new species of *Crocidura* from Scilly. *Ann. Mag. nat. Hist. (9).* **14**, 589.

84. [HOSKYNS, C.W.] (1852). *Talpa, or the Chronicles of a Clay Farm.* London.

85. HUNT, O. (1973). Factors affecting the survival of the large blue butterfly *Maculinea arion* L. in Devon and Cornwall. *Biol. J. Linn. Soc. Lond.* **5**, 360.

86. HURRELL, H.G. (1963). *Pine Martens.* Sunday Times Animals of Britain No. 22.

87. IMBRIE, J. & K.P. (1979). *Ice Ages: Solving the Mystery.* London.

88. JENNINGS, T.J. (1975). Notes on the burrow systems of woodmice (*Apodemus sylvaticus*). *J. Zool., Lond.* **177**, 500.

89. JEFFERIES, D.J. (1972). Organochlorine insecticide residues in British bats and their significance. *J. Zool., Lond.* **160**.

90. JOHNS, A.D. (1979). A comparative assessment of methods of individual tracking within a population of *Microtus agrestis* (Mammalia: Muridae) *J. Zool., Lond.* **189**, 333.

91. JOHNSON, E. (1979). Hair, fur and moult in mammals. *Biol. J. Linn. Soc. Lond.* **12**, 358.

92. JONES, F.W. (1929). *The Matrix of the Mind.* London.

93. KIND, C.M. (1975). The home range of the weasel (*Mustela nivalis*) in an English woodland. *J. Anim. Ecol.* **44**, 639.

94. — & MOORS, P.J. (1979). On co-existence, foraging strategy and bio-geography of weasels and stoats (*Mustela nivalis* and *M. erminea*) in Britain. *Oecologia (Berl.)* **39**, 129.

95. KIRKWOOD, T.B.L., & HOLLIDAY, R. (1979). The evolution of ageing and longevity. *Proc. roy. Soc. B* **205**, 531.
96. KRUUK, H. (1972). Surplus killing by carnivores. *J. Zool., Lond.* **166**, 233.
97. LANGLEY, P.J.W. & YALDEN, D.W. (1977). The decline of the rarer carnivores in Great Britain during the nineteenth century. *Mammal Rev.* **7**, 95.
98. LEVER, C. (1978). The not so innocuous mink? *New Scient.* **78**, 812.
99. LEVITICUS. **26**, 6.
100. LINN, I. (1962). *Weasels.* Sunday Times, Animals of Britain No. 14. London.
101. — & CHANIN, P. (1978). More on the mink 'menace'. *New Scient.* **80**, 38.
102. LOCKIE, J.D. (1966). Territory in small carnivores. *Symp. zool. soc. Lond.* **18**, 143.
103. LOIZOS, C. (1966). Play in mammals. *Symp. zool. Soc. Lond.* **18**, 1.
104. MacKINNON, K. (1978). Competition between red and grey squirrels. *Mammal Rev.* **8**, 185.
105. MALTHUS, T. (1798). *An Essay on the Principle of Population.* London.
105a. MELLANBY, K. 1971. *The Mole.* London.
106. MILLAIS, J.G. (1904). On a new vole from the Orkney Islands. *Zoologist* (**4**), **8**, 241.
107. MILLER, G.S. (1912). *Catalogue of the Mammals of Western Europe.* London.
108. MONTAGU, I.G.S. (1923). On a further collection of mammals from the Inner Hebrides. *Proc. zool. Soc. Lond.* **1922**, 929.
109. — & PICKFORD, G. (1923). On the Guernsey *Crocidura. Proc. zool. Soc. Lond.* **1923**, 1043.
110. MONTGOMERY, W.I. (1978). Intra- and interspecific interactions of *Apodemus sylvaticus* (L.) and *A. flavicollis* (Melchior) under laboratory conditions. *Anim. Behav.* **26**, 1247.
111. — (1978). Studies in the distributions of *Apodemus sylvaticus* (L.) and *A. flavicollis* (Melchior) in Britain. *Mammal Rev.* **8**, 177.
111a. — (1980). The use of arboreal runways by the woodland rodents, *Apodemus sylvaticus* (L.), *A. flavicollis* (Melchoir) and *Clethrionomys glareolus* (Schreber). *Mammal Rev.* **10**, 189.
112. MOORE, P.D. (1975). Origin of blanket mires. *Nature, Lond.* **256**, 267.
113. MYERS, K. (1975). Utilization of appetite for sodium salts to control rabbit populations by poisoning. *Aust. Wildlife Res.* **2**, 135.
114. NEAL, E.G. (1962). *Otters.* Sunday Times, Animals in Britain No. 8. London.
115. — (1977). *Badgers.* Poole.
116. OAKLEY, K.P. (1969). *Frameworks for dating fossil man.* Ed. 3. London.
117. OLDHAM, C. (1901). Observations on the noctule. *Zoologist* (**4**) **5**, 51.
118. OWEN, R. (1846). *A History of British Fossil Mammals and Birds.* London.
119. PAGE, N.R. (1972). On the age of the Hoxnian interglacial. *Geol. J., Lond.* **8**, 129.
120. PALAEONTOGR. SOC. MONOGRAPHS. 1847 to present.
121. PARSONS, B.T. & MIDDLETON, A.D. (1937). The distribution of the grey squirrel (*Sciurus carolinensis*) in Great Britain in 1937. *J. Anim. Ecol.* **6**, 286.
122. PENK, A. & BRÜCKNER, E. (1909). *Die Alpen in Eiszeiten.* 3 vols. Leipzig.
123. PENGELLEY, E.T. & FISHER, K.C. (1957). Onset and cessation of hibernation under constant temperature and light in the golden-mantled ground squirrel (*Citellus lateralis*). *Nature, Lond.* **180**, 1371.
124. POCOCK, R.I. (1936). The polecats of the genera *Putorius* and *Vormela* in the British Museum. *Proc. zool. Soc. Lond.* **1936**, 691.
125. POOLE, T.B. (1964). Observations on the facial pattern of the polecat. *Proc. zool. Soc. Lond.* **143**, 350.
126. — (1966). Aggressive play in polecats. *Symp. zool. Soc. Lond.* **18**, 23.
126a. QUILLIAM, T.A. (1966). The mole's sensory apparatus. In Quilliam, T.A. (Ed.) The mole: its adaptation to an underground environment. *J. zool. Soc. Lond.* **149**, 31.
127. SHOTTON, F.W. (1973). A reply to 'On the age of the Hoxnian interglacial' by N.R. Page. *Geol. J., Lond.* **8**, 387.
128. — (1977). The Devensian stage: its development, limits and substages. In MITCHELL, G.F. & WEST, R.G. The changing environmental conditions in Great Britain and Ireland during the Devensian (last) cold stage. *Phil Trans. roy. Soc. London. B*, **280**, 103.

129. SILVERTOWN, J.W. (1980). The evolutionary ecology of mast seeding in trees. *Biol. J. Linn. Soc. Lond.* **14**, 235.
130. SIMPSON, G.C. (1930). Climate during the Pleistocene period. *Proc. roy. Soc. Edin.* **50**, 262.
131. SIMPSON, G.G. (1945). The principles of classification and a classification of mammals. *Bull. Amer. Mus. Nat. Hist.* **85**.
132. SOUTHERN, H.N. (1940). The ecology and population dynamics of the wild rabbit *Oryctolagus cuniculus* (L). *Ann. Appl. Biol.* **27**, 509.
133. — (1948). Sexual and aggressive behavior in the wild rabbit. *Behaviour.* **1**, 173.
134. STEVENS, M.N. (1957). *The Natural History of the Otter.* UFAW. London.
135. STODDART, D.M. (1976). Mammalian Odours and Pheromones. *Inst. Biol. Studies in Biology No. 73.* London.
136. STUART, A.J. (1974). Pleistocene history of the British vertebrate fauna. *Biol. Rev.* **49**, 225.
137. SUMMERS, C.F. (1979). The scientific background to seal stock management in Great Britain. *NERC Pubs. Ser. C No. 21.* London.
138. SWIFT, S.M. (1980). Activity patterns of pipistrelle bats (*Pipistrellus pipistrellus*) in north-east Scotland. *J. Zool., Lond.* **190**, 285.
139. SZABO, B.J. & COLLINS, D. (1975). Ages of fossil bones from British interglacial sites. *Nature, Lond.* **254**, 680.
140. TANSLEY, A.G. (1939). *The British Isles and their Vegetation.* Cambridge.
141. TAYLOR, J.C. (1968). The use of marking points by grey squirrels. *J. Zool., Lond.* **155**, 246.
142. THOMAS, A.S. (1975). *The Follies of Conservation.* Ilfracombe.
143. THOMAS, J.A. (1973). The conservation of the large blue butterfly *Maculinea arion* L., and other rare invertebrates. *Biol. J. Linn. Soc. Lond.* **5**, 361.
144. TILDESLEY, M.L. (1924). Sir Thomas Browne: his skull, portraits, and ancestry. *Biometrika.* **15**, 1.
145. TINBERGEN, N. (1965). Von den Vorratskammern des Rotfuchses (*Vulpes vulpes* L.). *Z. Tierpsychol.* **22**, 119.
146. TUDGE, C. (1978). Dog's eye view. *New Scient.* **77**, 749.
147. TUMANOV, I.L. (1972). [Age changes and morphophysiological characters of some species of martens.] *Zool. Zh.* **51**, 694.
148. VINCENT, R.E. (1958). Observations of red fox behaviour. *Ecology.* **39**, 755.
149. WARWICK, T. (1940). Fieldmice (*Apodemus*) from the Outer Hebrides, Scotland. *J. Mammal.* **21**, 347.
150. WATERTON, C. (1838). *Essays on Natural History.* London.
151. WEST, R.G. (1977). *Pleistocene Geology and Biology.* 2 ed. London.
152. WHITE, G. (1788). *The Natural History and Antiquities of Selborne.* London.
153. WOODFORDE, J. (1924). *The Diary of a Country Parson 1758–1802.* Ed. J. BERESFORD. 5 vols. London.
154. YALDEN, D.W. (1980). Urban small mammals. *J. Zool., Lond.* **191**, 403.
155. ZEUNER, F.E. (1945). *The Pleistocene Period.* London.

INDEX